Combating Malnutrition in Ethiopia

AN EVIDENCE-BASED APPROACH FOR SUSTAINED RESULTS

AFRICA HUMAN
DEVELOPMENT SERIES

Combating Malnutrition in Ethiopia

AN EVIDENCE-BASED APPROACH FOR SUSTAINED RESULTS

AFRICA HUMAN
DEVELOPMENT SERIES

Andrew Sunil Rajkumar,
Christopher Gaukler,
and Jessica Tilahun

THE WORLD BANK
Washington, D.C.

© 2012 The International Bank for Reconstruction and Development / The World Bank
1818 H Street NW
Washington DC 20433
Telephone: 202-473-1000
Internet: www.worldbank.org

1 2 3 4 14 13 12 11

This volume is a product of the staff of the International Bank for Reconstruction and Development / The World Bank. The findings, interpretations, and conclusions expressed in this volume do not necessarily reflect the views of the Executive Directors of The World Bank or the governments they represent.

The World Bank does not guarantee the accuracy of the data included in this work. The boundaries, colors, denominations, and other information shown on any map in this work do not imply any judgment on the part of The World Bank concerning the legal status of any territory or the endorsement or acceptance of such boundaries.

ISBN: 978-0-8213-8765-8
eISBN: 978-0-8213-8766-5
DOI: 10.1596/978-0-8213-8765-8

Cover photo: Laura Buback

Library of Congress Cataloging-in-Publication Data
Rajkumar, Andrew Sunil.
  Combating malnutrition in Ethiopia : an evidence-based approach for sustained results / Andrew Sunil Rajkumar, Christopher Gaukler, and Jessica Tilahun.
      p. cm.
    Includes bibliographical references.
    ISBN 978-0-8213-8765-8 (alk. paper) — ISBN 978-0-8213-8766-5 (eISBN)
    1. Malnutrition—Ethiopia—Statistics. 2. Malnutrition in children—Ethiopia. 3. Cost effectiveness—Ethiopia. I. Gaukler, Christopher. II. Tilahun, Jessica. III. World Bank. IV. Title.
    [DNLM: 1. Malnutrition—Ethiopia—Statistics. 2. Child—Ethiopia. 3. Cost-Benefit Analysis—Ethiopia—Statistics. 4. Infant—Ethiopia. 5. International Cooperation—Ethiopia—Statistics. 6. Maternal Nutritional Physiological Phenomena—Ethiopia—Statistics. 7. Nutrition Policy—Ethiopia—Statistics. WS 115]
    RA645.N87R34 2011
    362.196'3900963—dc23

2011015871

Table of Contents

BOXES

FIGURES

MAPS

TABLES

Foreword

Historically overlooked and underfunded, malnutrition has emerged in recent years as a critical challenge on the global development agenda. It is now recognized as a major obstacle in the way of achieving some of the targets under the first Millennium Development Goal (MDG)—to eradicate extreme poverty and hunger—in many countries. At the spring meetings of the World Bank and International Monetary Fund in 2010, the governments of Canada and Japan, the U.S. Agency for International Development, and the World Bank co-hosted a high-level meeting on "Scaling Up Nutrition." Robert B. Zoellick, president of the World Bank Group, spoke about nutrition as a "forgotten MDG" and noted that it was "the critical multiplier MDG, because if you fell short on nutrition, it was going to hurt every one of the other goals."

We know that nutrition interventions are among those with the highest potential impact in the developing world for each dollar spent. Three years ago, in January 2008, *The Lancet* issued a special five-part series on nutrition. The series filled a long-standing gap by marshaling systematic evidence of the impact of malnutrition on infant and child mortality and the largely irreversible long-term effects on health and on cognitive and physical development. *The Lancet* highlighted a set of nutrition interventions that have been shown in a range of studies to be extremely cost-effective, with high returns to cognitive development, individual earnings, and economic growth. Yet resources to tackle malnutrition still fall far short of what is needed.

In Ethiopia, malnutrition indicators are among the worst in the world, and the country is one of the 36 that together account for about 90 percent of the world's stunted children. But there has been significant recent progress in Ethiopia, and the problem of malnutrition has been addressed with a different approach in recent years. In 2008, for the first time, Ethiopia developed a National Nutrition Strategy and launched the National Nutrition Program to implement it. The International Development Association has contributed US$30 million so far toward this program, which is also funded by the government and a range of other partners.

In this context, the book makes a valuable contribution. It provides the analytical underpinnings for implementation of the National Nutrition Program and more broadly for the efforts of the government and development partners to address malnutrition in Ethiopia in the short and medium term. The findings of the book are based on the authors' detailed analysis of data from several different sources, including household surveys and program data specific to Ethiopia. The book is intentionally pragmatic—its recommendations are based not just on technical analysis but also on practical considerations and delivery structures on the ground in Ethiopia.

Key findings include the need for a multisectoral approach to combat malnutrition that goes beyond addressing food insecurity alone and the high benefit-cost ratios of nutrition interventions in general—although some are identified as being of higher priority for introduction or scaling up. Ways to enhance effectiveness are also suggested, including improved program targeting, enhanced coordination among programs, and the establishment of an effective nutrition information and surveillance system.

I would like to extend special recognition and thanks to the Ethiopian partners who made this book possible, in particular Dr. Kesetebirhan Admasu, state minister of health; Dr. Shiferaw Teklemariam, former state minister of health and current minister of federal affairs; Dr. Tsehaynesh Messele, director general of the Ethiopia Health and Nutrition Research Institute; Dr. Cherinet Abuye, director of the Food Science and Nutrition Research Directorate, Ethiopia Health and Nutrition Research Institute; and Dr. Belaynesh Yifru, officer at the Dire Dawa case team, Urban Health Promotion and Disease Prevention Directorate, Ministry of Health. They have played an instrumental role in establishing and implementing the National Nutrition Program, along with Dr. Tewodros Adhanom, minister of health; Dr. Kebede Worku, state minister of health; Dr. Neghist Tesfaye, director of the Urban Health Promotion and Disease Prevention Directorate; and Dr. Ferew Lemma, senior nutrition adviser, Federal Ministry of Health.

The challenges in addressing malnutrition in Ethiopia are enormous, and sustained efforts as well as adequate financing will be needed over several years. If this is accomplished, Ethiopia may eventually be one of the leaders in addressing malnutrition in Sub-Saharan Africa and more generally in low-income countries. I believe that the insights offered in this book will support the policy dialogue and program implementation efforts that will be needed in order to make this happen.

Ritva Reinikka
Director
Human Development
Africa Region

Acknowledgments

This book was prepared by the authors Andrew Sunil Rajkumar (senior economist at the World Bank and team leader), Christopher Gaukler (social protection consultant at the World Bank), and Jessica Tilahun (nutrition adviser at the U.S. Agency for International Development), with contributions from Eskender Tesfaye (World Bank consultant), Jack Fiedler (World Bank consultant), David Lawson (Institute for Development Policy and Management), Hailay Teklehaimanot (Center for National Health Development), Yemane Yihdego (Center for National Health Development), Caroline Poeschl (World Bank consultant), and Rishi Mediratta (World Bank consultant).

The authors wish to express their special appreciation and gratitude to the many people and agencies who generously shared data and information with them and who facilitated the sharing of this information—in particular, personnel from the government agencies and other organizations administering the programs analyzed in the book (see tables 3.1, 3.2, and 3.3 for a full listing). The authors would like to especially thank the Ministry of Health of the government of Ethiopia, as well as the regional bureaus of health and the Ethiopia Health and Nutrition Research Institute for participating as active partners throughout preparation of this study, and, in particular, His Excellency Dr. Kesetebirhan Admasu, state minister of health; His Excellency Dr. Shiferaw Teklemariam, former state minister of health and current minister of federal affairs; Dr. Tsehaynesh Messele, director general of the Ethiopia Health and Nutrition Research Institute; Dr. Cherinet Abuye, director of the Food Science and Nutrition Research Directorate, Ethiopia Health and Nutrition Research Institute; and Dr. Belaynesh Yifru, officer at the Dire Dawa case team, Urban Health Promotion and Disease Prevention Directorate, Ministry of Health.

The book was prepared under the overall guidance of Laura Frigenti and Eva Jarawan (former and current sector managers, respectively, in charge of health for Ethiopia at the World Bank), as well as Kenichi Ohashi (country director for Ethiopia at the World Bank). Invaluable comments and input for the book were received from a range of people in the World Bank and outside, including the peer reviewers Meera Shekar and Menno Mulder-Sibanda, as well as Harold Alderman, Marito Garcia, Trina Haque, Ziauddin Hyder, Yuki Isogai, Frew Tekabe, Lisa Saldanha, Iqbal Kabir, Wendmsyamregne Mekasha, Sylvie Chamois, Teshome Desta, Abebe Hailemariam, Mathewos Tamiru, and Jakob Mikkelsen. Useful insights were also obtained from various members of the World Bank Ethiopia country team.

Abbreviations

AIDS	acquired immune deficiency syndrome
CBN	Community-Based Nutrition
CBRHA	Community-Based Reproductive Health Agent
CGP	Child Growth Promotion
ENCU	Emergency Nutrition Coordination Unit
EOS	Enhanced Outreach Strategy for Child Survival
EEOS	Extended EOS
ESHE	Essential Services for Health in Ethiopia
EWRD	Early Warning and Response Directorate
GDP	gross domestic product
HEP	Health Extension Program
HIV	human immunodeficiency virus
IFHP	Integrated Family Health Program
MDG	Millennium Development Goal
MERET	Managing Environmental Resources to Enable Transitions to More Sustainable Livelihoods (World Food Programme)
MUAC	mid-upper arm circumference
NCHS	National Center for Health Statistics
NGO	nongovernmental organization
SNNP	Southern Nations, Nationalities, and Peoples
TSFP	Targeted Supplementary Food Program
UNICEF	United Nations Children's Fund
USAID	United States Agency for International Development
WASH	Water, Sanitation, and Hygiene

Glossary

Anemia. Low level of hemoglobin in the blood leading to reduced capacity to carry oxygen to tissues and organs. Anemia can have various causes, but, most commonly, it is a consequence of iron deficiency. Symptoms are decreased energy, decreased mental capacity, and increased maternal mortality.

Body mass index. An index of fatness. It is calculated by dividing weight in kilograms by height in meters squared. Both high and low indexes are associated with poor health. The normal range for a healthy adult is 18.5 to 24.9. A BMI below 18.5 is considered too lean, while one above 25 is considered overweight. A BMI greater than 30 is considered obese, and one greater than 40 is considered morbidly obese.

Complementary foods. Formerly called "weaning foods." Complementary foods are introduced while a child continues to breast-feed. It is recommended that complementary foods be started at six months of life and be provided two to three times a day with increasing consistency as the child grows.

Exclusive breast-feeding. When an infant is fed only breast milk and is not fed water, tea, gruel, or other animal milk. Exclusive breast-feeding is recommended for the first six months of life.

Food security. Availability, access, and use of sufficient food by all people at all times for an active, healthy life (Benson 2006). See also *nutrition security.*

Gini coefficient. A measure of income inequality ranging from 0 (perfect equality) to 1 (perfect inequality).

Infant mortality rate. The number of infants out of every 1,000 live births who are expected to die at the age of exactly one year or less.

Iodine deficiency disorder. Disorder caused by a deficiency of iodine in the diet. The spectrum of disorders includes goiter, hypothyroidism, impaired mental function, stillbirths, abortions, congenital abnormalities, and neurological cretinism.

Kebele. A neighbourhood association or community in Ethiopia.

Low birthweight. An infant born weighing less than 2,500 grams (5.5 pounds). In rural areas, this is estimated by the infant's "relative size" to other babies, as assessed by the birth attendant or mother.

Malnutrition. An imbalance between the body's needs and its use and intake of nutrients. The imbalance can be caused by poor or lacking diet, poor hygiene, disease states, lack of knowledge, and cultural practices, among others. Underweight, stunting, wasting, obesity, and vitamin and mineral deficiencies are all forms of malnutrition.

Mid-upper arm circumference (MUAC). One of the anthropometric measures used in assessing nutritional status. It is always measured on the left arm. Measuring MUAC is easier and faster to use and train for than measuring weight and height.

Moderate malnutrition. A common benchmark used in health and nutrition studies that can be defined in more than one way. In this book, unless stated otherwise, "moderate malnutrition" refers to a child with a MUAC between 11 and 12 centimeters.

Neonatal mortality rate. The number of infants out of every 1,000 live births who are expected to die during the first 28 days of life.

Nutrition security. When a household attains secure access to food coupled with a sanitary environment, adequate health services, and knowledgeable care (Benson 2006). See also *food security.*

Severe acute malnutrition. A common benchmark used in health and nutrition studies. It refers to a child who has visible severe wasting or nutritional edema. In Ethiopia, children with a MUAC less than 11 centimeters are considered to have severe acute malnutrition.

Severe stunting, wasting, or underweight rate. A common benchmark used in health and nutrition studies. It is technically defined as the percentage of children under five years of age who suffer from severe stunting, wasting, or underweight, defined, respectively, as having a height-for-age, weight-for-height, or weight-for-age value that is equal to or smaller than the value corresponding to three standard deviations below the median of the global reference population—that is, the value corresponding to –3 Z-scores with respect to the global reference population (see also the definitions of stunting, wasting, and underweight).

Stunting. When a child has low stature compared to other children his or her age because of inadequate nutrition, care, and environment. A proxy measure for long-term malnutrition, it is defined as height-for-age that is equal to the value corresponding to or smaller than two standard deviations below the median of the global reference population—that is, the value corresponding to –2 Z-scores with respect to the global reference population (a population with a distribution of height-for-age values that is considered normal by international standards).

Total stunting, wasting, or underweight rate. Also referred to as the "stunting, wasting, or underweight rate." A common benchmark used in health and nutrition studies, it is technically defined as the percentage of children under five years of age who suffer from stunting, wasting, or underweight (see definitions of stunting, wasting, and underweight).

Under-five mortality rate. The number of children out of every 1,000 live births who are expected to die at the age of exactly five years or less.

Undernutrition. Failure to get enough nutrients for a healthy body. Undernutrition can result from low intake, malabsorption during disease, or extreme losses, such as during bouts of diarrhea.

Underweight. When a child has low weight compared to other children his or her age. "Underweight" is one way to measure acute malnutrition. It is defined as weight-for-age that is equal to or smaller than the value corresponding to two standard deviations below the median of the global reference population—that is, the value corresponding to –2 Z-scores with respect to the global reference population (a population with a distribution of weight-for-age values that is considered normal by international standards).

Vitamin A deficiency. A form of malnutrition resulting from inadequate intake or high loss of vitamin A. Symptoms include growth retardation, night blindness in mild deficiency, and xerophthalmia (drying of the cornea), which leads to complete blindness.

Wasting. When a child has a low weight for his or her current height. Wasting is used as a proxy measure of acute malnutrition. It is defined as weight-for-height that is equal to or less than the value corresponding to two standard deviations below the median of the global reference population—that is, the value corresponding to –2 Z-scores with respect to the global reference population (a population with a distribution of weight-for-height values that is considered normal by international standards).

Woreda. District with local government in the Ethiopian system.

Z-score. A unit of measure often used in the nutrition and health field. It is the deviation of an individual's value from the median value of the global reference population, divided by the standard deviation of the global reference population. The Z-score indicates where one observation lies in reference to the global population. A Z-score of −2 or less (that is, equal to or smaller than two standard deviations below the median of the global reference population) is considered low. (The global reference population is a population with a distribution of heights, weights, ages, or related measures that is considered normal by international standards.) The Z-score criteria always yield a greater prevalence of malnutrition than the percent-of-median criteria because the former takes into account variations in the standard deviation of weight at different heights, thereby making it more statistically valid. The World Health Organization recommends the use of Z-scores, because they are the most age-independent method of presenting indexes. In addition, individuals with indexes below the extreme percentiles can be classified more accurately.

Executive Summary

Malnutrition can be transient like an acute disease. More often, it is chronic—a lifelong, intergenerational condition beginning early in life and continuing into old age. Most undernutrition starts during pregnancy and the first two years of life. After a child reaches 24 months of age, damage from early malnutrition is irreversible.

Various indicators are commonly used to measure and monitor malnutrition, including rates of stunting, wasting, and underweight among children under five years of age (see the glossary for definitions and explanations). Stunting is a measure of long-term, chronic malnutrition. Wasting is a measure of more transient, acute, but reversible malnutrition. These two measures are often not highly correlated. Underweight is a composite index of stunting and wasting; an underweight child can be stunted, wasted, or both.

Successive Welfare Monitoring Surveys indicate a substantial decrease in the rate of stunting in urban and rural areas from 1996 to 2004. The national trend for wasting has been more mixed in the medium term, but the prevalence of underweight among children has declined steadily. Despite encouraging improvements, stunting rates in Ethiopia remain very high by developing country and regional standards. About half of all Ethiopian children are stunted. Wasting rates, however, are not especially high by regional and Sub-Saharan African standards.

The national estimates of child stunting and wasting prevalence mask significant urban-rural and regional variations. Perhaps the largest and most persistent disparities exist between rural and urban areas. Gender-based disparities are relatively small in Ethiopia, as in other countries.

Aside from stunting and wasting, the top micronutrient deficiencies—those of iron, vitamin A, and iodine—are rife in Ethiopia. Ethiopia will lose an estimated 10 percent of gross domestic product (GDP) from 2006 to 2015 (about US$12 billion) because of iron and iodine deficiency disorders and stunting alone. Large numbers of Ethiopian children—of whom almost half are stunted and many more suffer from other forms of malnutrition—experience the lifelong consequences of malnutrition, including increased risk of mortality and future illness, impaired cognitive ability, delayed enrollment and lower attainment in school, and overall loss of productivity.

The government of Ethiopia formulated and approved the first National Nutrition Strategy in February 2008 to concentrate efforts on reducing malnutrition. The National Nutrition Program was approved in December 2008 to implement the strategy following a programmatic approach. The Ministry of Health is the lead agency overseeing the program and implementing its key aspects; other ministries and sectors are also involved in the multisectoral effort to reduce malnutrition.

NUTRITION SECURITY VERSUS FOOD SECURITY

Many mistakenly believe that malnutrition is mainly due to a lack of food and that providing food is the ultimate solution. But, in fact, although nutrition security is affected by food security, the two are only moderately related. Nutrition security is also influenced strongly by many other factors such as health status, feeding and child care practices, and water and sanitation. A regression analysis of household data from Ethiopia's 2005 Demographic and Health Survey indicates that increasing a household's welfare status—which helps to lower the risk of food insecurity—reduces child wasting to some (limited) extent, but has no discernible effect on child stunting. Economic growth and higher household income alone will not substantially reduce child malnutrition. Nutrition security cannot be achieved by focusing only on interventions targeting the income or food security of households.

Data from Ethiopia's 2004 Welfare Monitoring Survey show a clear, positive relationship between under-five child wasting rates and the extent of self-reported household food insecurity (see figure 1). Thus, adequate provision of food to food-insecure households is necessary to alleviate wasting. But the data also show that child wasting rates are still very high even in households with no food insecurity, indicating that a significant amount of wasting results from factors other than food insecurity. These must be addressed through appropriate interventions other than the provision of food. The same data show no obvious relationship between child stunting rates and household food insecurity. These findings highlight the importance of addressing nonfood factors to reduce wasting and stunting.

Figure 1   Malnutrition Rates in Under-Five Children from Households with Varying Degrees of Self-Reported Food Insecurity, 2004

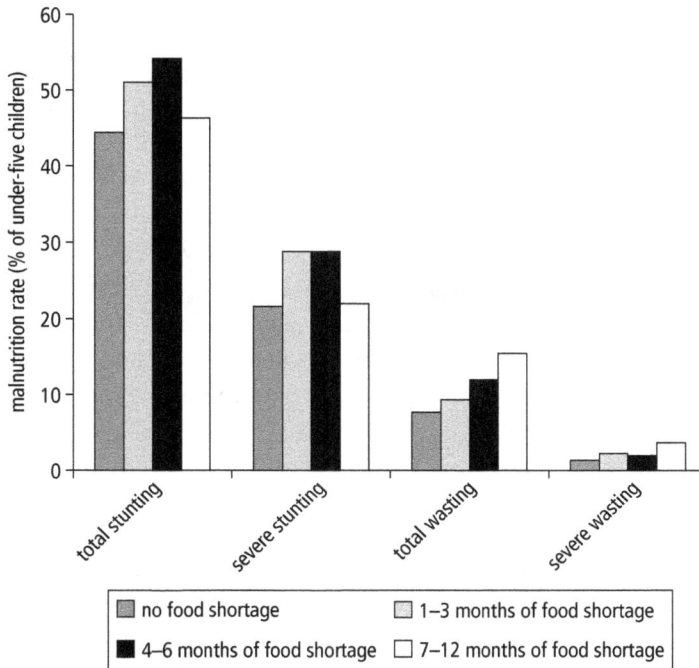

Source: Authors' calculations using data from the 2004 Welfare Monitoring Survey.
Note: Total wasting refers to moderate as well as severe wasting, and total stunting refers to moderate as well as severe stunting.

Increasing evidence from various countries shows that a multisectoral approach is most effective for reducing malnutrition and that the most successful programs do more than just reduce food insecurity. Malnutrition rates can often be substantially improved by educating mothers on appropriate feeding and child care behavior, providing immunizations for common childhood illnesses, ensuring access to a safe supply of clean water, and improving a household's sanitary conditions, among others. And every one of these interventions is achievable without changing the amount of food provided.

COST-EFFECTIVE INTERVENTIONS AND RECENT PROGRESS

A significant proportion of Ethiopian women do not breast-feed their babies correctly. An estimated 50,000 infant deaths, or 18 percent of all infant deaths, each year are attributable to poor breast-feeding habits.

Most inappropriate breast-feeding practices are due to lack of knowledge rather than practical or financial constraints. There is no evidence of a positive relationship between wealth and optimal breast-feeding. Community volunteer programs that teach optimal breast-feeding practices, among other interventions, have proven very successful in improving behavior. This intervention is highly cost-effective and has a large impact on reducing child mortality.

One of several community volunteer programs in Ethiopia, the Community-Based Nutrition (CBN) Program was introduced in 39 *woredas* (districts) in 2008 and has been scaled up gradually since then. This program is modeled on successful large-scale programs that have been implemented in countries such as Bangladesh and Thailand. These programs, when well implemented, have typically resulted in (a) a large initial reduction of up to several percentage points in the prevalence of underweight among under-two children in the first year or two, followed by (b) an additional reduction of around 1 to 2 percentage points a year on top of any reduction that would have occurred anyway, without the programs. Preliminary data indicate that the first batch of CBN *woredas* is exhibiting this pattern, with large initial reductions in the prevalence of underweight children in beneficiary *woredas* (see figure 2). But more data and analysis are needed before firm conclusions can be drawn.

Only about one-fifth of Ethiopian households used adequately iodized household salt in 2005, a *decrease* from 2000, when 28 percent used it, according to successive Demographic and Health Surveys. Iodine deficiency disorders in infants or in utero unequivocally decrease mental abilities, permanently reduce productivity, and result in congenital and other abnormalities. The cost of reducing iodine deficiency in Ethiopia is very low; universal salt iodization costs about US$0.05 per capita annually. Ethiopia recently took a critical first step toward this goal by starting iodization on a significant scale in Afar region, which produces most of Ethiopia's salt. But Ethiopia still has some way to go before reaching universal salt iodization. Program implementation has to be monitored carefully, with adjustments made as needed. In addition, legislation regarding obligatory salt iodization needs to be examined, strengthened as required, and adequately enforced.

NUTRITION INTERVENTIONS: HIGH COST-EFFECTIVENESS AND BENEFIT-COST RATIOS

This book presents the results of a cost-effectiveness and benefit-cost analysis for a range of interventions affecting Ethiopian nutrition by using

Figure 2 Prevalence of Underweight Children in _Woredas_ in the First Phase of the CBN Program, by Region, 2008–10

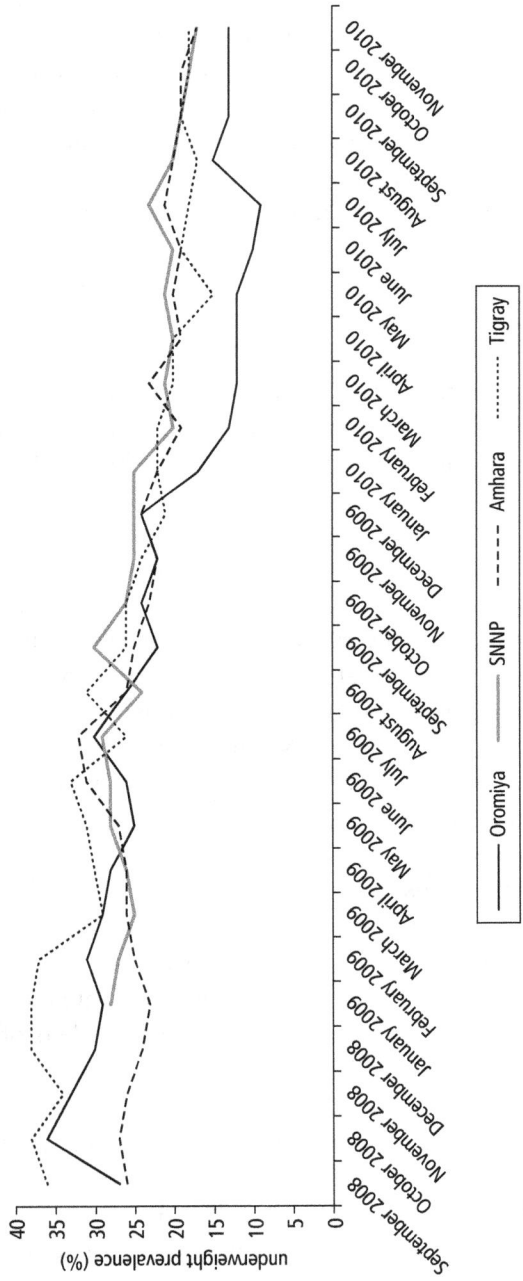

Source: Data from the CBN Program.
Note: The figure depicts the prevalence of total (moderate and severe) underweight among under-two children, based on data from the monthly weighing sessions in the 39 _woredas_ included in the first phase of the CBN Program.

Ethiopia-specific cost and impact data gathered from studies in Ethiopia and elsewhere. Existing interventions are included in the analysis as well as other "potential" interventions that have been proposed as possible candidates for introduction into national programming at some point. These potential interventions are mostly proven micronutrient interventions, including (a) supplementing children with iron and folate and with zinc; (b) fortifying foods with iron and vitamin A; and (c) providing deworming medicine to pregnant women.

Micronutrient interventions are found to be extremely cost-effective, with very high benefit-cost ratios (see figure 3). Of the 10 interventions examined that have benefit-cost ratios above the median, five are micronutrient interventions. Micronutrient interventions increase economic gains by reducing mortality, increasing productivity, and increasing child ability. Iodine does all three; salt iodization has a very high benefit-cost ratio of 81.

Providing deworming medicine and bed nets are not micronutrient interventions, but their economic benefits are substantial. Distributing bed nets and providing deworming medicine to pregnant women result in economic gains that are, respectively, 26 and 648 times higher than the costs. They also have the potential to save large numbers of lives when scaled up (see figure 4).

The analysis illustrates the effectiveness of the community volunteer programs that focus in particular on educating mothers and caregivers on appropriate breast-feeding, child care, and other practices. The promotion of optimal breast-feeding, analyzed as part of the Community Health Promoters Volunteer Program, is a high-ranking intervention. Overall, the volunteer programs that were examined show benefits that exceed costs by seven to 27 times.

All of the interventions considered return high levels of benefits relative to costs. The analysis finds that the benefit-cost ratio is greater than 1 for all interventions studied, and for many it is much greater. Interventions that provide food are relatively expensive compared to other interventions, but they have the potential to save large numbers of under-five lives when scaled up nationwide (figure 4).

One clear conclusion that emerges is that several of the potential interventions that are analyzed here but not being implemented in Ethiopia should be implemented. This is particularly true for the provision of deworming medicine to pregnant women. This intervention would reach a large fraction of the affected population with little additional cost if it were included in the existing structure of the Enhanced Outreach Strategy for Child Survival (EOS) and the Extended EOS (EEOS) programs. There is also a strong case for introducing in Ethiopia (perhaps initially on a pilot

Figure 3 Benefit-Cost Ratios for Current and Potential Interventions

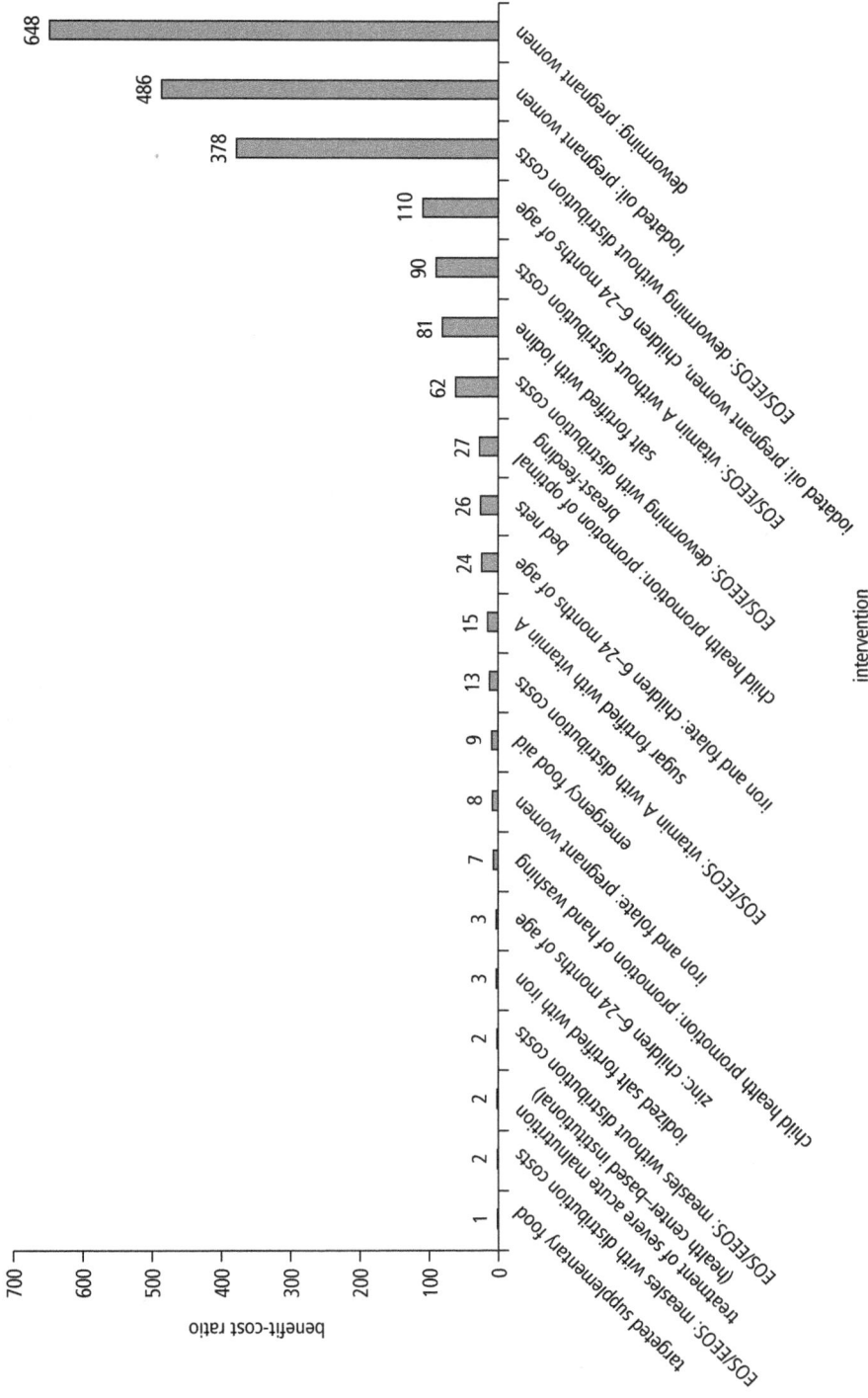

Horizontal bar chart. Y-axis: benefit-cost ratio (0 to 700). X-axis: intervention.

intervention	benefit-cost ratio
deworming: pregnant women	648
iodated oil: pregnant women	486
iodated oil: pregnant women, children 6–24 months	378
EOS/EOS: deworming without distribution costs	110
salt fortified with iodine	90
EOS/EOS: vitamin A without distribution costs	81
EOS/EOS: deworming with distribution costs	62
bed nets	27
child health promotion: promotion of optimal breast-feeding	26
iron and folate: children 6–24 months of age	24
sugar fortified with vitamin A	15
EOS/EOS: vitamin A with distribution costs	13
emergency food aid	9
iron and folate: pregnant women	8
child health promotion: promotion of hand washing	7
zinc: children 6–24 months of age	3
iodized salt fortified with iron	3
child health promotion: iodized salt fortified without distribution costs	2
EOS/EOS: measles without institutional	2
treatment of severe acute malnutrition (health center–based institutional)	2
EOS/EOS: measles with distribution costs	1
targeted supplementary food	1

Source: Authors' calculations based on program data.
Note: Of the interventions depicted, the following do not currently exist in Ethiopia: iron in iodized salt, zinc for children 6–24 months of age, iron or folate for children 6–24 months of age, sugar fortified with vitamin A, and deworming for pregnant women. EOS = Enhanced Outreach Strategy for Child Survival; EEOS = Extended EOS.

Figure 4   Under-Five Deaths Averted and Cost per Capita for Various Interventions

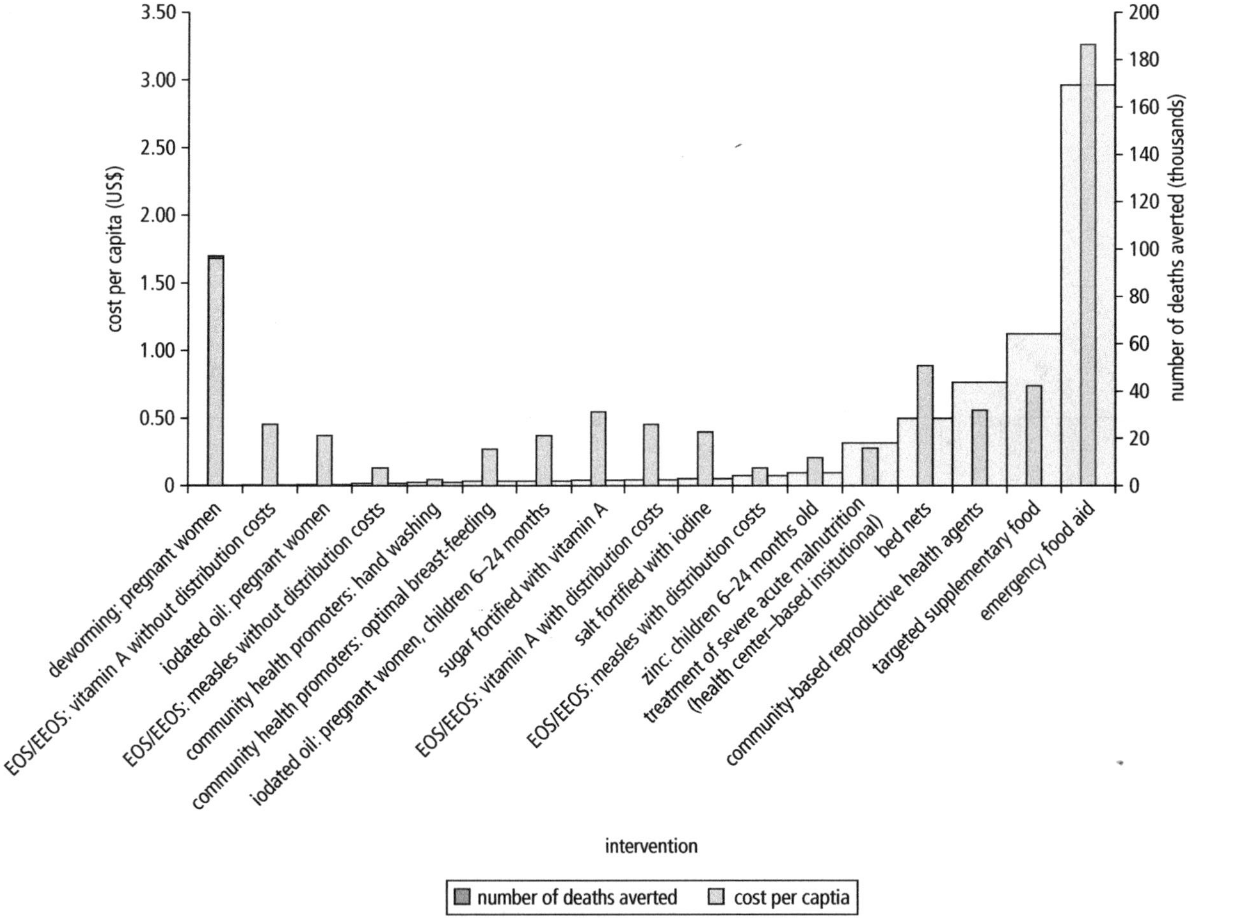

Source: Authors' calculations based on program data.

Note: The baseline for under-five deaths is the number for 2005. For each program, the number of deaths averted was computed under a scenario of scaling up the program nationwide.
EOS = Enhanced Outreach Strategy for Child Survival; EEOS = Extended EOS.

basis) certain interventions that were not included in the analysis but that elsewhere have had high impacts relative to their costs. These include home fortification of complementary foods with micronutrient powder.

Quantitative measures such as benefit-cost ratios, cost-effectiveness estimates, and estimates of the number of lives that could potentially be saved are not the only important factors to consider when one is deciding whether to implement nutrition interventions. Others include the short-term and long-term funding situation; availability of supplies and the delivery structure; the political environment; and various programmatic, feasibility, and sustainability considerations.

NEED TO IMPROVE LINKAGES BETWEEN DIFFERENT PROGRAMS AND SECTORS

Because nutrition is affected by so many different multisectoral interventions, a harmonized approach that links different sectors, subsectors, and programs is necessary to combat malnutrition effectively. Currently, different programs affecting nutrition typically operate in isolation, with little or no coordination. Each program independently chooses its own *woredas* of focus. When two or more programs overlap in the same *woreda*, they often suffer from a lack of harmonization, including in the selection of beneficiary households.

If two or more uncoordinated programs coexist in the same *woreda* or *kebele* (community), the result may lead to diminishing returns by stretching existing local capacity and reducing instead of increasing the impact of each program. This is evident from the current situation where many health extension workers are required to play a coordinating role for several programs, which means that they are overstretched and not performing optimally.

A key goal of the National Nutrition Strategy and National Nutrition Program is to strengthen the linkages between the different programs, sectors, and agencies working on nutrition-related areas. Among other things, the strategy called for establishing a national nutrition coordination committee. This high-level cross-sectoral coordinating body was formed in late 2008 to ensure that different agencies work together in addressing malnutrition.

Some of the difficulties in coordination and linkages have been addressed in part by creation of the Emergency Nutrition Coordination Unit (ENCU) at the federal level. Regional ENCUs have also been created and are fully functional, with a full complement of staff, in several regions. There is some evidence that the regional ENCUs have played a role in harmonizing the various nutrition-related programs in the regions.

A small pilot project with a specific focus on strengthening linkages between core nutrition interventions and the activities of the Productive Safety Net Program is now under way. The pilot activities fall under different sectors (health and agriculture) and different government agencies; hence, intersectoral coordination is necessary for implementation of the pilot. More such pilots involving other sectors are needed; after careful evaluation, successful pilots should be scaled up in the future.

NEED TO DEVELOP AN ENHANCED NUTRITION INFORMATION AND SURVEILLANCE SYSTEM

Although the amount of nutrition data collected in Ethiopia is relatively large, its usefulness is currently limited for programming purposes, including for program design, program evaluation, and targeting. Strengthening the country's nutrition information and surveillance system is a key goal of the National Nutrition Program, as doing so would improve the ability to track nutritional trends in different parts of the country and within population subgroups, facilitate a better understanding of the impacts of different interventions, and generally facilitate programming to fight malnutrition.

NEED TO IMPROVE TARGETING OF PROGRAMS COMBATING MALNUTRITION

Localized data on nutrition indicators are limited because of an inadequate nutrition information and surveillance system. As a result, targeting programs to the most nutritionally insecure *woredas* is difficult, if not impossible. Nutrition-related programs often fall back on measures of food insecurity or other vulnerabilities, such as the chronic vulnerability index, despite their only partial correlation or lack of correlation with nutrition insecurity. The most common scenario is for programs aimed at reducing malnutrition to target areas that already regularly receive food aid and are designated as being "food insecure."

The need for emergency food aid is determined with the help of the Early Warning System *belg* and *meher* (crop season) assessments. But coverage in some parts of the country is poor, especially in certain areas with pastoral, nonfamine-prone, nomadic, historically marginalized, and urban populations.

Moreover, the system used to provide food aid in Ethiopia is inflexible and has a certain inertia. *Woredas* that were labeled as being food insecure years ago have retained the label, even though it may not apply today, and they appear to receive food aid consistently, even in years when weather conditions are not especially bad. Conversely, *woredas* labeled as being food secure are much less likely to receive food aid overall, despite recent shocks that have plunged some of them into food insecurity.

With this inflexibility in the targeting of food aid, it is not surprising to find that large numbers of food-insecure households are not being reached in the *woredas* designated as food secure. Data from the 2004 Welfare Monitoring Survey show that about 25 percent of all households in the *woredas* designated as fully food secure report experiencing some food shortages within the previous 12 months (see figure 5). The corresponding percentages for households in *woredas* designated as partially food insecure and food insecure is not much higher (32 and 35 percent, respectively).

The prevalence of large numbers of food-insecure households, even in *woredas* designated as food secure, is one reason for the startling finding that there is little difference in stunting and wasting rates among the *woredas* designated as food insecure, partially food insecure, and fully food secure, based on 2004 Welfare Monitoring Survey data (see figure 6). Another reason for this surprising finding is that a substantial component

Figure 5 Percentage of Households Reporting Food Shortage within Previous 12 Months in *Woredas*, by Food Security Designation

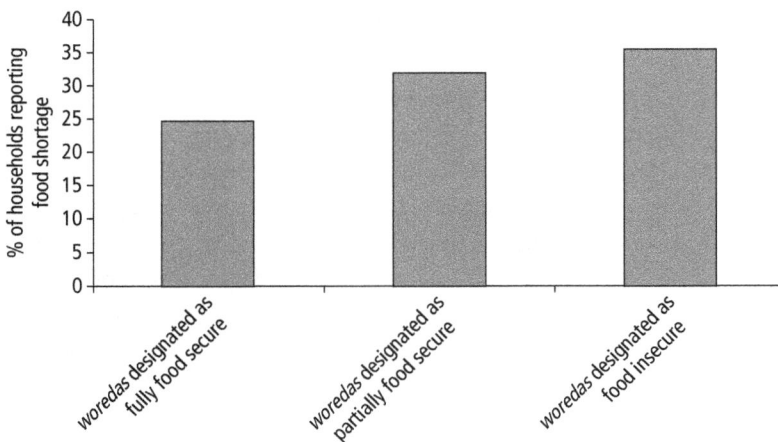

Source: Authors' calculations using data from the 2004 Welfare Monitoring Survey and food aid data from the Disaster Risk Management and Food Security Sector.

Figure 6   Total Stunting and Wasting Rates in *Woredas*, by Food Security Designation, 2004

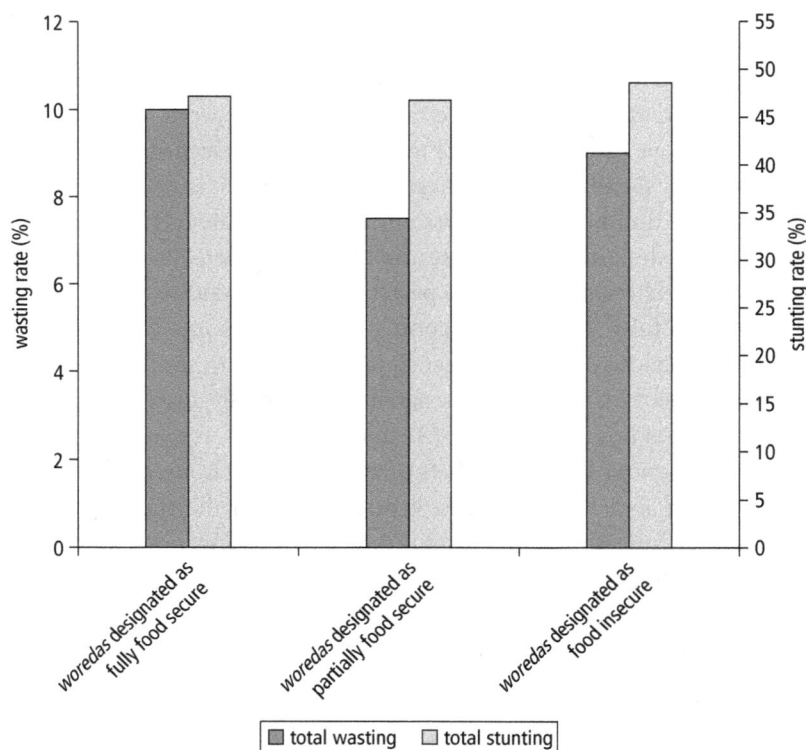

Source: Authors' calculations using data from the 2004 Welfare Monitoring Survey and food aid data from the Disaster Risk Management and Food Security Sector.
Note: Total wasting refers to moderate as well as severe wasting, and total stunting refers to moderate as well as severe stunting.

of both wasting and stunting is due to factors other than household food shortages (figure 1), and these factors may be driving the results depicted in figure 6. These factors include poor health status, inadequate safe water and sanitation, and inappropriate child care and child-feeding practices.

The targeting of nutrition-related programs thus falters on two counts. First, food aid targeting is flawed, often missing large swaths of the food-insecure population who reside in *woredas* designated as food secure. Second, even if food aid were targeted perfectly, basing the targeting of nutrition programs on the targeting of food aid would still be problematic because the correlation between food insecurity and malnutrition is only partial and is especially weak if malnutrition is measured by stunting rates.

Poor coordination among different programs operating in the same *woreda* compounds the problem. The *woredas* designated as food insecure tend to be the main beneficiaries not just of food aid but also of several different and often overlapping major programs addressing malnutrition. These programs are, in general, not coordinated with each other, and they sometimes overburden the health extension workers working in those *woredas*. Many of the less favored *woredas* that are designated as food secure benefit from disproportionately fewer programs or have no programs at all, in spite of their often high prevalence of malnutrition (see figure 7).

A geographic analysis helps to illustrate the weaknesses in the targeting of beneficiary *woredas* by programs aiming to combat malnutrition. Maps 1 and 2 show that large parts of the country had high rates of stunting in 2004 (map 2), but a low concentration of programs affecting nutrition—or no such programs at all—in 2007 (map 1). A similar pattern is seen for wasting. Ethiopia's malnutrition rate would probably be substantially reduced if some of the programs were shifted from *woredas* with a high concentration of major programs into *woredas* with high malnutrition rates but no major programs.

A harmonized method of selecting *woredas* for all programs needs to be created and urgently implemented. And *woredas* that are not often included in programming on the grounds of their being designated as food secure need to be reassessed and considered for programming. The selection of beneficiary *woredas* also needs to address another

Figure 7   Stunting and Wasting Rates in *Woredas* Grouped by the Number of Major Programs Affecting Nutrition, 2004

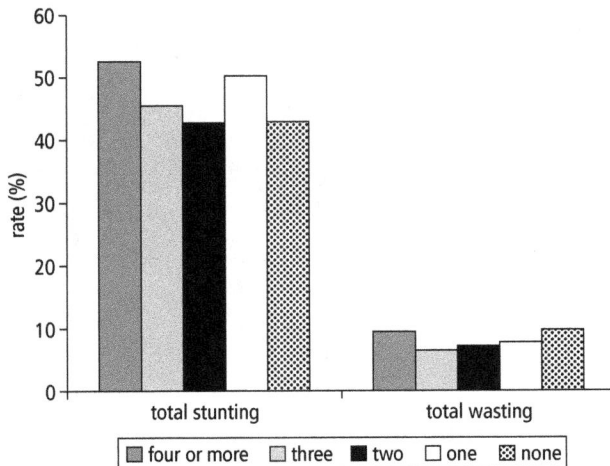

Source: Authors' calculations using program data and data from the 2004 Welfare Monitoring Survey.
Note: The Water, Sanitation, and Hygiene (WASH) programs and emergency food aid are excluded from the programs considered. Total wasting refers to moderate as well as severe wasting, and total stunting refers to moderate as well as severe stunting.

Map 1   Concentration of Major Programs in Ethiopia Affecting Nutrition (Excluding Food Aid and WASH) and Location of _Woredas_ Regularly Receiving Food Aid, 2007

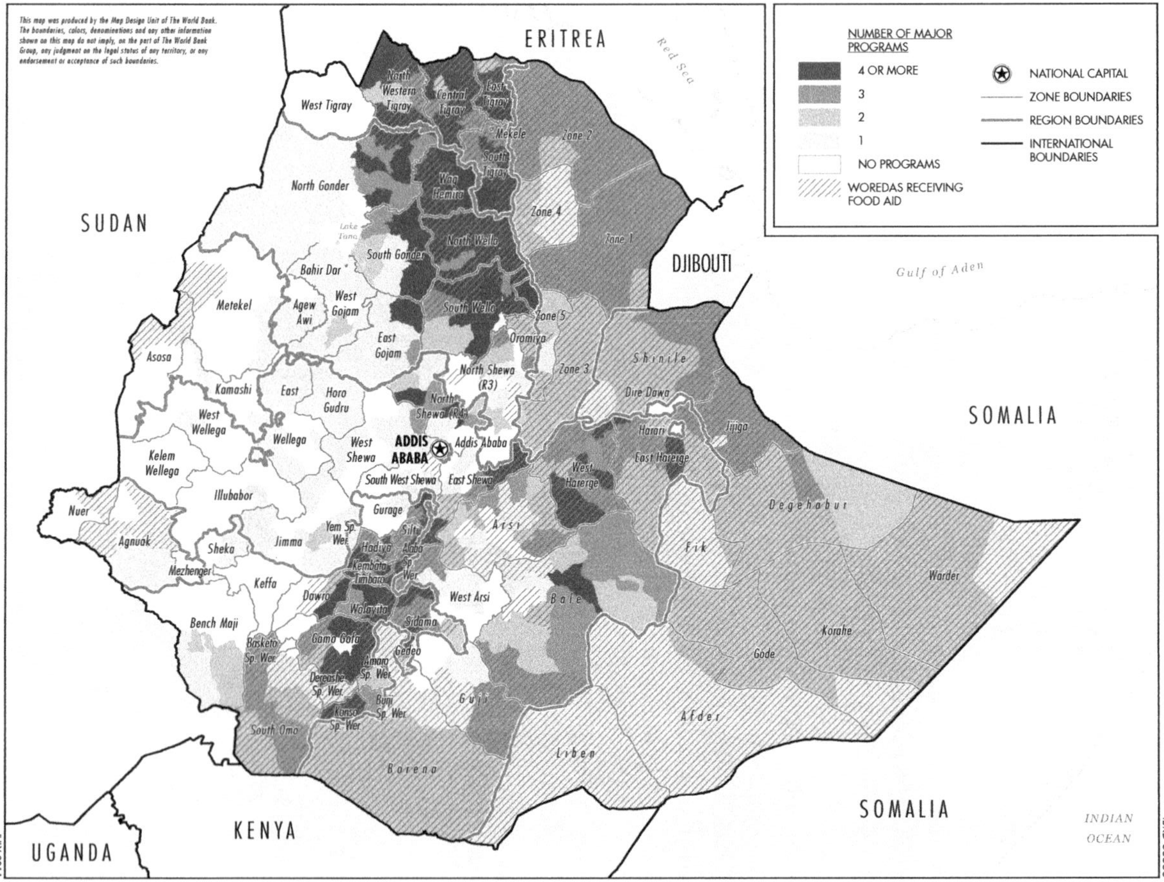

Source: Generated from program data and food aid data from the Disaster Risk Management and Food Security Sector (DRMFSS).

Map 2   Stunting Prevalence in Ethiopia, at Zonal Level, 2004

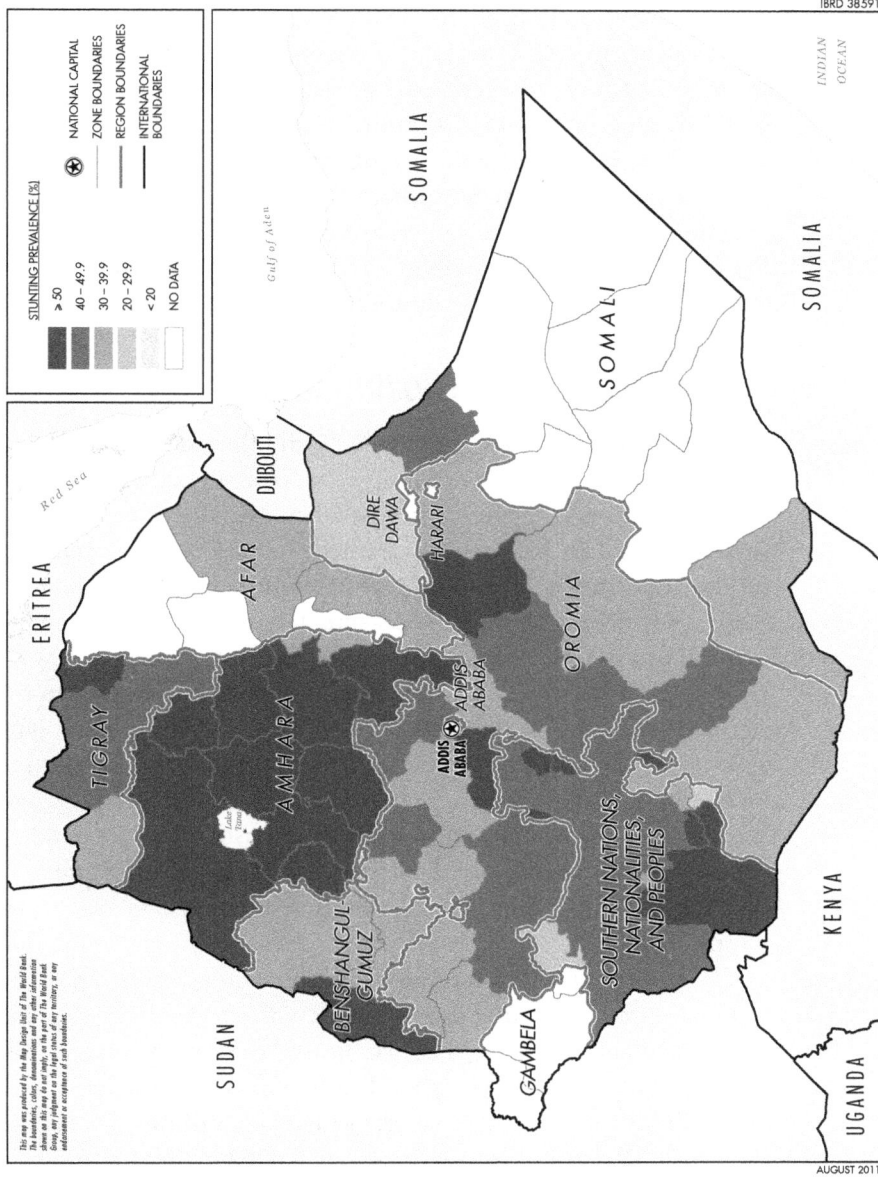

Source: Estimates generated from data from the 2004 Welfare Monitoring Survey (CSA 2004).

weakness: the tendency to focus disproportionately on the larger regions and on rural areas, often ignoring the smaller, emerging regions and the urban poor, who also suffer from high rates of malnutrition. In addition, improvements could be made in targeting programs to the correct population subgroups, households, and members within households.

On the bright side, however, the analysis shows that programs with a strong community volunteer focus appear to be better targeted than the food-providing programs, if stunting is the indicator of focus. Furthermore, although stunting and wasting rates vary across the country, they are generally high almost everywhere. Despite the poor targeting of many programs, most nevertheless operate in *woredas* with high rates of malnutrition and thus have the potential to have a large impact in their focus *woredas*, even though the maximum potential may not be realized.

NEW APPROACHES AND LOOKING TO THE FUTURE

The Health Extension Program, the EOS, and the Extended EOS are critical nutrition programs in the country. The core strength of the landmark Health Extension Program is its mostly female cadre of health extension workers; more than 30,000 have now been trained and deployed throughout the country. The EOS and EEOS feature large-scale biannual campaigns providing vitamin A supplementation, deworming, and other interventions to under-five children and pregnant and lactating women.

The Ministry of Health is interested in pursuing a transition of EOS and EEOS program activities to the Health Extension Program. But first, appropriate preparatory activities need to be undertaken to ensure that the system is ready to assume responsibility for such large-scale activities. These include (a) analysis of how health extension workers handle their current workload and (b) implementation of a support structure in which sufficient and adequately trained community volunteers are in place to support them.

The prevailing institutional approach to treating severe acute malnutrition has revolved around health centers with a focus on inpatient rather than outpatient treatment. Because health centers are inaccessible for many Ethiopians, the Ministry of Health and its nutrition partners have started shifting treatment of severe acute malnutrition to health posts, where health extension workers are being trained in the community management of acute malnutrition on an outpatient basis. This change is expected to improve access to treatment for severe acute malnutrition because there are many more health posts than health centers in the country—one in every rural *kebele*. There would also be a significant reduction in the unit costs of treatment, which would enable more patients to be treated with the same amount of resources.

Public-private partnerships need to be explored and developed to strengthen many nutrition interventions. Such partnerships could develop interventions to fortify foods with micronutrients and to produce food and food products to treat moderate and severe malnutrition—such as ready-to-use therapeutic food and ready-to-use supplementary food. Complementary foods could also be developed using locally available inputs. In addition, public-private partnerships could support the entire value chain for the relevant inputs needed to produce these products.

POLICY RECOMMENDATIONS FOR NUTRITION INTERVENTIONS

The book offers the following recommendations for improving nutrition interventions in Ethiopia:

- Adequate monitoring and implementation of salt iodization activities are needed in the Afar region. The existing legislation for obligatory iodization of household salt needs to be reviewed, strengthened, and enforced.
- Except for a few urban areas, the EOS and EEOS programs have been scaled up to most parts of the country. Their very high benefit-cost ratios warrant their implementation everywhere.
- Deworming should be provided to pregnant and lactating women through the EOS and EEOS (potentially reaching most pregnant and lactating women in the country because of the wide coverage of these programs). This intervention has a very high benefit-cost ratio of 648.
- Before transition from the EOS and EEOS programs to the Health Extension Program can occur, adequate research is needed, and a well-functioning system of community volunteers who provide adequate support to health extension workers needs to be implemented.
- Advocacy and policy should be used to disseminate the message that nutrition security is affected by many other factors besides food security, including those related to health, water and sanitation, and appropriate child care and breast-feeding practices.
- Existing community volunteer programs should be scaled up with an emphasis on promoting good household practices (for example, optimal child care, breast-feeding, complementary feeding, and hand washing); these types of programs are highly beneficial relative to the

costs. They include the Community-Based Nutrition program, which so far has shown impressive results in Ethiopia and is modeled on large-scale successful programs implemented in countries like Thailand and Bangladesh.

- Most of the interventions and programs reviewed in this book have high benefit-to-cost ratios and should continue to be supported at current levels or expanded (if they are already being implemented in Ethiopia). In cases where the interventions are not currently being implemented in the country, one could consider introducing them. But factors such as on-the-ground feasibility as well as legislative and programmatic concerns also need to be considered.

- Certain interventions that were not reviewed as part of the benefit-cost analysis, but which have been shown elsewhere to have high impacts relative to their costs, should also be supported or introduced, perhaps initially on a pilot basis. They include home fortification of complementary foods with micronutrient powder and various cost-effective interventions in sectors other than health (for example, education, agriculture, and water and sanitation).

- The use and interpretation of nutrition data need to be improved by streamlining the collection and flow of data collected under the EOS and Community-Based Nutrition programs. These data need to be linked with agro-economic data as part of the country's Early Warning System. Also, the use of surveys and different sources of data needs to be enhanced to improve the capture and analysis of nutrition-related information (for example, by including additional indicators for priority nutrition areas in the Welfare Monitoring Surveys and Demographic and Health Surveys and by "triangulating" different sources of data—collected from surveys, health facilities, community volunteer activities, mass mobilizations, and other sources).

- A more flexible system of food aid targeting should be implemented that is more responsive to shocks and less focused on the division between the *woredas* designated in the past as food insecure and those designated as food secure.

- Vigorous efforts are needed to improve the coordination and harmonization of the different programs affecting nutrition in the country and the process of selecting beneficiary *woredas*. Gains could often be obtained by shifting some of the programs from *woredas* with a high concentration of major programs into *woredas* with high malnutrition rates but no major programs. When programs must overlap in a *woreda* or *kebele*, a harmonized process is needed for selecting the target beneficiaries for each program, as well as other harmonization efforts. A more equitable approach also needs to be designed for selecting beneficiary *woredas* rather than concentrating on a subset of highly favored *woredas* designated as food insecure.

- Pilot projects that focus on strengthening the linkages between programs in different sectors that affect nutrition should be implemented, such as the pilot project (mentioned above) that links core nutrition interventions with the Productive Safety Net Program. These pilots could then be evaluated with a view to scaling up successful ones in the future.

- Support of the Federal Emergency Nutrition Coordination Unit should be continued, as should support of regional ENCUs, tasking each of these with improving coordination and strengthening linkages among the different programs affecting nutrition in their region.

- Efforts to bring the institutional approach to treating severe acute malnutrition to the health post level should be continued, as should efforts to enhance the focus of this approach on outpatient treatment and the use of community volunteers. Pilot attempts to test new modalities along these lines should be implemented and evaluated carefully.

- Public-private partnerships should be enhanced to produce food and food products by using locally available resources for the treatment of moderate and severe malnutrition as well as for complementary feeding. Also, more work is needed to support the value chain of relevant food products and to develop interventions to fortify foods with micronutrients.

CHAPTER 1

Introduction

Ethiopia is Africa's oldest independent country and the second most populous country in Sub-Saharan Africa. Although it is perhaps best known for its periodic droughts and famines, civil conflicts, and the border war with neighboring Eritrea, Ethiopia has made significant progress in key indicators of human development over the past two decades: primary school enrollments have increased almost threefold, and child mortality has been cut in half. The poverty headcount, which stood at 60.5 percent in 1995, fell to 39 percent in 2005, the last year for which data are available.[1] Gross domestic product (GDP) per capita also remained steady for a decade beginning in 1994, increasing sharply more recently (see table 1.1). But income inequality has persisted in rural areas and worsened in urban areas (see figure 1.1).[2] The country ranks a dismal 157 out of 169 according to the United Nations Development Programme's human development index (UNDP 2010), and its population of 74 million in 2007 (based on the census conducted that year) is expected to grow about 60 percent by 2030 (World Bank 2007).

Ethiopia is divided into 11 geographic areas composed of nine regions and two city administrations. They are Addis Ababa, Afar, Amhara, Benshangul-Gumuz, Dire Dawa, Gambela, Harari, Oromia, Somali, Southern Nations, Nationalities, and Peoples (SNNP), and Tigray. Each region is divided into zones, which are further subdivided into *woredas* (equivalent to districts with local government) and then into *kebeles*, which are neighborhood associations or communities. On average, each *kebele* has a population of about 5,000.

Ethiopia is endowed with many natural resources, a varied climate, and diverse agro-ecological zones where a rich variety of agricultural products grow. Most Ethiopians (about 85 percent) live in rural areas, and

Table 1.1 GDP and Official Development Assistance in Ethiopia, 1994–2008

Year	GDP per capita (US$)	Official development assistance (US$ millions)
1994	112	1,063
1995	116	876
1996	126	816
1997	126	578
1998	118	660
1999	121	643
2000	124	686
2001	131	1,104
2002	129	1,297
2003	123	1,594
2004	136	1,806
2005	149	1,910
2006	161	1,947
2007	174	1,924
2008	189	2,508

Source: World Bank 1995–2009.
Note: GDP per capita is in constant 2000 U.S. dollars.

Figure 1.1 Gini Coefficient in Rural and Urban Areas in Ethiopia, 1995–2005

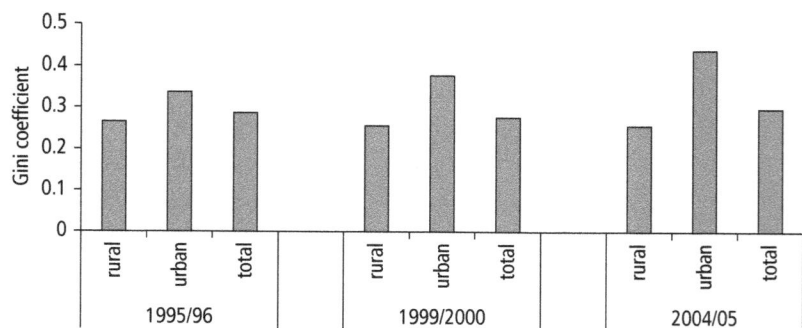

Source: Ethiopia, Ministry of Finance and Economic Development 2007.

most rely for their livelihood on rain-fed agriculture and rearing of live-stock. Without a doubt, Ethiopia has the capacity to produce sufficient food for its population and even for export (Benson 2006). Nevertheless, Ethiopia currently must import food to feed its people.

MALNUTRITION: DEFINITION, CAUSES, AND CONSEQUENCES

Malnutrition is the "nonincome face of poverty." The first United Nations Millennium Development Goal, which calls on countries to halve the number of people living in poverty between 1990 and 2015,[3] uses reducing malnutrition (that is, halving the percentage of children under five who are underweight) as one of the indicators of progress. Undernourished children are more likely to have lower educational achievement, and maternal and child undernutrition is associated with lower economic status in adulthood, with effects that spill over to future generations.

The term "malnutrition" is often associated with images of starving children who are suffering from severe acute malnutrition—with their bellies bloated and their arms and legs painfully boney. Malnutrition can indeed refer to short-term acute malnutrition. But more often, malnutrition is chronic and lifelong, a highly preventable condition that begins in early childhood and continues into old age, devastating one generation and passing the miserable legacy on to the next.

Chronic malnutrition occurs when insufficient nutrients are ingested to sustain the body. More than just calories, fat, and protein, nutrients also include the vitamins and minerals required for proper body function. For example, a child may consume sufficient calories for energy, but insufficient zinc for proper growth and immune function. This deficiency could be due to a diet lacking in variety or to recurrent bouts of diarrhea, resulting in the depletion of key minerals. The most common conditions related to malnutrition include intrauterine growth restriction, stunting (low height-for-age), wasting (low weight-for-height), deficiency in micronutrients (especially folic acid, vitamin A, iodine, iron, and zinc), low birthweight, high maternal mortality, various types of anemia, failure to grow, xerophthalmia (vitamin A deficiency blindness), and even obesity. All of these conditions can have negative consequences for health, physical growth, mental function, reproduction, and even future work productivity and capacity.

This study uses underweight as an indicator of nutrition status and disaggregates this indicator into its component parts of stunting and wasting. Stunting is a measure of long-term, or chronic, malnutrition, while wasting is a measure of more transient, or short-term, acute malnutrition. Stunting is a permanent condition after a certain point. A stunted child *will* become a stunted adult. Wasting is a transient and reversible condition. Its onset may be due to a sudden shortage or withholding of food, among other causes. Underweight is a composite measure of stunting and wasting. When measures of stunting and wasting are available, they are reported separately.

Most undernutrition begins during pregnancy—referred to as intrauterine growth retardation—and the first two years of life, leading to higher infant mortality rates, stunting, low birthweight, and premature delivery. Early damage is irreversible after the child reaches 24 months of age; after that time, the rates of increase in stunting and underweight prevalence level off (Bryce and others 2008; see figure 1.2). In Ethiopia, the height deficits in malnourished children can be as much as 11 centimeters by 24 months of age (Ethiopia PROFILES and AED 2005). The two-year "window of opportunity" is therefore a universal key period for nutrition interventions.

For adults, a malnourished woman is more likely than an adequately nourished one to have a low-birthweight baby and to die during delivery. Low-birthweight babies are more likely to become stunted, and a stunted girl has a greater likelihood of complications during pregnancy and delivery, as well as a greater chance of having a low-birthweight baby—thus continuing the intergenerational cycle of malnutrition (see figure 1.3).

The underlying causes of malnutrition are many and basic. A child's health has a great impact on potential nutritional intake. Infectious disease plays a large role in determining a child's nutrition status because

Figure 1.2   Stunting and Underweight Rates in Under-Five Children in Ethiopia, by Age, 2005

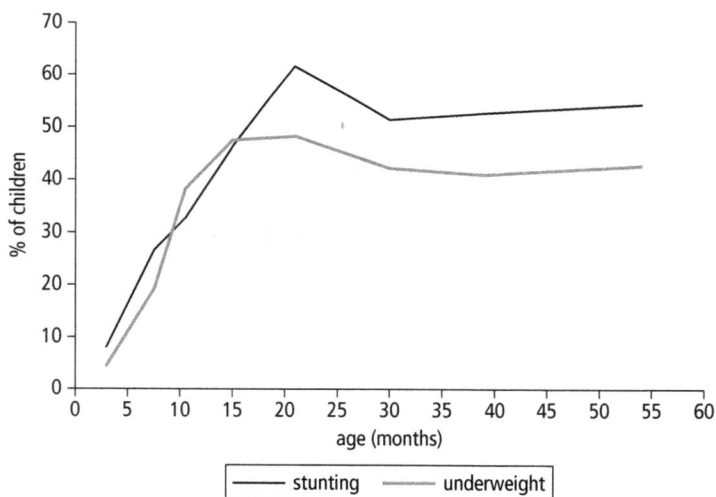

Source: CSA and ORC Macro 2006.
Note: Figure depicts total stunting and total underweight rates (percentage of children with height-for-age and weight-for-age, respectively, that is equal to or smaller than the value corresponding to two standard deviations below the median of the global reference population).

Figure 1.3   Intergenerational Link of Malnutrition

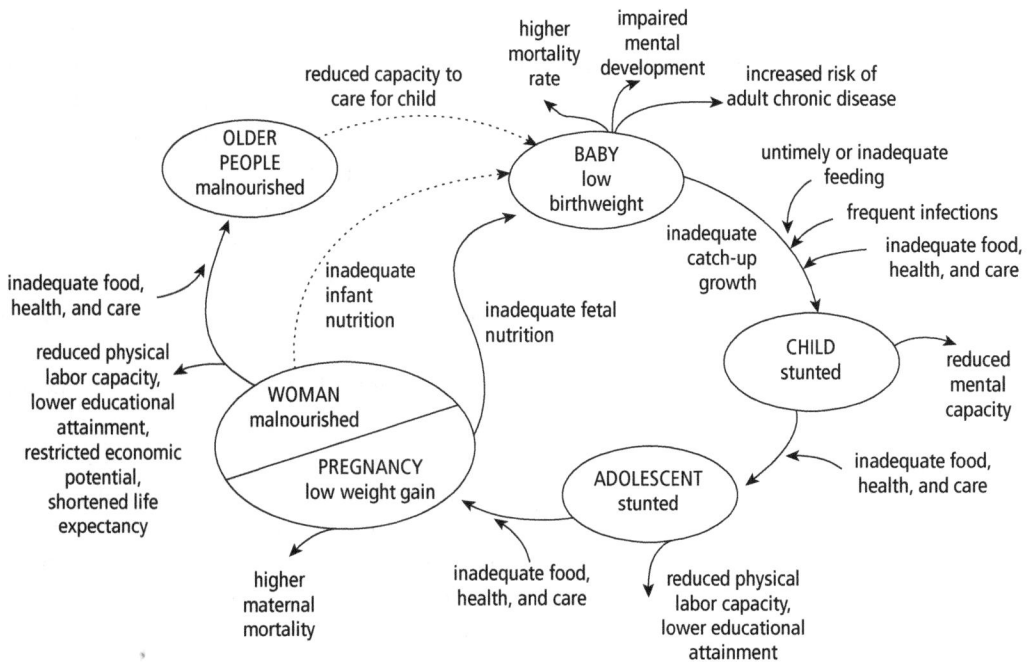

Source: UN ACC-SCN and IFPRI 2000.

continual bouts of disease deplete the store of nutrients in the body and can affect the quality and quantity of nutrient absorption. Environmental factors also make Ethiopia a hazardous environment for children. Livestock are housed in the same room where children sleep, and smoke hangs in the air from cooking fires burned in the home. A mother's education level, rural infrastructure, access to information, cultural beliefs and practices, and access to health care and potable water are all important factors affecting nutrition status.

Because malnutrition has many causes and manifestations, a range of indicators is necessary to measure it accurately and assess its prevalence. Rates of stunting, wasting, and underweight among children less than five years of age are commonly used indicators, referring, respectively, to abnormally low height-for-age, weight-for-height, and weight-for-age. The extent of stunting in a population or population subgroup is typically measured using either (a) the total stunting rate (alternatively termed the global stunting rate or simply the stunting rate) or (b) the severe stunting rate. Wasting and underweight rates have similar refinements.[4] The total stunting rate is the percentage of children under five with height-for-age equal to or smaller than the value corresponding to two standard deviations below the median of the global reference population. The severe stunting rate is the percentage of children under five with height-for-age equal to or smaller than the value corresponding to three standard deviations below the median of the global reference population.[5] Similar definitions apply for the rates of wasting and underweight. The reference population for these definitions is based on a distribution of heights, weights, and ages considered normal by international standards. The standardized measures are used worldwide, so rates of wasting and stunting are comparable across countries and regions. Unless otherwise stated, the rate of stunting, wasting, or underweight in this book refers to the total rate for children under five.

The internationally accepted definition of a "normal" reference population, with associated "normal" age-specific distributions of height and weight, originally was based on standards developed by the National Center for Health Statistics (NCHS) in the United States. Although the World Health Organization has recently developed new malnutrition standards, NCHS standards are often still used, especially to examine trends or to make comparisons across time. The malnutrition statistics cited throughout this book are all based on NCHS standards.

While some correlation exists between stunting and wasting rates, the correlation can vary by region. Areas with high stunting rates often have relatively low wasting rates and vice versa, as shown by the data presented in chapter 2. Nevertheless, stunting and wasting are related. A child's normal linear growth (or retarded growth, often leading to stunting) is adversely affected by repeated bouts of illness and inadequate dietary intake, as well as deficiencies in essential micronutrients, including zinc. Stunting is therefore an indicator of the cumulative impact of illness and poor dietary intake over time in a surviving child. Acute weight loss in a child, or wasting, is caused by insufficient intake of food or poor absorption of nutrients, mostly due to acute illness. Wasting directly affects linear growth and, in the absence of catch-up growth, ultimately leads to stunting. Therefore, while geographic correlation may be weak, the two indicators are related, and the correlation potentially can be demonstrated in a longitudinal analysis.

FOOD SECURITY VERSUS NUTRITION SECURITY

To understand malnutrition and its consequences properly, one must understand the difference between food security and nutrition security. Food security is the "availability, access, and utilization of sufficient food by all people at all times for an active healthy life" (Benson 2006). Nutrition security is more complex. It occurs "when a household attains secure access to food coupled with a sanitary environment, adequate health services, and knowledgeable care" (Benson 2006). Although a family's nutrition security is affected by its ability to access food, other factors also affect nutrition security, including appropriate breast-feeding, other feeding and child care practices, hygiene, health status and health interventions, immunizations, the perceived status of women in society, and adequate water and sanitation.

While food security plays a crucial role in the nutrition status of a country, alleviating and preventing malnutrition require sustained multisector interventions that address the range of factors affecting an individual's nutrition status. Successful interventions focus on food issues, proper child care behavior, optimal breast-feeding and complementary feeding for children under two, hygiene, education, improved access to potable water, medical care, and mosquito nets, among other interventions. Programs focused on improving food security have a better chance of decreasing malnutrition in a targeted area if the associated nutrition security factors are assessed and addressed concurrently. For example, providing more food to vulnerable households will increase the available calories per person, but will not resolve the problem of contaminated water causing high rates of diarrhea or any other factors leading to malnutrition in vulnerable households.

Stunting and wasting rates—which are commonly used indicators of malnutrition—are linked to food security. Wasting is provoked by food scarcity or withholding and by poor absorption of food; it is often transient in nature. Highly food-insecure areas tend to have higher wasting rates than food-secure areas. However, stunting rates in poorer countries are often equally high in food-insecure *and* food-secure areas because stunting incorporates the cumulative impact of illness and inadequate dietary intake in a surviving child over time. The weak correlation between food security and nutrition security—especially as measured by the rate of stunting—is described in chapter 2 using Ethiopia-specific data.

Stunting and even wasting rates can often be substantially improved— even without changing the amount of food provided—by teaching appropriate feeding and child care practices, providing immunizations, and improving water and sanitation, among other interventions. Large-scale nutrition programs in Thailand and several states in India and Bangladesh have demonstrated the success of a range of interventions other than food provision (Mason and others 2006). For example, in many of these large-scale programs, children are typically weighed by trained community volunteers every one to three months. If a child is underweight, the immediate recourse is not to provide food but rather to counsel the mother and other caregivers on appropriate breast-feeding, other feeding, hygiene, and child care. The situation is monitored over time, and if the child continues to be abnormally underweight, only then is food provided.

A SNAPSHOT OF MALNUTRITION IN ETHIOPIA

Malnutrition is a major health problem affecting children and adults in Ethiopia (Benson 2006). In poorer countries like Ethiopia, it is a contributing factor in more than 50 percent of all child deaths (Pelletier and Frongillo 2003).

There are many causes of malnutrition in Ethiopia. Some are related to altitude and climate. Ethiopia is a unique mix of highland and arid areas. In arid or semiarid areas, which are less than 1,600 meters above sea level and cover nearly 40 percent of the country, agricultural production levels can be low, and the dry climate has a negative impact on food availability, which in turn has a negative impact on nutrition security. Ethiopia's arid and semiarid areas are in the northern, northeastern, and eastern lowland regions. Another 54 percent of the country is made up of submoist, moist, and subhumid highland zones. These mid- to high-altitude areas fall in the northern, central, western, and eastern regions, enjoy a growing period of 61 to 240 days, and are the most important rain-fed agriculture and livestock production areas (although some important agricultural zones in the highlands are suffering from serious natural resource degradation). More than 80 percent of the rural population lives in highland areas, where harsh living conditions can lead to higher numbers of low-birthweight babies due to the increased need of women and children for calories and iron (see map 1.1).

Many other factors also affect malnutrition levels in Ethiopia. Recurrent shocks such as droughts, floods, and civil unrest disrupt and diminish livelihoods and, therefore, a population's resilience to shocks.[6] Agricultural practices are often inadequate or inappropriate. The majority of agriculture is rain-fed despite the great potential for irrigation systems (see map 1.2), and more than 60 percent of farming households cultivate less than 1 hectare of land, which is too small to sustain a family. Furthermore, inadequate transportation prevents access to markets and employment opportunities. An estimated 80 percent of Ethiopians live a half-day walk from the nearest all-weather road (Development Researchers' Network and others 2004).

Map 1.1 Elevation Map of Ethiopia

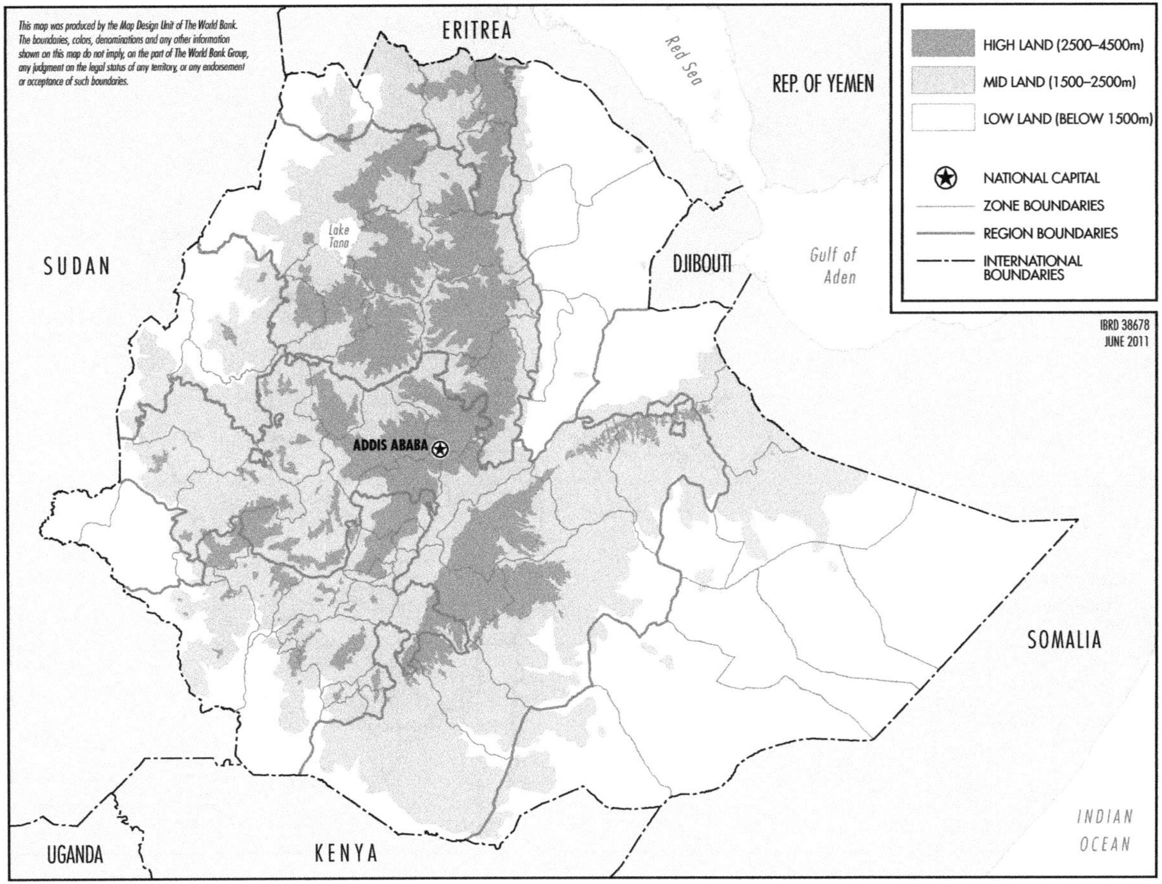
This map was produced by the Map Design Unit of The World Bank. The boundaries, colors, denominations and any other information shown on this map do not imply, on the part of The World Bank Group, any judgment on the legal status of any territory, or any endorsement or acceptance of such boundaries.
ERITREA
Red Sea
REP. OF YEMEN
SUDAN
Lake Tana
DJIBOUTI
Gulf of Aden
ADDIS ABABA
SOMALIA
UGANDA
KENYA
INDIAN OCEAN
HIGH LAND (2500–4500m)
MID LAND (1500–2500m)
LOW LAND (BELOW 1500m)
NATIONAL CAPITAL
ZONE BOUNDARIES
REGION BOUNDARIES
INTERNATIONAL BOUNDARIES
IBRD 38678
JUNE 2011

Source: World Bank.

Map 1.2 Irrigation Potential in Ethiopia

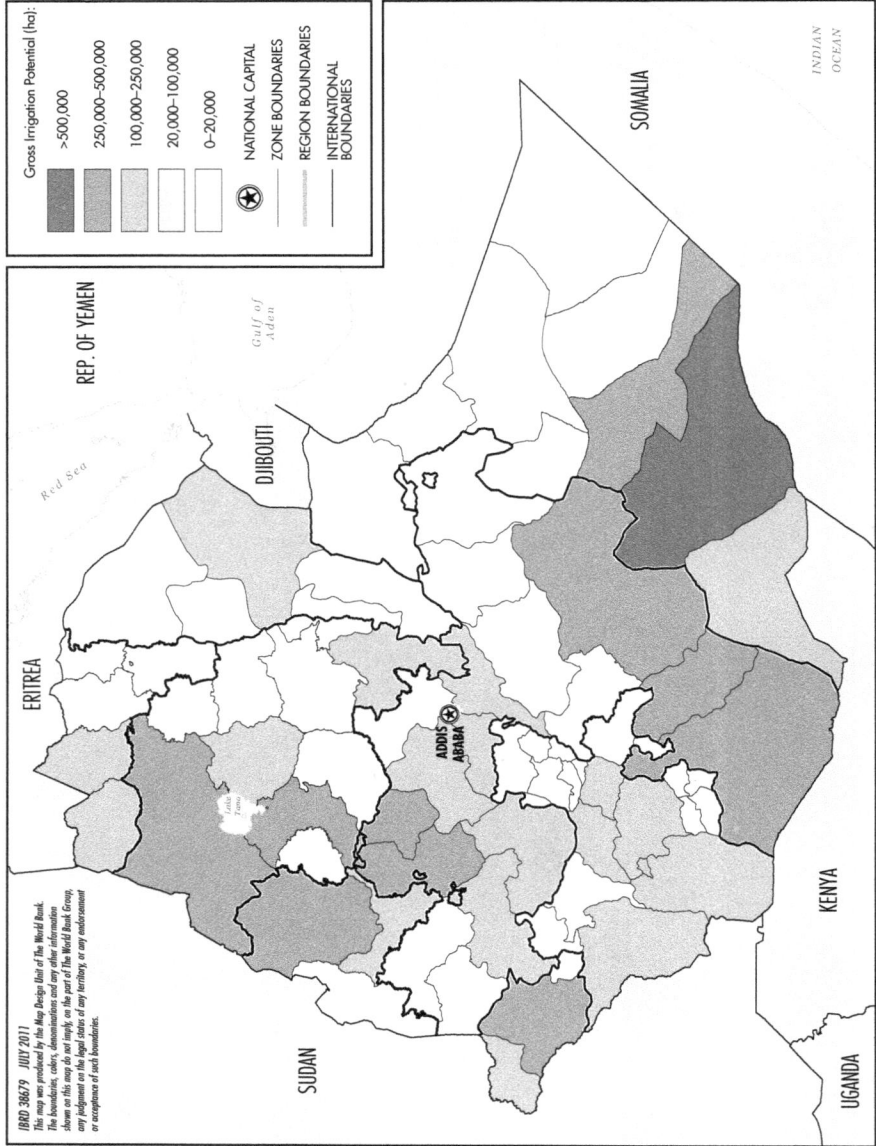

Source: World Bank, drawing from work by the Ministry of Water Resources, Ethiopia.

Figure 1.4 presents the United Nations Children's Fund (UNICEF) conceptual framework illustrating the causes of childhood malnutrition in Ethiopia. It confirms a central theme of this book: *nutrition insecurity is related to—but is not the same as—food insecurity.* A multisectoral approach is therefore needed to address nutrition insecurity.

MICRONUTRIENT INDICATORS

Some of the most widespread disorders in Ethiopia are micronutrient deficiencies, all of which result in illness and billions of dollars in lost earnings for the poorest households. A high proportion of the population is afflicted with iodine deficiency disorders, vitamin A deficiency, and iron deficiency anemia. Iron deficiency anemia, iodine deficiency disorders, and stunting alone are projected to cost Ethiopia about 10 percent of GDP

Figure 1.4   UNICEF Conceptual Framework for Causes of Childhood Malnutrition, Adapted for Ethiopia

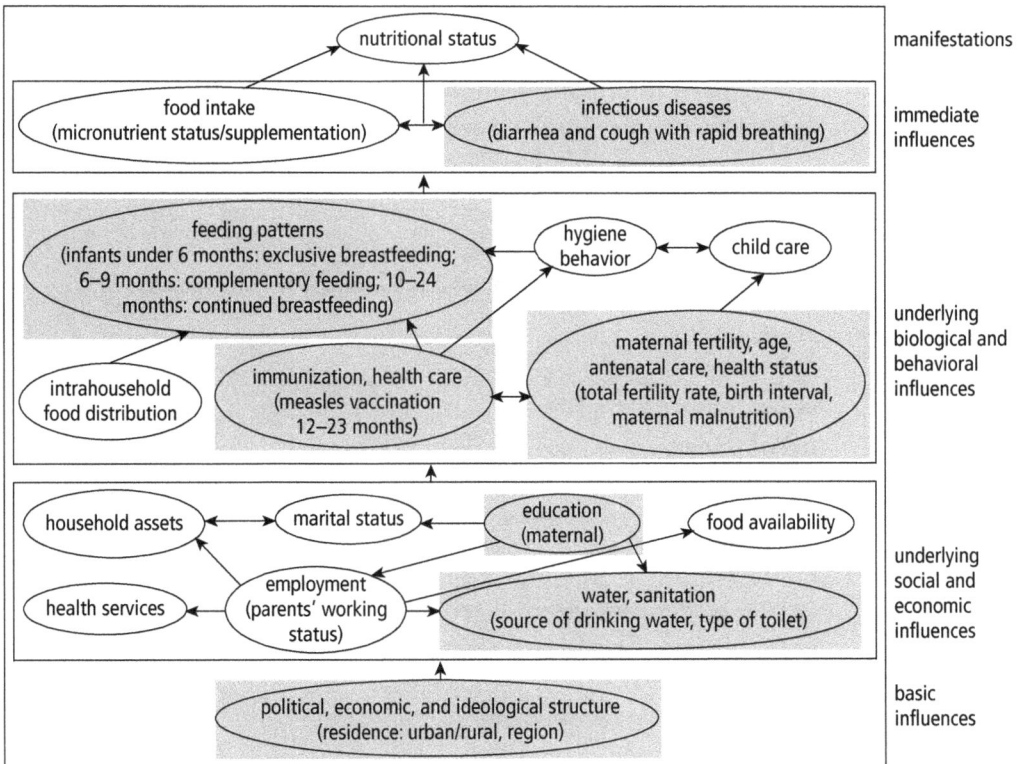

Source: CSA, USAID, and ORC Macro 2001.

(about US$12 billion) between 2006 and 2015.[7] Using data from the 2005 Ethiopia Demographic and Health Survey, table 1.2 provides a nutritional snapshot of the country's rural and urban populations, based on the latest available data.

Iodine deficiency disorders decrease individuals' mental abilities and permanently affect their mental capacity, thus diminishing the productive capacity of a society as well (see table 1.3). Although iodine deficiency disorders can be prevented by the use of iodized salt—a simple and cost-effective intervention—Ethiopia's current use is very low. Only about one-fifth of households used adequately iodized salt in 2005,[8] a *decrease* from 2000, when about 28 percent did, according to successive Demographic and Health Surveys. A separate survey conducted in 2005 by the Ethiopian Health and Nutrition Research Institute concluded that only 4 percent of households used adequately iodized salt (EHNRI 2005). While a discrepancy exists between these different sources of data on the use of iodized salt in Ethiopia, clearly the use is extremely low, whichever data source is used. According to the Ethiopian Health and Nutrition Research Institute survey, the prevalence of iodine deficiency disorders—based on measurement of urinary iodine levels, which are considered a more reliable method of detection than the prevalence of goiter—was alarmingly high at 80 percent.

Vitamin A contributes significantly to immune system function. Vitamin A deficiency can lead to growth retardation, susceptibility to infection, and blindness (see table 1.3). Distributing vitamin A biannually has great

Table 1.2 Nutrition Indicators in Rural and Urban Areas of Ethiopia, 2005
% of the population

Indicator	Urban	Rural
Adequately iodized salt in the home	21.0	19.7
Children 6–35 months of age (last-born only) who ate foods rich in vitamin A in the previous 24 hours	44.2	24.5
Women with children less than three years of age who ate foods rich in vitamin A in the previous 24 hours	54.4	31.5
Children 6–59 months of age who received a vitamin A supplement in the six months preceding the survey	62.0	44.5
Women who reported night blindness (a sign of vitamin A deficiency) in previous pregnancy	3.1	6.4
Children 6–59 months of age with anemia	46.8	54.0
Women with anemia	17.8	28.2

Source: 2005 Demographic and Health Survey (CSA and ORC Macro 2006).

Table 1.3 Consequences of Malnutrition in Ethiopia

Indicator	Health consequences	Economic consequences
Stunting	Decelerated growth, decelerated brain development, lower productivity as a stunted adult, higher rate of maternal mortality for stunted women, 1.4% decrease in activity for 1% decrease in height	Br 18 billion (about US$2 billion) was lost between 2000 and 2005 from stunting;[b] an estimated 3% of GDP will be lost between 2006 and 2015 due to stunting.
Vitamin A deficiency	Night blindness and spontaneous abortion in women; retarded growth; greater susceptibility to infection, night blindness, and total blindness in children; 23% of child deaths attributed to vitamin A deficiency	61% of Ethiopian children suffer from vitamin A deficiency.
Iodine deficiency disorders	Goiter, hypothyroidism, impaired mental function, stillbirths, abortions, congenital abnormalities, and neurological cretinism;[a] lower IQ by 10–15 points	4.1 million Ethiopian children were born with intellectual disabilities between 2000 and 2005. Another 15 million will be born with intellectual disabilities between 2006 and 2015. Between 2000 and 2005, Br 11.3 billion (about US$1.3 billion) were lost due to iodine deficiency disorders, and an estimated 4.4% of GDP will be lost due to these disorders between 2006 and 2015.
Iron deficiency anemia	Decreased blood flow to body organs and tissues resulting in decreased energy, decreased ability to concentrate and impaired cognitive development, increased maternal mortality, lower IQ by about 9 points	54% of children 6–59 months old and 27% of women in Ethiopia have iron deficiency anemia; an estimated 2.5% of GDP will be lost between 2006 and 2015 due to iron deficiency anemia.
Zinc deficiency	Loss of appetite, stunting, skin rashes, slower wound healing	Zinc status is very difficult to assess; however, an estimated 21.7% of the population is at risk for deficiency (Hotz and Brown 2004).

Source: Ethiopia PROFILES and AED 2005.
a. Neurological cretinism is an untreatable or irreversible form of iodine deficiency that is passed on to a fetus and leads to mental handicap, stunted growth, malformations in the bones, and early death.
b. Ethiopia's currency is the birr (Br).

potential to reduce child deaths; meta-analysis of field trials indicates that this protocol can reduce overall child mortality by 23 percent (Bhutta and others 2008).

The prevalence of vitamin A deficiency in Ethiopia is strikingly high, estimated at 27 percent (Ethiopia PROFILES and AED 2005). Despite the availability of foods rich in vitamin A such as pumpkin, spinach, eggs, mangos, carrots, and organ meats, the percentage of Ethiopians who consume these foods is relatively low, especially in rural areas. According to the 2005 Demographic and Health Survey, only 24.5 percent of rural children 6–35 months of age among last-born children consumed foods rich in vitamin A in the 24 hours preceding the survey (table 1.2). The corresponding percentage for women with children less than three years of age was only slightly higher, at 31.5 percent. Low intake of vitamin A by women with young children implies low levels of vitamin A in breast milk.

Iron deficiency anemia is the primary cause of anemia and is found in 53.5 percent of children 6–59 months of age and 26.6 percent of women in Ethiopia. Iron deficiency anemia leads to lower productivity and decreased ability to concentrate, both of which have costly economic consequences (see table 1.3). While the prevalence of iron deficiency anemia in Ethiopia is high, it is not as high as in some other Sub-Saharan African countries, probably due to Ethiopians' consumption of *teff*, a local grain rich in iron.

BREAST-FEEDING INDICATORS

An estimated 50,000 Ethiopian infants die each year because of poor breast-feeding practices with a range of harmful effects—18 percent of all infant deaths annually (Ethiopia PROFILES and AED 2005). The World Health Organization and other experts recommend that (a) breast-feeding should be initiated within one hour of delivery and no other liquids or foods should be given to the child, (b) no other foods or liquids aside from breast milk should be given until the age of six months, and (c) at the age of six months, complementary foods should be introduced while breast-feeding continues.[9] But child-feeding practices are heavily and sometimes adversely influenced by culture, tradition, and the availability of alternatives to breast milk.

A large proportion of women in Ethiopia do not undertake appropriate breast-feeding practices. About a third of babies are not breast-fed within one hour of birth (see table 1.4), and significant proportions of women continue to breast-feed exclusively (that is, without complementary feeding) well after their babies turn six months old, even though at that age breast milk alone cannot provide sufficient calories, protein, vitamins, and minerals to the infant.

Table 1.4 Breast-Feeding Practices in Rural and Urban Areas of Ethiopia, 2005
percent

Indicator	Urban	Rural
Babies ever breast-fed	95.0	96.0
Babies breast-fed within one hour of birth	64.8	69.5
Babies given prelacteal feeds	38.3	28.0

Source: 2005 Demographic and Health Survey (CSA and ORC Macro 2006).
Note: Prelacteal feeds are defined here as anything other than breast milk given to a newborn before the initiation of breast-feedings (for example, animal milk, water, and tea).

Urban babies tend to fare worse than rural babies in Ethiopia (see table 1.4). Where breast milk alternatives are more readily available (mostly in urban areas), they are more often used. Most inappropriate breast-feeding behavior is therefore due to lack of knowledge rather than to practical or financial constraints. In the absence of public information on the benefits of breast-feeding, women will continue to undertake sub-optimal breast-feeding practices, even though exclusive breast-feeding is the cheapest and healthiest alternative up to six months of age.

Figure 1.5 compares breast-feeding practices in 2000 and 2005 and shows a mix of trends. The percentage of mothers providing complementary foods to infants after six months of age improved over time, but the number of infants exclusively breast-fed for the first six months of life decreased. The increase in the percentage of children six to nine months of age who were not breast-fed at all is a worrisome trend.

Figure 1.5   Infant Feeding Practices in Ethiopia, by Age, 2000 and 2005

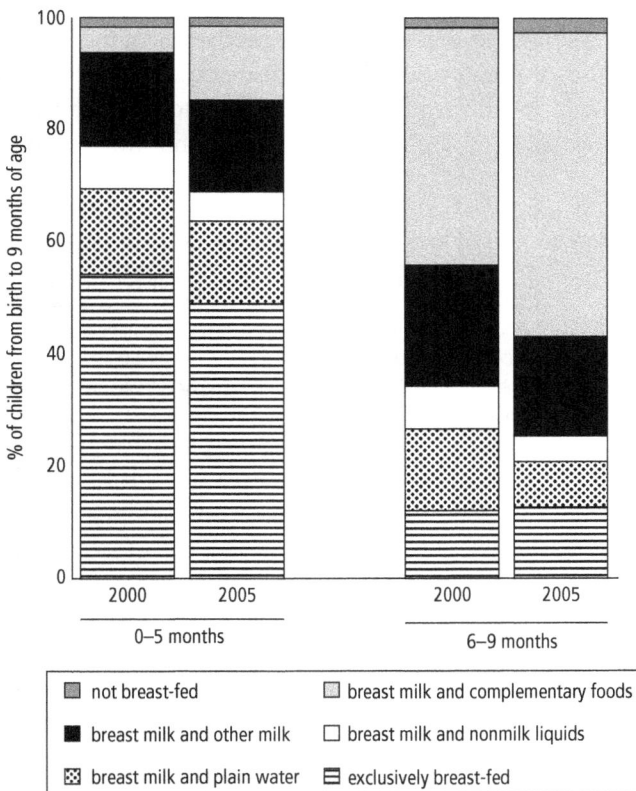

Source: 2000, 2005 Demographic and Health Survey (CSA and ORC Macro 2006).

Although difficult to quantify, the negative consequences of inappropriate breast-feeding practices are far-reaching and extensive, yet nonetheless remain underrepresented in the data. Table 1.5 shows the three key optimal breast-feeding practices and the associated negative consequences when they are not practiced.

Community volunteer programs that educate women about appropriate breast-feeding practices have been effective in changing behavior and are quite cost-effective. For example, chapter 3 shows how breast-feeding practices have been successfully changed by community health promoters who are part of Essential Services for Health in Ethiopia, a nongovernmental organization.

ETHIOPIA FROM A REGIONAL AND WORLD PERSPECTIVE

Ethiopia's level of nutrition security—or rather its level of nutrition insecurity—is best understood in the context of neighboring countries. In table 1.6, indicators of water supply, sanitation, and immunization coverage are presented for Ethiopia, its neighbors, Sub-Saharan Africa as a whole, and other developing countries. While the percentage of the Ethiopian population with access to safe drinking water increased from 1996 to 2004 (see figure 1.6), table 1.6 shows that access to adequate water and sanitation is significantly worse in Ethiopia than in most neighboring countries.

Table 1.5 Consequences of Inappropriate Breast-Feeding Practices

Optimal practices	Consequence of suboptimal practices
Initiation of breast-feeding within one hour of birth	Precious colostrum is lost, depriving an infant of immune-boosting antibodies and other substances critical for initial development; dehydration and other problems result if a child is given nothing or is given prelacteal feeds, which can induce diarrhea.[a]
Exclusive breast-feeding for six months	Introduction of other liquids or foods before the gut is developed increases intestinal bleeding, food infections, and diarrhea. Nonsterile water introduces infectious microbes to a newborn baby's system before it is sufficiently developed.
Introduction of complementary foods	At six months of age and afterward, breast milk alone is no longer a sufficient source of calories, fat, protein, vitamins, and minerals. Growth failure begins at six months if there is inadequate nutrition and energy intake from complementary foods.

Source: Authors.
a. Colostrum is the "first milk" that comes from the mother. It is critical for a newborn's development and includes, among others, key antibodies, nutrients, components of the innate immune system, growth factors, and antimicrobial factors. Prelacteal feeds are defined here as anything other than breast milk given to a newborn before the initiation of breast-feeding, such as animal milk, water, and tea.

Table 1.6 Water Supply, Sanitation, and Immunization Indicators for Ethiopia and Elsewhere

Country or region	% of population using improved water source, 2006	% of population using improved sanitation facilities, 2006	% of children at age one year with these immunizations, 2008		
			DPT3[a]	Polio3	Measles
Ethiopia	42	11	81	75	74
Eritrea	60	5	97	96	95
Kenya	57	42	85	85	90
Somalia	29	23	31	24	24
Sudan	70	35	86	85	79
Sub-Saharan Africa	58	31	72	71	72
Least developed countries	62	33	78	77	76

Source: UNICEF 2009.
a. Diphtheria, pertussis, and tetanus.

Figure 1.6 Percentage of the Population in Rural and Urban Areas of Ethiopia with Access to Safe Water Sources, 1996–2004

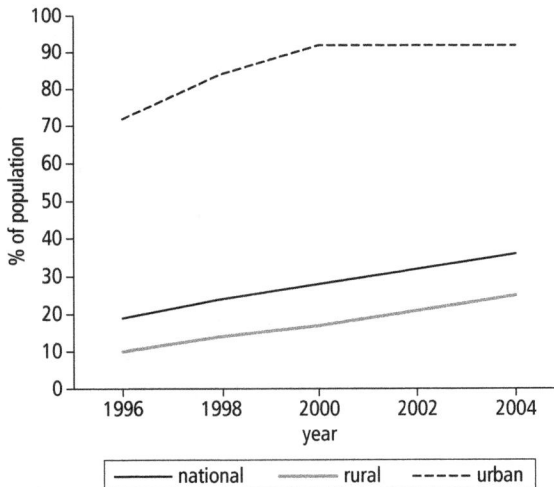

Source: Ethiopia, Ministry of Finance and Economic Development 2007.

Table 1.7 shows nutrition and health indicators for various countries and regions before the recent global food price and financial crises. The neonatal mortality and stunting rates were already substantially higher in Ethiopia before the crisis than in neighboring and other developing countries. Wasting, however, was not especially high by regional and Sub-Saharan African standards. The under-five mortality rate is lower in Ethiopia

Table 1.7   Health and Nutrition Indicators for Ethiopia and Elsewhere

Country or region	Under-five mortality rate (per 1,000 live births), 2008	Infant mortality rate (per 1,000 live births), 2008	Neonatal mortality rate (per 1,000 live births), 2004	Stunting rate (%)	Wasting rate (%)
Ethiopia	109	69	41	47	11
Eritrea	58	41	21	44	15
Kenya	128	81	34	35	8
Somalia	200	119	49	42	13
Sudan	109	70	27	40	16
Sub-Saharan Africa	144	86	40	42	10
Least developed countries	129	82	40	45	11

Source: UNICEF 2009.

than in Kenya and Somalia and is lower than the Sub-Saharan African average. Infant mortality rates fare slightly worse, with only Somalia and Sudan having higher rates. Ethiopia is among the few countries worldwide with especially high overall malnutrition rates (see maps 1.3 and 1.4).

For many indicators, the most recent available data are for the years before the global food price crisis of 2007 and the first half of 2008. During the crisis, food prices in Ethiopia rose sharply, but they have fallen significantly since then. Increases in food prices generally lead to a deterioration in the quality of diet and a reduction in the consumption of micronutrient-rich foods (Action Against Hunger 2009). Detailed analysis of the long- and short-term effects of the food crisis should be done in the near future using data, when available, from the nationally representative Demographic and Health Surveys and Welfare Monitoring Surveys, among other sources.

The figures on stunting and wasting for Ethiopia that are presented in table 1.7 were taken from the 2005 Demographic and Health Survey. These health and nutrition indicators are the most suitable for cross-country comparisons, but not for comparisons over a long period of time because surveys were conducted only in 2000 and 2005. Data from successive Welfare Monitoring Surveys—which use the same nutritional indicators and reference population as the Demographic and Health Survey (with minor differences in data collection methods)—were used to compare outcomes over long periods of time (for example, table 1.9 and figures 1.7 to 1.9). The figures for stunting from the latest 2004 Welfare Monitoring Survey are similar to those from the 2005 Demographic and Health Survey. But according to the 2004 Welfare Monitoring Survey, the wasting rate is 8.3 percent, significantly lower than the 10.5 percent rate found in the 2005 Demographic and Health Survey.

Map 1.3   Prevalence of Underweight among Under-Five Children, Worldwide

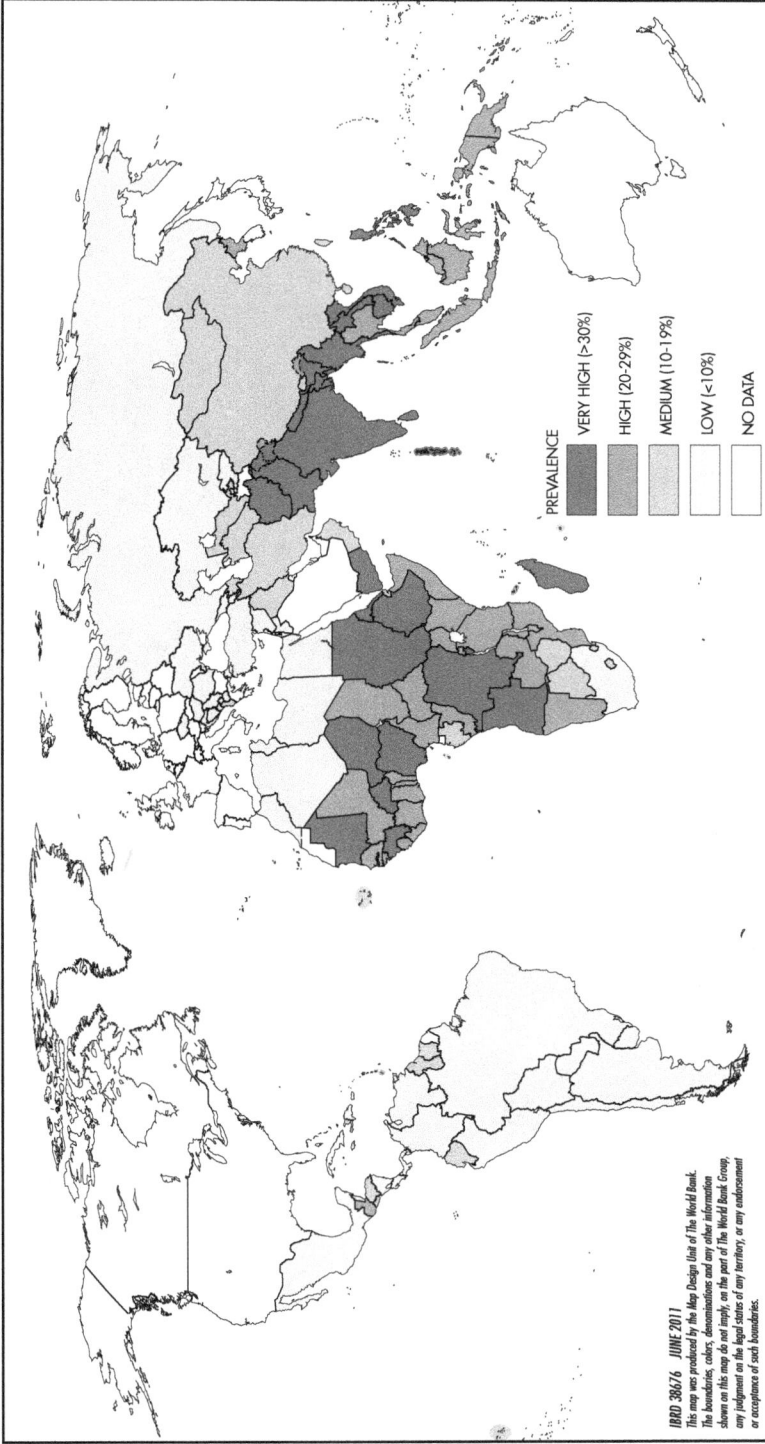

PREVALENCE

VERY HIGH (>30%)

HIGH (20–29%)

MEDIUM (10–19%)

LOW (<10%)

NO DATA

IBRD 38676   JUNE 2011

This map was produced by the Map Design Unit of The World Bank.
The boundaries, colors, denominations and any other information
shown on this map do not imply, on the part of The World Bank Group,
any judgment on the legal status of any territory, or any endorsement
or acceptance of such boundaries.

Source: World Health Organization, Global Database on Child Growth and Malnutrition.

Map 1.4 Prevalence of Stunting among Under-Five Children, Worldwide

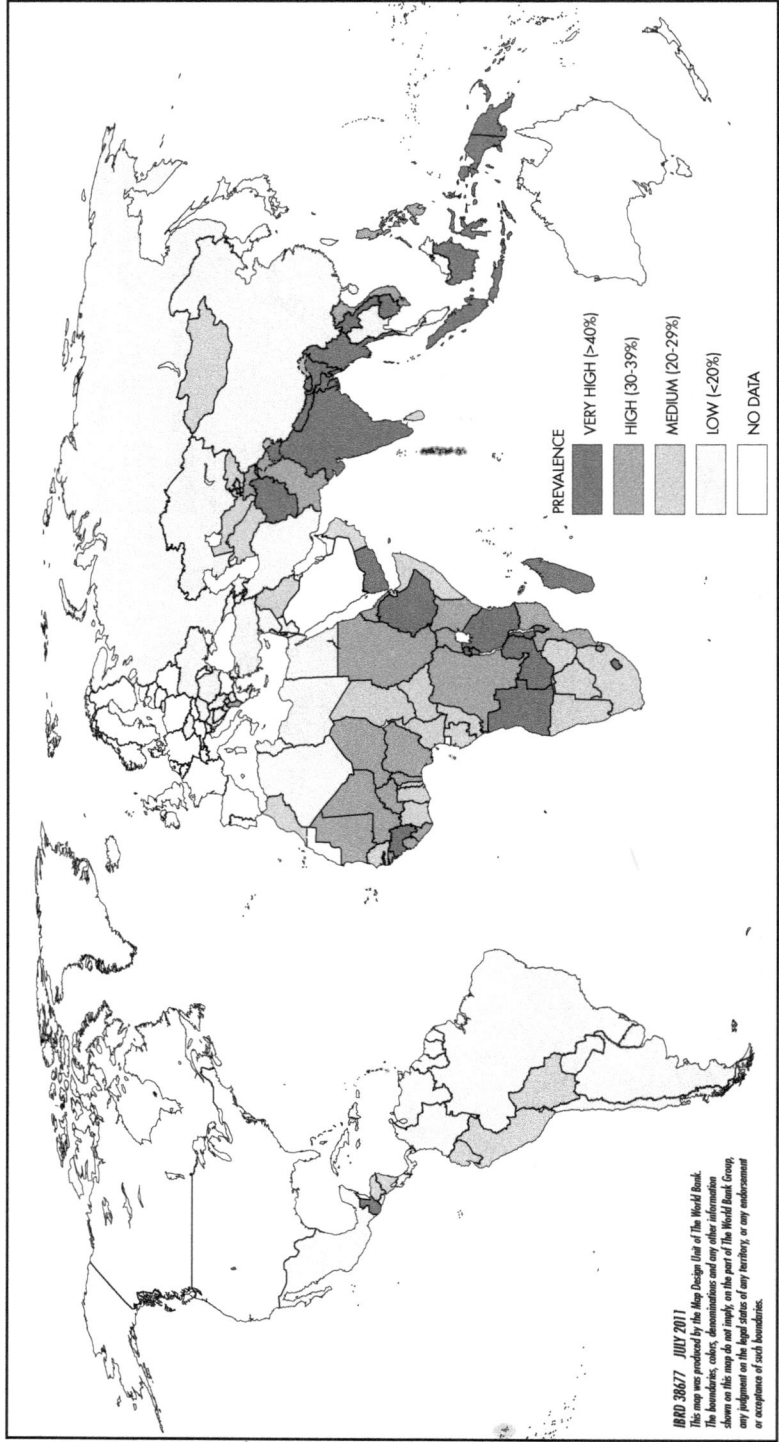

PREVALENCE

VERY HIGH (>40%)

HIGH (30-39%)

MEDIUM (20-29%)

LOW (<20%)

NO DATA

IBRD 38677 JULY 2011
This map was produced by the Map Design Unit of The World Bank.
The boundaries, colors, denominations and any other information
shown on this map do not imply, on the part of The World Bank Group,
any judgment on the legal status of any territory, or any endorsement
or acceptance of such boundaries.

Source: World Health Organization, Global Database on Child Growth and Malnutrition.

ETHIOPIA'S NUTRITION INDICATORS OVER TIME

Over time, Ethiopia's indicators have improved. In 1960, the under-five mortality rate was an astounding 294 deaths per 1,000 live births. By 2008, it had decreased 63 percent to 109 (see table 1.8). Despite this precipitous drop in child deaths, Ethiopia's under-five mortality rate remains at unacceptably high levels.

Stunting rates in both urban and rural areas have declined substantially over the past 10 years (see table 1.9 and figure 1.7), according to data from successive Welfare Monitoring Surveys.[10] This decline occurred more rapidly in urban than in rural areas. However, the national trend for wasting has been mixed in the medium term (table 1.9 and figure 1.8). The national prevalence of child wasting rose slightly from 7.3 percent in 1996 to 9.6 percent in 2000, before falling to 8.3 percent in 2004. The favorable trend in stunting prevalence, which fell from 65.7 percent in 1996 to 46.9 percent in 2004, is encouraging, given that the stunting rate was stubbornly high—among the highest in the world (Christiaensen and Alderman 2004)—for most of the 1980s and 1990s. Data from earlier Welfare Monitoring

Table 1.8 Mortality Rate among Under-Five Children in Ethiopia, 1960–2008

deaths per 1,000 live births

Year	Under-five mortality rate
1960	294
1995	195
1996	177
1997	175
1998	173
1999	176
2001	172
2002	171
2003	169
2004	166
2005	164
2006	123
2007	119
2008	109

Source: UNICEF 1997–2009.

Table 1.9   Prevalence of Wasting, Stunting, and Underweight among Under-Five Children in Rural and Urban Areas of Ethiopia, by Gender, 1996–2004
percent

Year	Wasting			Stunting			Underweight		
	Boys	Girls	Both	Boys	Girls	Both	Boys	Girls	Both
National									
1996	7.8	6.9	7.3	67.6	63.8	65.7	47.8	42.9	45.4
1998	10.7	8.4	9.6	55.9	53.5	54.7	46.5	43.2	44.9
2000	10.2	8.9	9.6	58.1	55.3	56.7	45.9	44.1	45.0
2004	8.6	7.9	8.3	48.3	45.4	46.9	37.6	36.1	37.1
Rural									
1996	8.0	7.2	7.6	68.4	64.8	66.6	49.3	44.0	46.7
1998	10.8	8.6	9.7	57.4	55.0	56.2	47.9	44.7	46.3
2000	10.4	9.2	9.8	59.4	56.3	57.9	47.6	45.6	46.7
2004	8.8	8.1	8.4	49.9	47.1	48.5	39.1	38.3	38.7
Urban									
1996	6.4	4.1	5.3	61.0	55.5	58.4	35.1	33.6	34.4
1998	9.8	7.2	8.5	42.1	38.9	40.5	32.8	28.7	30.7
2000	7.0	5.8	6.4	44.2	44.7	44.4	26.7	27.4	27.0
2004	6.9	6.0	6.5	31.1	27.9	29.6	21.5	20.0	20.8

Source: Successive Welfare Monitoring Surveys (CSA 2004).

Figure 1.7   Stunting Rates among Under-Five Children in Rural and Urban Areas of Ethiopia, by Gender, 1996–2004

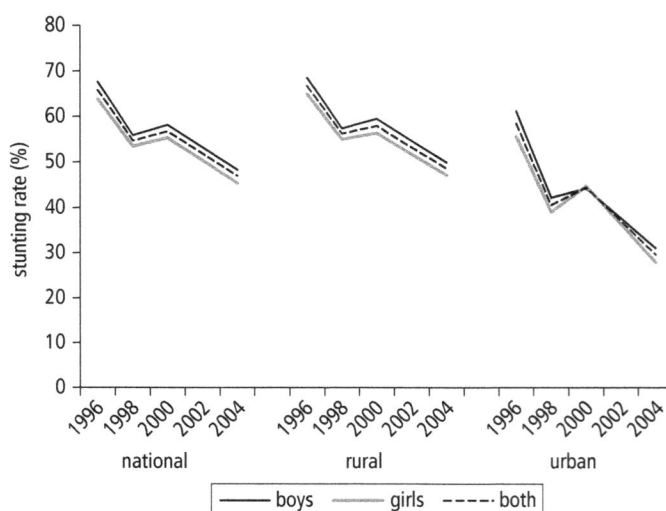

Source: Successive Welfare Monitoring Surveys (CSA 2004).

Figure 1.8   Wasting Rates among Under-Five Children in Rural and Urban Areas of Ethiopia, by Gender, 1996–2004

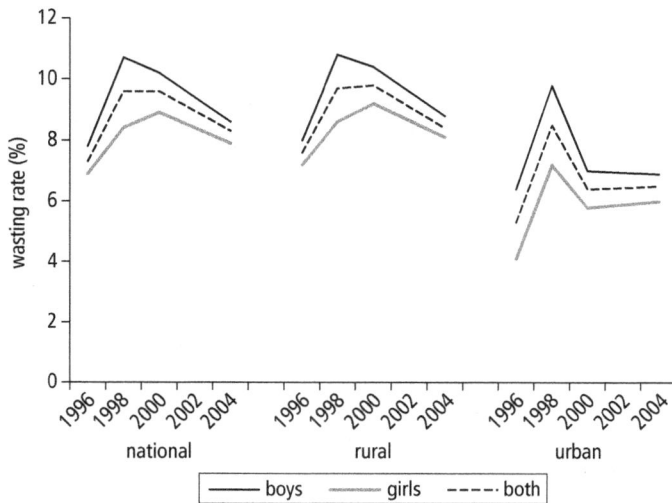

Source: Successive Welfare Monitoring Surveys (CSA 2004).

Figure 1.9   Underweight Rates among Under-Five Children in Rural and Urban Areas of Ethiopia, by Gender, 1996–2004

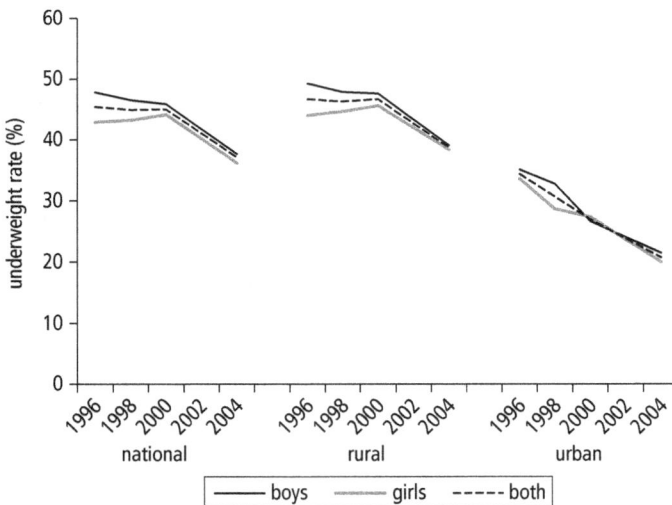

Source: Successive Welfare Monitoring Surveys (CSA 2004).

Surveys show that the stunting rate rose from 60 percent in 1983 to 65.7 percent in 1996.

Underweight prevalence, like stunting prevalence, declined substantially from 2000 to 2004 (table 1.9; figure 1.9). The two indicators are linked. The decline in underweight prevalence was affected by the sharp decline in stunting prevalence because underweight prevalence is a composite indicator incorporating both stunting and wasting.

These encouraging improvements do not warrant complacency, however. Stunting rates in Ethiopia remain high compared to those in other low-income countries and the region (table 1.7). Wasting prevalence, while comparing favorably with that of some of Ethiopia's neighbors, remains unacceptably high.

NOTES

1. Based on data from the World Bank, World Development Indicators. Figures are for 1990 to 2008 for the primary school enrollment rate and for 1990 to 2009 for the under-five mortality rate. The poverty headcount is the percentage of the population living below US$1.25 a day at purchasing power parity.

2. Inequality is measured by the Gini coefficient computed with data from various household income, consumption, and expenditure surveys over the past 10 years. A score of 0 means perfect equality, while a score of 1 means perfect inequality.

3. The goal is to halve from 1990 to 2015 the following: (a) the proportion of the population with less than US$1 of income a day (in terms of purchasing power parity), (b) the poverty gap ratio; (c) the share of the poorest quintile in total national consumption, (d) the percentage of children under five who are (moderately or severely) underweight, and (e) the proportion of the population below the minimum level of dietary energy consumption.

4. See the glossary for definitions and explanations.

5. For example, if a child's height-for-age is two and a half standard deviations below the median of the global reference population, then the child would be considered stunted, but not severely stunted. So he or she would be included in the total stunting rate, but not the severe stunting rate.

6. Children 6–24 months of age were found to experience about 0.9 centimeter less growth over a six-month period in communities where half the crop area was damaged due to a weather shock, compared to areas without crop damage (Yamano, Alderman, and Christiaensen 2005).

7. Calculated from (a) an estimate of the total loss in Ethiopian birr taken from Ethiopia PROFILES and AED (2005) and (b) data on GDP in previous years and figures for projected GDP until 2015.

8. At least 15 parts per million of iodine.

9. Complementary feeding are additional foods added to a child's diet starting at about six months of age to complement breast milk.

10. The Welfare Monitoring Surveys are nationwide household surveys conducted once every few years by Ethiopia's Central Statistical Agency.

CHAPTER 2

Who Is Malnourished in Ethiopia and Why? Findings from a Disaggregated Analysis

Chapter 1 provides a snapshot of malnutrition in Ethiopia, presenting data on indicators of different types of malnutrition over time at an aggregate level and comparing Ethiopia's indicators with those of other countries. This chapter examines the available data on these same indicators at a more disaggregated level, looking at disparities across regions within Ethiopia and across wealth quintiles. Using the results of regression analysis, this chapter also discusses the determinants of certain types of malnutrition in Ethiopia.

The analysis uses the latest available data at the time of writing, generally from 2004 and 2005, but some of the indicators may have worsened since then as a result of the recent food price and financial crises.

STUNTING, WASTING, AND UNDERWEIGHT: DISPARITIES BY REGION AND LEVEL OF WEALTH

In Ethiopia, while national estimates show that gender-based disparities in nutrition are relatively small, disparities in child nutritional outcomes are large and persistent between rural and urban areas. Regional disparities are also large, as shown in table 2.1, which presents relatively detailed and disaggregated data from successive Welfare Monitoring Surveys from 1983 to 2004 on Ethiopia's national prevalence of malnutrition. The regional disparities are also depicted in figures 2.1, 2.2, and 2.3.

The prevalence of wasting is highest for children in Afar (16.2 percent; table 2.1 and figure 2.1). Somali and Tigray each have a wasting rate of more than 10 percent, and Addis Ababa has the lowest wasting rate, at about 5 percent. Oromia and Benshangul-Gumuz have moderate wasting rates among children (about 9 percent).

Table 2.1 Child Malnutrition in Ethiopia, by Gender, Place of Residence, and Region, 1983–2004
percent

Indicator	Stunting						Underweight						Wasting					
	1983	1992	1996	1998	2000	2004	1983	1992	1996	1998	2000	2004	1983	1992	1996	1998	2000	2004
Gender																		
Male	61.0	65.7	67.0	55.9	58.1	48.3	38.2	49.3	47.8	46.5	45.9	37.6	9.0	8.7	7.8	10.7	10.2	8.6
Female	58.6	62.7	63.8	53.3	55.3	45.5	36.5	45.9	42.9	43.2	44.1	36.7	7.8	7.2	6.9	8.4	8.9	7.9
Residence																		
Urban	—	—	58.4	40.5	44.4	29.6	—	—	34.4	30.7	27.0	20.8	—	—	5.3	8.5	6.4	6.7
Rural	59.8	64.2	66.6	56.2	57.9	48.5	37.8	47.6	46.7	46.3	46.7	38.7	8.3	8.0	7.6	9.7	9.8	8.4
Region																		
Tigray	—	—	74.8	60.3	58.7	45.0	—	—	57.0	57.6	53.3	40.3	—	—	9.6	14.4	11.9	12.2
Afar	—	—	58.8	51.4	42.1	35.8	—	—	39.0	36.4	29.2	37.7	—	—	14.8	8.3	11.3	16.2
Amhara	—	—	72.2	65.5	64.5	58.3	—	—	55.6	54.8	52.6	45.4	—	—	9.7	10.5	10.7	7.9
Oromia	—	—	60.8	50.3	53.6	42.4	—	—	37.4	41.0	40.4	33.6	—	—	6.8	9.2	8.9	8.5
Somali	—	—	58.3	54.8	48.2	37.0	—	—	41.2	43.1	37.2	33.5	—	—	3.7	10.3	11.5	12.7
Benshangul-Gumuz	—	—	57.3	49.3	51.1	41.0	—	—	43.8	49.9	43.7	39.2	—	—	7.8	13.9	11.5	9.4
SNNP	—	—	69.3	55.9	56.3	47.0	—	—	49.6	43.2	46.2	36.2	—	—	5.9	8.2	8.9	7.0
Gambela	—	—	47.7	50.2	40.5	—	—	—	33.4	42.4	32.0	—	—	—	9.7	9.1	13.3	—
Harari	—	—	60.2	47.8	46.6	30.0	—	—	27.8	27.6	28.3	24.8	—	—	2.6	6.9	5.0	6.4
Addis Ababa	—	—	47.2	34.2	36.7	22.7	—	—	20.5	20.3	18.2	12.7	—	—	5.1	4.5	5.3	5.4
Dire Dawa	—	—	47.1	30.5	39.7	26.0	—	—	42.5	29.4	31.0	24.3	—	—	11.4	10.1	11.9	8.4
Total	59.8	64.2	66.6	54.7	56.7	46.9	37.8	47.7	46.7	44.9	45.0	37.1	8.3	8.0	7.6	9.6	9.6	8.3

Source: Rural Nutrition Survey (CSA 1983, 1992); Welfare Monitoring Survey (CSA 1996, 1998, 2000, 2004).

Note: — = not available; SNNP = Southern Nations, Nationalities, and Peoples. No data exist from 1983 and 1992 for present-day regions, which were established in 1995, following implementation of a new federal constitution. The data for the regions for 1996 and 1998 were sampled from rural areas except for Addis Ababa, and Gambela was excluded from the 2004 Welfare Monitoring Survey.

Figure 2.1   Wasting Rates among Under-Five Children in Rural and Urban Areas of Ethiopia, by Region, 2004

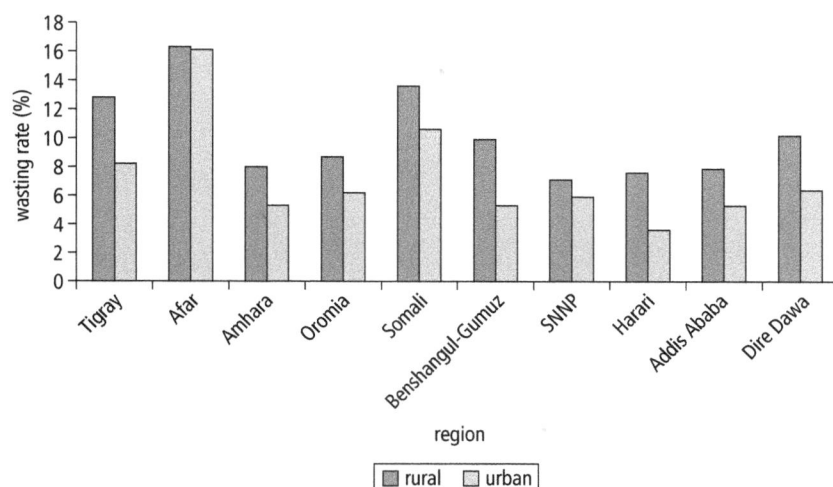

Source: 2004 Welfare Monitoring Survey (CSA 2004).
Note: SNNP = Southern Nations, Nationalities, and Peoples.

Figure 2.2   Stunting Rates among Under-Five Children in Rural and Urban Areas of Ethiopia, by Region and Location, 2004

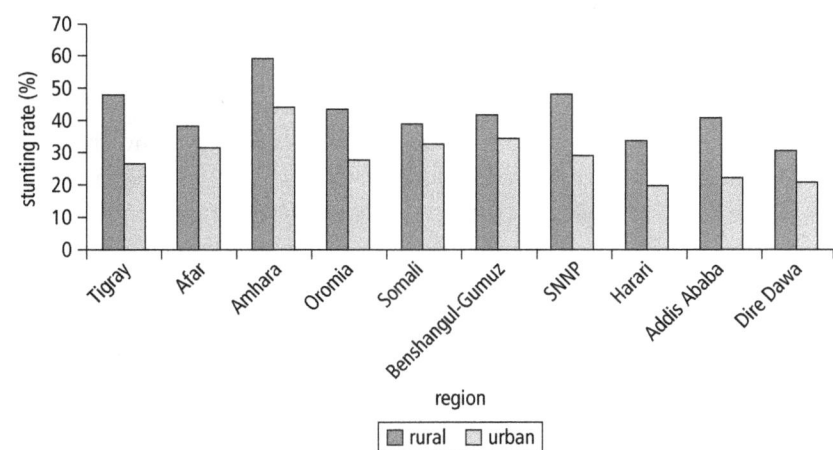

Source: 2004 Welfare Monitoring Survey (CSA 2004).
Note: SNNP = Southern Nations, Nationalities, and Peoples.

The prevalence of stunting is highest in Amhara (58.3 percent) followed by Southern Nations, Nationalities, and Peoples (SNNP, 47 percent) and Tigray (45 percent; see table 2.1 and figure 2.2). Addis Ababa has the lowest stunting rate (22 percent). In the rest of the country, the

Figure 2.3 Underweight Rates among Under-Five Children in Rural and Urban Areas of Ethiopia, by Region, 2004

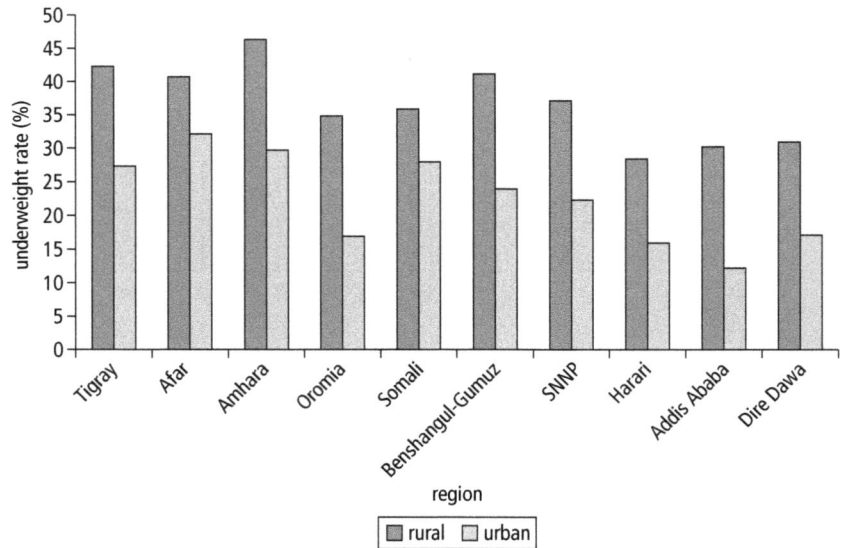

Source: 2004 Welfare Monitoring Survey (CSA 2004).
Note: SNNP = Southern Nations, Nationalities, and Peoples.

proportion of stunted children ranges from 26 percent in Dire Dawa to 42 percent in Oromia.

The prevalence of underweight by region is shown in figure 2.3. As expected, these figures reflect the regional prevalence of stunting and wasting, since both are incorporated in the underweight indicator for malnutrition. The prevalence of underweight is 12.7 percent in Addis Ababa; it soars as high as 45.4 percent in Amhara. The prevalence of underweight differs significantly between urban and rural areas within regions. The prevalence of underweight in rural children ranges from 28.4 percent in Harari to 46.3 percent in Amhara. In urban areas, it ranges from 12.2 percent in Addis Ababa to 32.1 percent in Afar.

As shown in figures 2.4 and 2.5, the prevalence of underweight and stunting, respectively, by wealth quintile for 2000 and 2005 improved between surveys. The level of underweight is much lower for each wealth quintile in 2005 than in 2000, although this is not the case for stunting. Households within the two highest wealth quintiles have a substantially lower prevalence of underweight than those in the other three wealth quintiles. Among the lower three quintiles, however, there is no relationship between household wealth and malnutrition levels.

Figure 2.4 Underweight Rates among Under-Five Children in Ethiopia, by Wealth Quintile, 2000 and 2005

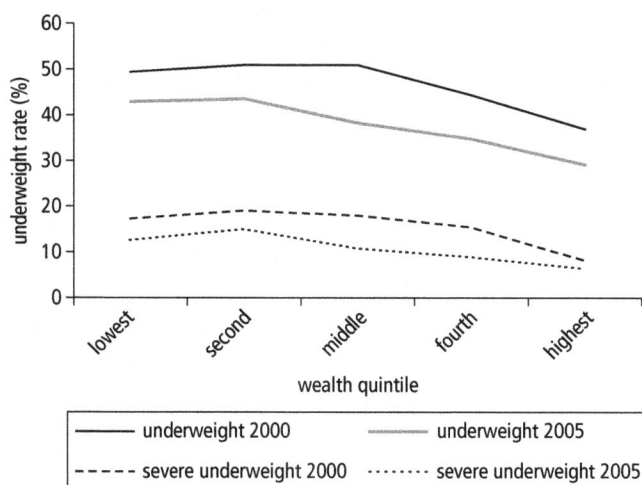

Source: 2000, 2005 Demographic and Health Survey (CSA and ORC Macro 2001, 2006); Gwatkin and others 2007.
Note: The wealthiest are in the highest wealth quintile, while the poorest are in the lowest quintile.

Figure 2.5 Stunting Rates among Under-Five Children in Ethiopia, by Wealth Quintile, 2000 and 2005

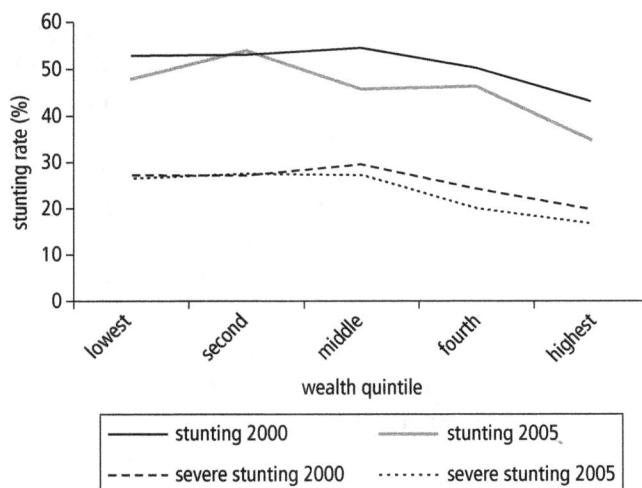

Source: 2000, 2005 Demographic and Health Survey (CSA and ORC Macro 2001, 2006); Gwatkin and others 2007.
Note: The wealthiest are in the highest wealth quintile, while the poorest are in the lowest wealth quintile.

Regional data show a weak interregional correlation between stunting and wasting. Stunting is both more widespread than wasting and most prevalent in areas that do not necessarily have a high prevalence of wasting. This finding supports the principle that long-term chronic malnutrition, as measured by stunting, differs from shorter-term acute malnutrition, as measured by wasting. Wasting occurs largely in food-insecure areas—and improving food security is thus likely to reduce wasting—but stunting occurs even in areas that are food secure. Thus, food is unlikely to be the decisive factor in attaining overall nutrition security. Because wasting is more strongly associated with food security than is stunting, improving food security is more likely to reduce wasting than stunting (as shown below according to survey data). Reducing stunting and wasting, as well as all other aspects of malnutrition, can only be accomplished by improving Ethiopia's food security *and* nutrition security.

DETERMINANTS OF CHILD STUNTING AND WASTING

Prior nutrition research about the determinants of child malnutrition in Ethiopia has been dominated by the use of Welfare Monitoring Surveys and adopted models focusing on children under five years of age. The key determinants of long-term child nutrition outcomes in Ethiopia have been commonly found to include household income, female adult education, community nutritional knowledge, and food prices. Previous research has used data from close to the start of the decade 2000–10. This book provides findings from more updated regression analysis done using 2005 Demographic and Health Survey data.

Two anthropometric measures—height-for-age and weight-for-height—are used as dependent variables in the regressions. Some may question the use of weight-for-height as an appropriate variable for this type of analysis because the onset of severely low weight-for-height is very rapid, while the variables against which it is regressed are relatively unchanged over time. Nevertheless, the information extracted from such an analysis can provide useful insights. A third anthropometric measure, weight-for-age, is commonly used in nutrition analysis and is examined in the descriptive sections of this book. However, as weight-for-age combines the information from both weight-for-height and height-for-age, it generally provides little additional information and therefore is not used in this book for analytical purposes.

In previous anthropometric regression analyses, a child's age was typically included as a single continuous right-hand-side variable. The analysis here goes one step further and breaks down the age of children into six-month categories. The key regression results underlying the analysis are presented in appendix A. The results indicate that the incidence of wasting is particularly high among Ethiopian children in the first 24 months of life, when they are in their formative years (see appendix A, table A.1). This can also be seen in figure 2.6, which shows the percentage of wasted children in different age groups. The extent of wasting peaks at 18.6 percent for children 12–17 months of age. It falls slightly to 16.8 percent for children 18–23 months of age and then falls sharply to below 10 percent for all older age groups.

The relationship between stunting prevalence and age is somewhat different. The regression results indicate that the percentage of stunted children rises with age over the first 24 months of life or so and remains at a high level thereafter (see appendix A, table A.2). This is also evident in figure 2.7, which shows the percentage of stunted children in different age groups. This pattern reflects the fact that child height is an indicator of long-term or accumulated health and nutrition status and is commonly found in developing countries. Past episodes of disease or poor nutrition may continue to affect height, even when the child is currently unaffected by disease or dietary deficiencies.

Figure 2.6 Wasting Rates among Under-Five Children in Ethiopia, by Age Group, 2005

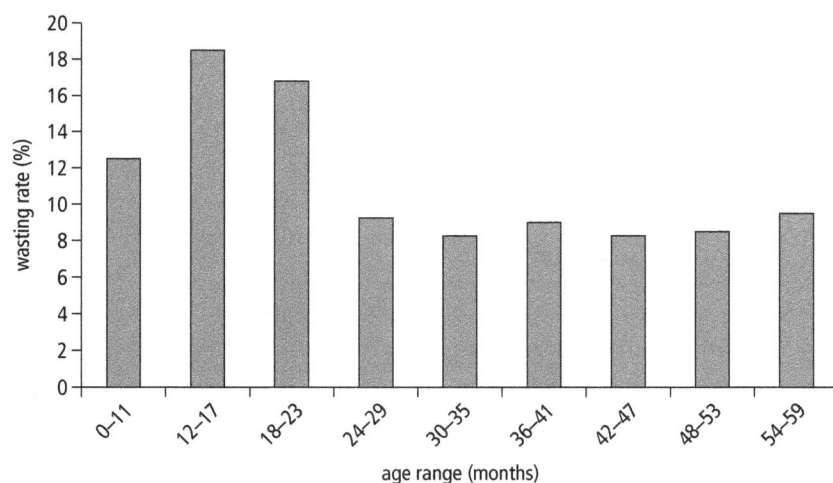

Source: Authors' calculations from 2005 Demographic and Health Survey data.
Note: The age group 0–5 months has only 11 children in the sample, so this group is combined with the group 6–11 months of age (which has 390 children in the sample). The number of children in the samples for the other age groups ranges from 299 to 459.

Figure 2.7 Stunting Rates among Under-Five Children in Ethiopia, by Age Group, 2005

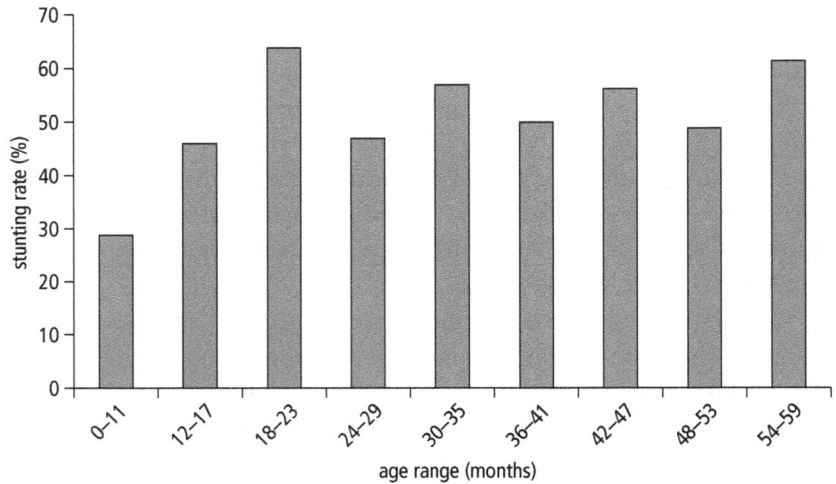

Source: Authors' calculations from 2005 Demographic and Health Survey data.
Note: The age group 0–5 months has only 11 children in the sample, so this group is combined with the group 6–11 months of age (which has 390 children in the sample). The number of children in the samples for the other age groups ranges from 299 to 459.

The regression results reported in appendix A suggest that higher welfare status of a child's household (as measured by household wealth) leads to less wasting, but the impact is not especially large (appendix A, table A.1). In the case of stunting, there is no statistically significant association between household wealth and the extent of stunting (appendix A, table A.2).

These findings highlight an increasingly frequent observation: *economic growth alone is insufficient to reduce child malnutrition*. And since wealthier households generally purchase and consume larger quantities of food, this finding also supports a theme of this book: *while food security correlates with nutrition security, the correlation is not particularly large*. Food aid is a critical component of nutrition security, but food alone does not automatically lead to improved nutrition. Therefore, multifaceted interventions are needed in Ethiopia to ensure nutrition security and not just to reduce food insecurity. To achieve nutrition security, policies are needed to increase parental, and especially female, adult education; strengthen households' ability to reduce crop damage caused by pests and droughts; and improve sanitary conditions and health infrastructure.

LINKS BETWEEN FOOD SECURITY STATUS AND MALNUTRITION

Understanding the links between food security status and malnutrition in Ethiopia is critically important for planning nutrition-related programming. This section describes the quantitative relationship between food security and nutrition security as assessed from analysis of *woreda*-level (district-level) food aid data and household- and individual-level data from the national 2004 Welfare Monitoring Survey.[1]

The analysis of food security in Ethiopia benefits in particular from one question in the 2004 Welfare Monitoring Survey: Has this household suffered from food shortage during the last 12 months? If the answer was yes, the respondent was asked the number of months of food shortage. Despite the subjectivity associated with self-reported data, in the absence of better alternatives, these data provide a rough but useful indicator of household food security status. And although the number of months of food shortage is self-reported, the wasting and stunting rates are based on anthropometric measurement.[2]

The Welfare Monitoring Survey data show that total and severe wasting rates among children under five years of age are clearly related to a household's self-reported number of months of food shortage during the previous 12 months (see table 2.2 and figure 2.8). In 2004, the total wasting rate among children from households with 7–12 months of self-reported food shortage was about double the rate for households with no reported food shortage. The severe wasting rate among this first category of children was about two-and-a-half times that of the second. These findings highlight the importance of wasting as an acute measure of malnutrition among children under five years of age, who are highly sensitive to bouts of short-term food insecurity.

Table 2.2 Malnutrition Rates among Under-Five Children in Households with Varying Degrees of Self-Reported Food Insecurity in Ethiopia, 2004
% of children under five years of age, unless otherwise noted

Household experience in previous 12 months	Number of children in sample	Stunting rate		Wasting rate	
		Total	Severe	Total	Severe
No food shortage	8,406	44.4	21.6	7.7	1.4
1–3 months of food shortage	1,634	51.0	28.8	9.4	2.3
4–6 months of food shortage	826	54.2	28.8	12.0	2.0
7–12 months of food shortage	311	46.3	22.0	15.5	3.7

Source: Authors' calculations using self-reported data from the 2004 Welfare Monitoring Survey.

Figure 2.8   Wasting Rates among Under-Five Children in Households with Varying Degrees of Self-Reported Food Insecurity in Ethiopia, 2004

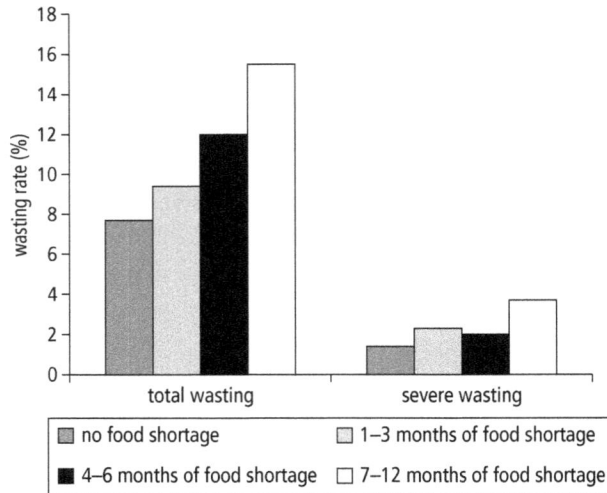

Source: Authors' calculations using 2004 Welfare Monitoring Survey data.

The data show a strong correlation between food insecurity and wasting rates. Therefore, programs providing food must be properly targeted to food-insecure households to alleviate wasting. However, wasting rates are still very high among children from households experiencing no reported food shortage within the previous 12 months. In 2004, the rates of total and severe wasting among children from households reporting no food shortage during the previous 12 months were 7.7 and 1.4 percent, respectively—still high by international standards. It is clear from these data that *a significant amount of wasting in Ethiopia results from factors other than food insecurity.* To reduce malnutrition, these factors need to be addressed through appropriate interventions other than the provision of adequate food, such as those related to health, water and sanitation, child care, and appropriate child-feeding practices.

The data show no clear relationship between stunting rates among children under five years of age and the self-reported number of months of food shortage experienced by a household during the previous 12 months (see table 2.2 and figure 2.9). This could be because the food shortage variable in the analysis measures shortage only within the previous 12 months and not medium- or longer-term food shortage. Yet stunting among children under five years of age reflects the impact of an accumulation of factors over the previous few years—specifically up to five

Figure 2.9 Stunting Rates among Under-Five Children in Households with Varying Degrees of Self-Reported Food Insecurity in Ethiopia, 2004

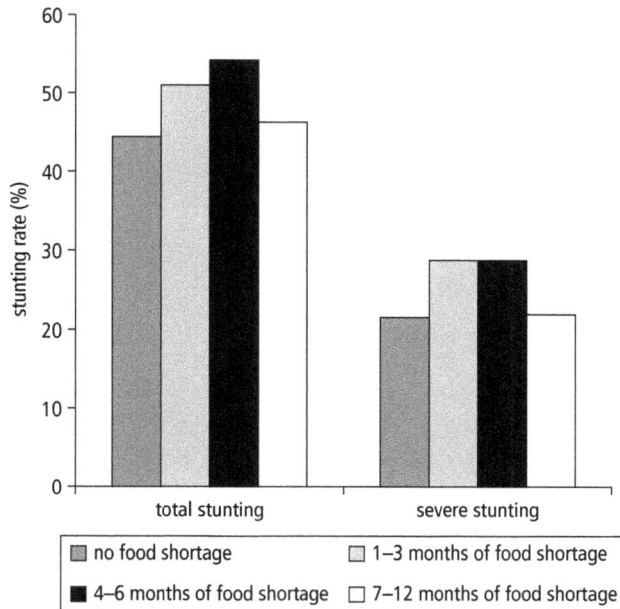

Source: Authors' calculations using 2004 Welfare Monitoring Survey data.

years, depending on the age of each child at the time of the survey. Restricting the analysis to children less than one or two years of age at the time of the survey would better illustrate whether a correlation exists.

But even when the analysis is restricted to children under two years of age or children under one year of age, the data still show no clear relationship between stunting rates and the self-reported number of months of food shortage during the previous 12 months (see table 2.3). These results support the fact that addressing nonfood factors is especially important to reduce the high rates of stunting in Ethiopia. That the relationship between food shortage and wasting is much more apparent than the relationship between food shortage and stunting should come as no surprise. However, this does not mean that food shortages do not affect stunting. Rather, the relationship between the two is more complex and indirect than the relationship between food shortage and wasting. Also, the results are less reliable for households experiencing 7–12 months of food shortage due to the small number of households sampled in this category (108 for children under two years of age and 49 for children under one year of age). There is a positive relationship between stunting rates

Table 2.3 Stunting Rates among Under-Two and Under-One Children from Households with Varying Degrees of Self-Reported Food Insecurity in Ethiopia, 2004
% of children with stunting, unless otherwise noted

Household experience in previous 12 months	Children under two years of age			Children under one year of age		
	Number of children	Total stunting	Severe stunting	Number of children	Total stunting	Severe stunting
No food shortage	2,890	43.2	21.3	1,332	30.0	13.2
1–3 months of food shortage	549	52.0	29.5	244	42.8	24.8
4–6 months of food shortage	256	56.2	29.5	127	42.3	19.0
7–12 months of food shortage	108	45.1	20.4	49	35.4	10.5

Source: Authors' calculations using 2004 Welfare Monitoring Survey data.

and the extent of food shortage if this category is ignored. And a significant degree of subjectivity likely exists in household estimates of the number of months of food shortage, which could possibly skew the results.

These findings are corroborated by previous analysis of Ethiopia and poorer countries and echo the findings of the seminal work by Pelletier and others (1995), illustrated in box 2.1.

A clear finding of the above analyses—and an overarching theme of this book—is that Ethiopia's high malnutrition rates are only partly explained by food shortages. *Nonfood factors are a major cause of high malnutrition rates in Ethiopia.* This finding is critical to consider when one is selecting the most effective interventions for reducing malnutrition in Ethiopia.

SUBOPTIMAL BREAST-FEEDING PRACTICES: SCOPE OF THE PROBLEM AND CAUSES

Proper breast-feeding practices are critically important to child health status and nutrition. This section builds on the information presented in chapter 1 regarding optimal breast-feeding practices in Ethiopia. Data from the 2005 Demographic and Health Survey are used to examine the breast-feeding practices of different subgroups of women and to assess the determinants of optimal breast-feeding practices based on regression analysis.

Geographically, across the country, there is some variation in the median duration of breast-feeding according to the 2005 Demographic and Health Survey (see figure 2.10 and table 2.4). Overall, the median duration of breast-feeding was 25.8 months, with relatively little difference in duration by sex of the child. Rural children appear to be breast-fed

BOX 2.1   PREVIOUS ANALYSIS OF THE RELATIONSHIP BETWEEN NUTRITION
SECURITY AND FOOD SECURITY

Pelletier and others (1995) used results from the 1992 Rural Nutrition Survey to
demonstrate that the nutrition status of children, as measured by stunting and
wasting prevalence, is "weakly and inconsistently associated with the size of the
family's cultivated area" and that "high levels of chronic malnutrition exist in
food-deficit and food-surplus regions alike" (see figure B2.1, panels a and b).
(Figure B2.1, panel a, does indicate that the prevalence of wasting is overall nega-
tively associated with the size of cultivated area, but this relationship is not even
across the four size categories. Furthermore, and more important, the association
between the prevalence of wasting and the size of cultivated area is not consistent
across regions; it is actually *positive* in several regions and often statistically
insignificant even when it is negative.) The weak relationship between the extent
of food security and the prevalence of malnutrition reveals that food alone is an
insufficient predictor of nutrition status.

Figure B2.1 Wasting and Stunting Rates in Ethiopia, by Size of Family's Cultivated Area, 1992

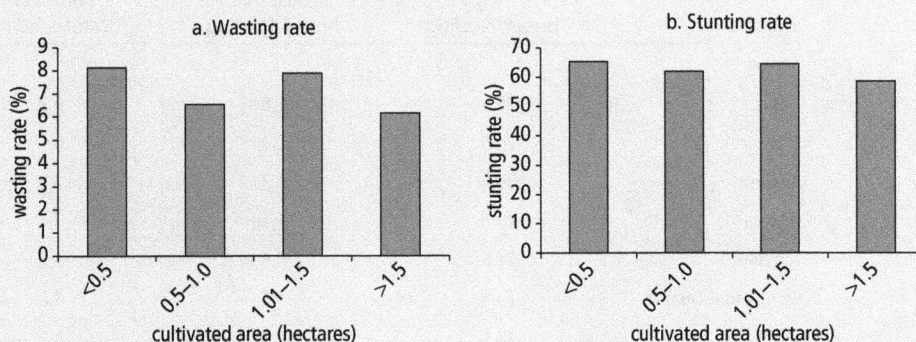

Source: Pelletier and others 1995.

for a slightly longer period than urban children, as are children in Amhara
and Gambela compared with children in other regions.

Perhaps paradoxically, the 2005 Demographic and Health Survey data
show that optimal breast-feeding practices are more common among less
educated mothers than among better-educated ones. There also appears
to be a weak negative relationship between wealth and optimal breast-
feeding practices; mothers in the lower wealth quintiles have slightly better use of optimal practices than mothers in the higher wealth quintiles
(see figures 2.11 to 2.13).

Figure 2.10   Median Duration of Breast-Feeding in Ethiopia, by Region

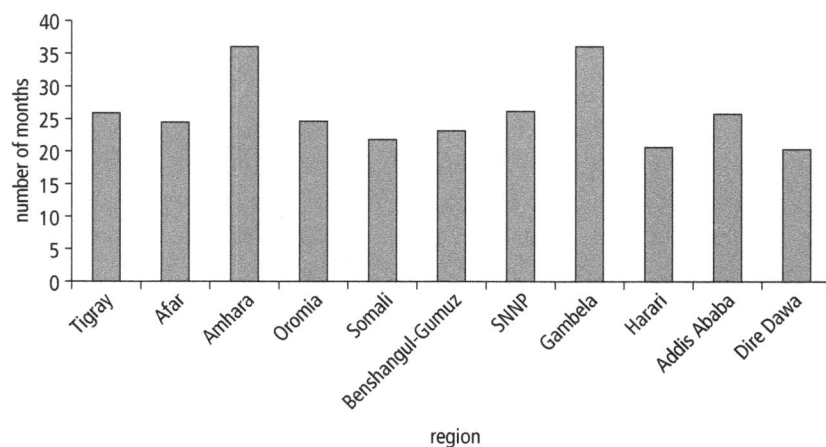

Source: 2005 Demographic and Health Survey (CSA and ORC Macro 2006).

Table 2.4   Breast-Feeding Practices in Ethiopia, by Region and Wealth Quintile, 2005
median duration (months)

Indicator	Any breast-feeding	Exclusive breast-feeding	Predominant breast-feeding
Region			
Tigray	25.9	1.6	6.3
Afar	24.5	0.4	0.7
Amhara	36.0	4.3	7.1
Oromia	24.6	1.6	3.4
Somali	21.8	0.5	2.9
Benshangul-Gumuz	23.1	1.6	4.0
SNNP	26.1	1.8	3.2
Gambela	36.0	1.6	4.0
Harari	20.6	0.8	3.1
Addis Ababa	25.7	0.6	0.9
Dire Dawa	20.3	0.5	5.0
Wealth quintile			
Lowest	25.1	0.7	3.4
Second	27.1	2.6	5.2
Middle	25.4	3.0	4.6
Fourth	25.9	2.4	4.5
Highest	25.3	3.2	2.2

Source: 2005 Demographic and Health Survey (CSA and ORC Macro 2006).

Figure 2.11   Initiation of Breast-Feeding in Ethiopia, by Education of Mother

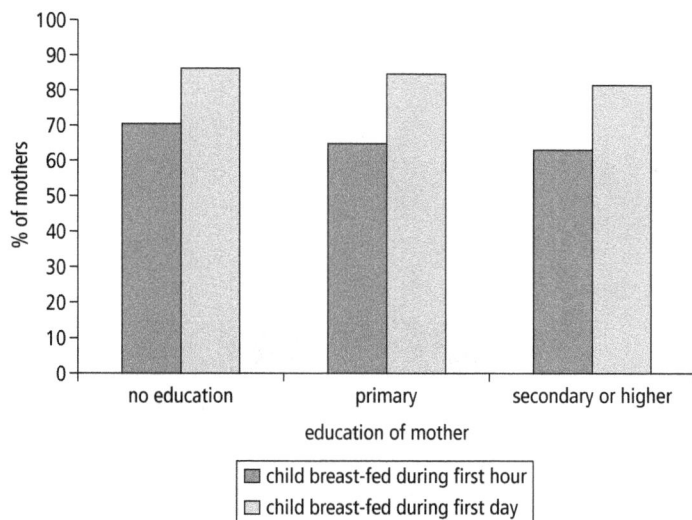

Source: 2005 Demographic and Health Survey (CSA and ORC Macro 2006).

Figure 2.12   Initiation of Breast-Feeding in Ethiopia, by Wealth Quintile of Mother

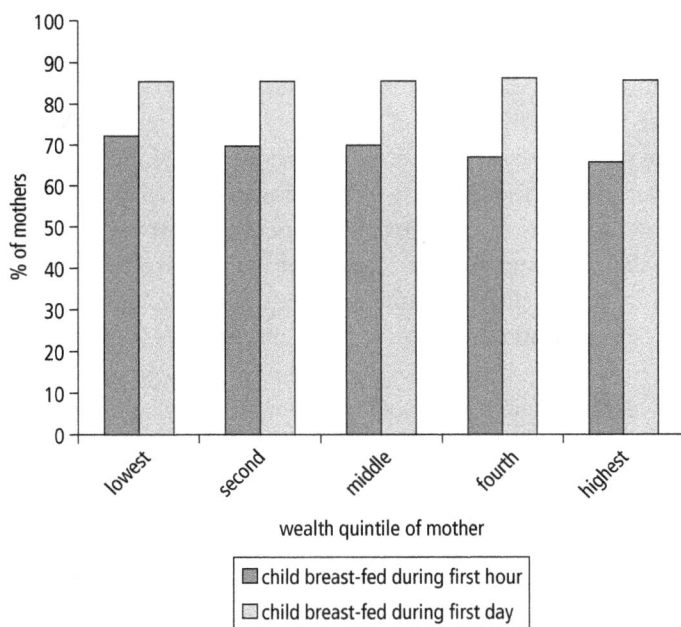

Source: 2005 Demographic and Health Survey (CSA and ORC Macro 2006).

Figure 2.13 Duration of Breast-Feeding Practices in Ethiopia, by Education of Mother

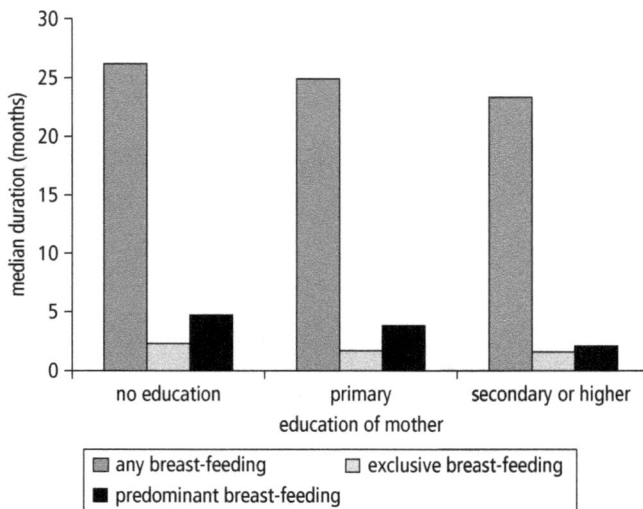

Source: 2005 Demographic and Health Survey (CSA and ORC Macro 2006).

Figures 2.11 and 2.12 show that the proportion of mothers breast-feeding their child within the first hour of birth—a key component of optimal breast-feeding practices—is highest among mothers with the lowest levels of formal education and the poorest mothers.[3]

As shown in figure 2.13, the median amount of time spent exclusively breast-feeding is lowest among the most educated mothers. According to the World Health Organization and other health authorities, mothers should spend six months exclusively breast-feeding. Table 2.4 shows that the median period spent breast-feeding varies relatively little by wealth index. The median amount of time spent exclusively breast-feeding increases slightly from the first to the third wealth quintile, but it peaks there and then falls slightly from the third to the fifth quintile.

This descriptive analysis of breast-feeding practices is further enhanced by quantitative analysis. The results of econometric regressions conducted for breast-feeding issues, presented in appendix A (see table A.3), indicate that a higher duration of breast-feeding is associated with an older head of household, a female head of household, and a smaller household. The findings regarding education and wealth from the descriptive analysis are echoed here. The regression analysis finds that, generally, children with more educated parents experience a *shorter* duration of breast-feeding, but the impact of household wealth on the duration of breast-feeding is not statistically significant.

Women practicing suboptimal breast-feeding are probably doing so because they lack knowledge of optimal breast-feeding practices, rather than because of financial or other constraints. The data presented here demonstrate that teaching mothers about appropriate practices can save tens of thousands of lives yearly. Figure 2.14 shows the number of child deaths that would be averted if recommended practices were followed. The first column is the baseline, or the number of under-five deaths in Ethiopia per year. The second column is the number of child deaths if one presupposes that breast-feeding is initiated within the first hour of life; this number is 29,000, or 7.6 percent less than the baseline. The third column reflects outcomes when breast-feeding is initiated within the first hour of life and is complemented with exclusive breast-feeding for the first six months. In this case, the number of child deaths per year would decrease by a further 29,000, or 7.6 percent. The final column presupposes appropriate breast-feeding (as assumed in the third column) as well as the introduction of proper complementary feeding at the age of six months. As a result, 22,000 more lives of under-five children would be saved every year; that is, 5.8 percent more child deaths would be averted annually.[4] In total, if the three types of optimal child-feeding practices were followed, 80,000 child deaths (21 percent of all child deaths) would be averted. See box 2.2 for a case study of breast-feeding practices.

Figure 2.14 Potential Decrease in Deaths of Under-Five Children in Ethiopia with Proper Feeding Practices

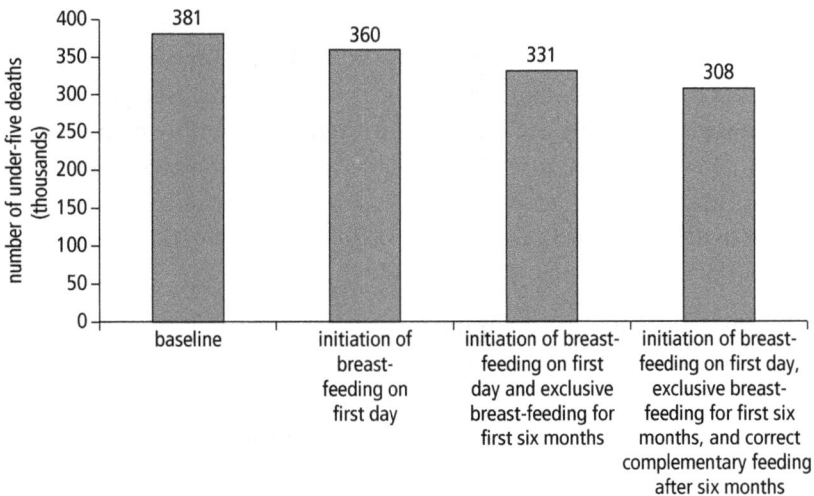

Source: Estimates based on the authors' calculations using results from Jones and others (2003) and Edmond and others (2006) and assuming about 3.2 million births a year for five years.

BOX 2.2 BREAST-FEEDING PRACTICES IN NORTH WOLLO, ETHIOPIA, 2002

A nutrition study from Gubalafto *woreda* in the North Wollo zone of Amhara surveyed 1,471 households with children under age two. The children were weighed and measured, and their mothers' mid-upper arm circumference was recorded. The following are the major findings from a series of focus group discussions about breast-feeding and complementary food with the surveyed mothers.

Breast-feeding. Approximately 60–70 percent of mothers with infants five months of age reported that they exclusively breast-fed their infants. Overall, infants less than six months of age who were not exclusively breast-fed were five times more likely to be malnourished than infants of the same age who were exclusively breast-fed. A small percentage of mothers (somewhat less than 10 percent) reported giving newborn babies butter or sugar water (prelacteal feeds) in the first few days of life.

Complementary food. Only 49 percent of all mothers knew the correct age to start complementary feeding. Of the mothers interviewed, 20 percent stated that in the 24 hours prior to the interview, their child 8–10 months of age had received only breast milk. During focus group discussions, some mothers said a reason for the delay in supplementing breast milk with complementary foods is the risk of diarrhea. Some mothers said that breast milk is less expensive than complementary foods.

The typical first complementary food offered to infants is liquid-softened bread (*kita, chibito,* or *injera*) made from sorghum, teff, or wheat. Either sesame seeds or linseeds are added to *chibito* bread flour. When queried, about two in three mothers (68 percent) stated that they gave green vegetables to young children.

Mothers' absence from child. The study found that whether a child was exclusively breast-fed was associated with a mother's absence from her infant for two or more hours a day. Women of poor and medium economic status spent on average 20 hours a week more away from home and their infants than better-off women. Although women of all economic statuses in Gubalafto *woreda* participate in farm work, the study concluded that women of poor and medium economic status are far more likely to be involved in cash-producing activities outside the home, such as collecting firewood or dung for sale.

The study also indicated that mothers in the poor economic group on average return to farm work about three to four months postpartum. Mothers in the better-off economic group return to farm work about six months after giving birth, permitting more time for both optimal breast-feeding and other infant care.

Source: Kuhl 2006.

VITAMIN A INTAKE: A DISAGGREGATED FOCUS

Chapter 1 presents summary data from the 2005 Demographic and Health Survey on indicators of vitamin A intake by women and young children in Ethiopia. This section provides a more disaggregated picture of the same data. Table 2.5 summarizes the essential consumption and supplementation data on vitamin A, disaggregated by region and wealth. Overall consumption of foods rich in vitamin A is higher among mothers in the highest wealth quintile. There are also significant differences across regions.

Table 2.5 Vitamin A and Micronutrient Intake in Under-Five Children in Ethiopia, by Age Group, Region, and Wealth Quintile
% of children

Indicator	Children under three years of age who consumed fruits and vegetables rich in vitamin A in past 24 hours	Last-born child 6–35 months of age who consumed food rich in vitamin A in past 24 hours	Children 6–59 months of age given vitamin A supplement in past six months
Region			
Tigray	9.5	25.1	65.3
Afar	11.4	9.3	33.3
Amhara	13.2	19.2	43.2
Oromia	33.2	26.4	43.0
Somali	4.6	7.9	38.8
Benshangul-Gumuz	27.8	31.1	27.4
SNNP	57.4	35.4	49.9
Gambela	56.5	38.2	39.1
Harari	42.7	33.9	36.7
Addis Ababa	35.9	37.9	53.2
Dire Dawa	28.8	23.9	46.7
Wealth quintile			
Lowest	19.7	16.9	39.5
Second	31.6	26.1	42.1
Middle	31.3	24.0	45.6
Fourth	26.0	28.9	49.6
Highest	39.8	37.9	55.4
Overall	31.1	26.0	45.8

Source: 2005 Demographic and Health Survey (CSA and ORC Macro 2006).

About 46 percent of children 6–59 months of age received a vitamin A supplement in the six months before the 2005 Demographic and Health Survey. However, this percentage is likely to have substantially increased since then, as the Enhanced Outreach Strategy for Child Survival (EOS) and the Extended EOS (EEOS) are being implemented in most parts of the country. As described in chapter 3, the EOS/EEOS programs aim to provide vitamin A supplements to all under-five children in most parts of the country through mass mobilizations twice a year. A meta-analysis of randomized trials found a 23 percent reduction in the mortality rates of children between 6 and 59 months of age due to vitamin A supplementation (Beaton and others 1993).

IODINE INTAKE AND SALT IODIZATION

Lack of iodine in utero has a range of negative effects, including reduced IQ, spontaneous abortions, and congenital abnormalities. Yet, as discussed in chapter 1, only about 20 percent of Ethiopian households use adequately iodized salt,[5] according to the 2005 Demographic and Health Survey (table 1.2). This section examines the same data at a more disaggregated level (see table 2.6). The place of residence appears to make relatively little difference in iodine fortification levels, and no substantive correlation is observed between higher utilization levels of adequately iodized salt and greater wealth. But there are large variations across regions. Households in Dire Dawa are most likely to consume adequately iodized salt (62 percent), while households in Benshangul-Gumuz are least likely to do so (14 percent).

The iodization of salt is a politically sensitive issue. Historically, Ethiopia had a limited capacity to produce its own iodized salt and relied heavily on Eritrea to supply it. After the 1998–2000 Ethiopian-Eritrean border conflict, Ethiopia lost access to Eritrea's iodized salt. In response, the government of Ethiopia initiated and supported efforts to explore inland sources of salt. Now most salt consumed in the country is produced domestically, predominately in Afar, which accounts for about 80 percent of all domestic production.

In September 2008, an Ethiopian federal and regional delegation participated in the East Africa regional conference on iodine deficiency disorders in Arusha, Tanzania. The purpose of the conference was to share experiences for consolidating efforts toward achieving universal salt iodization. The Ethiopian delegation also visited an iodization factory. The delegation's experience was fruitful. After a series of national consultative and regional meetings in Afar, consensus was obtained to iodize salt

Table 2.6 Iodine Content of Salt Consumed in Households in Ethiopia, by Region and Wealth Quintile
percent

Indicator	None	Inadequate	Adequate
Region			
Tigray	43.7	28.3	28.0
Afar	39.0	38.0	23.0
Amhara	53.4	31.7	14.9
Oromia	40.3	37.7	22.0
Somali	41.8	33.6	24.7
Benshangul-Gumuz	58.7	27.7	13.6
SNNP	45.9	35.6	18.5
Gambela	34.9	27.4	37.6
Harari	41.5	29.7	28.8
Addis Ababa	50.4	31.7	17.9
Dire Dawa	8.3	29.4	62.3
Wealth quintile			
Lowest	43.4	34.5	22.1
Second	48.0	33.4	18.7
Middle	44.0	36.2	19.8
Fourth	45.9	35.0	19.1
Highest	46.9	33.3	19.9

Source: 2005 Demographic and Health Survey (CSA and ORC Macro 2006).
Note: None = 0 parts of iodine per million; inadequate = less than 15 parts of iodine per million; and adequate = 15 or more parts of iodine per million.

in Ethiopia. A national iodization launch took place on April 11, 2009, and key stakeholders (composed of the government, international agencies, the private sector, and donors) signed an agreement outlining their responsibilities.

Salt iodization then commenced in Afar in April 2009, but stopped soon afterward and was stalled for several months. This apparently was due to the emergence of issues surrounding implementation, ownership, ensuring that sufficient benefits accrue to all stakeholders, and ensuring that these benefits are well understood and communicated. Some changes in the implementation mechanisms were made, and salt iodization in Afar was restarted in April 2010. The current modalities for implementation are expected to be more sustainable than before, and the quantity of salt iodized every month is expected to continue to increase over time. But close and continuous monitoring is needed, as well as other possible adjustments along the way. And while addressing programmatic efforts on the ground, the existing legislation regarding obligatory iodization of household salt needs to be examined, strengthened, and enforced.[6]

There is general agreement that Ethiopia still has some way to go before reaching universal salt iodization, which is a key goal of the National Nutrition Program (see chapter 5). However, the efforts and progress to date are very significant, when compared to the situation in 2008 and before. It is hoped that continued progress will be made and that universal salt iodization will be reached at some point in the near future.

IRON DEFICIENCY ANEMIA: A DISAGGREGATED FOCUS

Chapter 1 presents data from the 2005 Demographic and Health Survey showing that 53.5 percent of children and 26.6 percent of women in Ethiopia have iron deficiency anemia. This section provides further breakdowns of these data. Figure 2.15 shows the prevalence of iron deficiency anemia by wealth quintile broken down by degree of severity: mild, moderate, and severe. While mild iron deficiency anemia afflicts a roughly

Figure 2.15   Prevalence of Iron Deficiency Anemia in Under-Five Children in Ethiopia, by Degree of Severity and Wealth Quintile

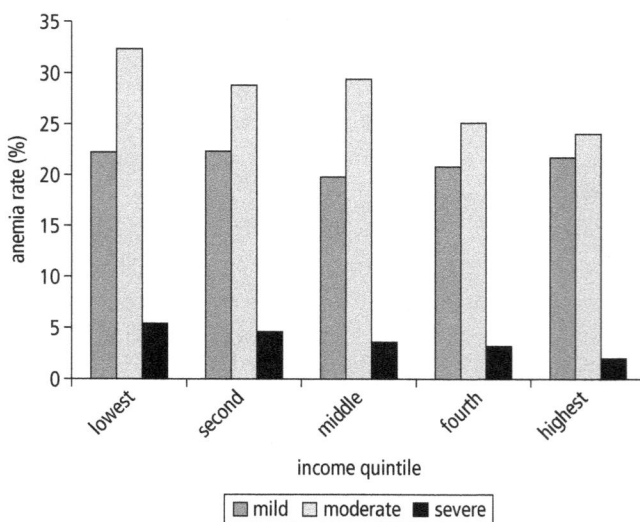

Source: 2005 Demographic and Health Survey (CSA and ORC Macro 2006).

Figure 2.16 Prevalence of Iron Deficiency Anemia in Under-Five Children in Ethiopia, by Region

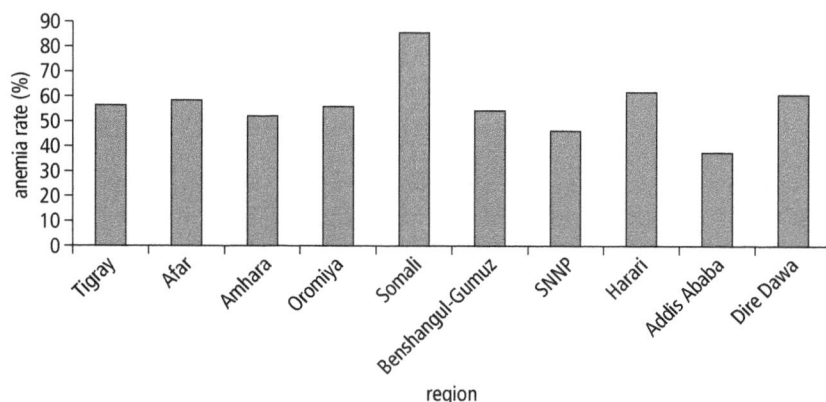

Source: 2005 Demographic and Health Survey (CSA and ORC Macro 2006).
Note: Figures include children with mild, moderate, and severe anemia.

equal proportion of children from each wealth quintile, moderate and severe anemia are relatively higher among the lower wealth quintiles.

The prevalence of iron deficiency anemia by region, according to the 2005 Demographic and Health Survey data, varies significantly across regions (see figure 2.16). The prevalence among children in Somali (85.6 percent) is much higher than the national rate (53.5 percent), while the prevalence in Addis Ababa is much lower (37.5 percent).

NOTES

1. More precisely, all regions were covered except Gambela.

2. The regressions whose results are reported in the previous section were done by using data from the 2005 Demographic and Health Survey. Unfortunately, unlike the 2004 Welfare Monitoring Survey, the 2005 Demographic and Health Survey did not include any question that could be used to evaluate the food security status of a household. However, the 2005 Demographic and Health Survey is more complete in other respects and was thus selected (rather than the 2004 Welfare Monitoring Survey) to perform the regressions in the previous section.

3. Prelacteal feeding, although common, has several negative effects. Prelacteal feeds are defined as anything other than breast milk given to a newborn before the initiation of breast-feeding, such as animal milk, water, and tea. The negative effects include delays in colostrum feeding, the potential to introduce bacteria, and, if the infant is fed animal milk, the possibility of introducing large proteins that can cause intestinal bleeding. Colostrum—yellow milk vital to newborns—contains maternal antibodies that boost the child's immune system and elements to help the infant's gut to finish developing. Nonsterile water introduces bacteria,

viruses, and other infectious microbes to a newborn baby's system before it is sufficiently developed.

4. As mentioned in chapter 1, suboptimal breast-feeding causes about 50,000 infants (under one year of age) to die each year. The number of children under five years of age who would be saved if optimal breast-feeding were practiced is larger, because suboptimal breast-feeding increases the risk of death not only during infancy but also in the later under-five years.

5. At least 15 parts per million of iodine.

6. Issued in 2000, Proclamation 200/2000 states, "Any person who produces or distributes salt for human consumption shall ensure that it meets the standard requirement of iodine content" (see Federal Negarit Gazeta, March 9, 2000). In general, there has been little compliance with this proclamation, and enforcement has been weak.

CHAPTER 3

Current Programs in Ethiopia

There are hundreds of programs in Ethiopia aimed at affecting malnutrition or targeting its underlying causes. Because of the nature of malnutrition, with its many causes and manifestations, the programs focus on a variety of issues—food distribution, environmental cleanup, access to water, veterinary care, primary education, primary health care, and adult literacy, among others. Only some programs seek to improve nutrition as an explicit program objective. But although "decreasing malnutrition" is not among the objectives of most of these programs, the end results will positively affect the nutrition status of children and their mothers. This chapter highlights a few of these programs, specifically the larger programs affecting malnutrition or health outcomes.

These programs are discussed to provide background for the quantitative analysis presented in chapter 4 that uses pre-2008 data, the most recent available at the time of analysis. After providing summary information about programs, the chapter takes a closer look at four programs that are among the most widespread and critical for nutrition. Some of the programs discussed underwent major changes in or after 2008. Specifically, the Essential Services for Health in Ethiopia (ESHE) and the Community-Based Reproductive Health Agent (CBRHA) programs merged to become the Integrated Family Health Program in 2008. Similarly, the Food Security Project, including its Child Growth Promotion (CGP) component, was phased out in June 2010 and replaced by the Community-Based Nutrition (CBN) Program and the Household Asset Building Program.

PROGRAMS THAT GIVE FOOD OR CASH

Programs giving beneficiaries food and cash for food have diverse objectives. Some give food or cash because one of their stated primary objectives is to improve nutritional indicators, but this is not a primary objective of all of the programs discussed in this section. Only the Targeted Supplementary Food Program (TSFP) and the program for treatment of severe acute malnutrition state that improving nutritional indicators is the primary reason for giving food and cash for food. For the other programs, improvements in nutritional indicators are a by-product of their main objective, which is usually related to reducing food insecurity or supplying food to beneficiaries. Table 3.1 lists each of the programs discussed in this section.

GOVERNMENT FOOD SECURITY PROGRAM

The Government Food Security Program is a key program to help vulnerable, food-insecure communities to increase their incomes and build their assets. It helps by providing communities with funds and technical assistance to support household-level asset-building interventions (financed through grants to households). Families can choose (a) a package encouraging diversification and income generation by growing vegetables and fruits and raising livestock for sale or (b) a package providing assistance in the identification and development of off-farm income-generating activities, including assistance in developing a business plan using technology and in monitoring household investments. Interventions at the community level focus on capitalizing local-level finance providers, such as microfinance institutions, through the provision of matching grants that are owned and managed by the community.

FOOD SECURITY PROJECT

Until June 2010, the Ministry of Agriculture and Rural Development implemented a Food Security Project with support from several donors, including the World Bank, the Canadian International Development Agency, Italian Cooperation, and the U.K. Department for International Development. The project began in 2002 and operated in food-insecure *woredas* (districts) in the regions of Amhara; Oromia; Tigray; and Southern Nations, Nationalities, and Peoples (SNNP). It included a CGP component, which began in 2005. (This component is classified and described below as a separate intervention because it was self-standing and operated using community volunteers and without providing food or cash for food.) Since June 2010, the CGP component has been taken over by the Community-Based Nutrition Program (described below). The asset-building aspects have been rolled into the Household Asset

Table 3.1 Programs That Give Food or Cash in Lieu of Food

Program or intervention	Managing agencies	Year began	Brief description	Woredas covered (at time of writing)	Target beneficiaries	Estimated number of beneficiaries (at time of writing)
Government Food Security Program	Government of Ethiopia	2003	Aims to help chronically food-insecure households reach a level of food security necessary for an active and healthy life	Chronically food-insecure woredas in all regions	All members of chronically and transitory food-insecure households	13.7 million in 2010
Food Security Project	Government of Ethiopia	2002	Aimed to (a) support chronically poor rural households, (b) increase employment and incomes, (c) reduce food costs, and (d) improve nutrition in children less than two years of age and in pregnant and lactating women	Phased out in 2010	Members of chronically food-insecure households	Phased out in 2010
Emergency food aid	World Food Programme	1973	Provides food for relief and livelihood protection in times of crisis	Woredas throughout the country, identified through needs assessments conducted twice a year	Vulnerable households facing a shock	5.2 million in 2010
Protracted Relief and Recovery Operation	World Food Programme	2000	Provides food for refugees in Ethiopia unable to procure their own	Woredas throughout the country with refugees in camps and communities	Refugees	147,000 in 2010

(continued)

Table 3.1 *(continued)*

Program or intervention	Managing agencies	Year began	Brief description	*Woredas* covered (at time of writing)	Target beneficiaries	Estimated number of beneficiaries (at time of writing)
Targeted Supplementary Food Program	Government of Ethiopia, United Nations Children's Fund (UNICEF), World Food Programme	March 2004	Provides supplementary food to beneficiaries identified through EOS screenings; each beneficiary receives a ration of 25 kilograms of blended food (Famix or corn soya blend) and three liters of vegetable oil every three months	Vulnerable *woredas* identified by UNICEF; 163 of the EOS *woredas* in seven regions receive targeted supplementary food (in 2010)	Children under five years of age with mid-upper arm circumference (MUAC) between 11 and 12 centimeters or bilateral edema and pregnant and lactating women with MUAC less than 17 centimeters (or less than 18 centimeters together with recent weight loss or chronic illness)	625,000 children under five years of age and 294,000 pregnant and lactating women in 2010
Productive Safety Net Program	Government of Ethiopia	February 2005	Focuses on asset creation at the household level via two components: (a) labor-intensive public works programs and (b) direct support for household heads, who can participate in other programs at the same time	Chronically food-insecure *woredas* in most regions	Vulnerable households within food-insecure *woredas,* defined by number of times the *woreda* has received emergency aid in the previous five years; targeting is done using community task forces to create a list of households	7.5 million in 2010

Program	Partners	Year	Description	Coverage	Target	Beneficiaries
School Feeding or Children in Local Development	Government of Ethiopia, World Food Programme	1994	Provides meals (Famix or corn soya blend) and, at times, take-home rations to primary schoolchildren in order to increase their school attendance and ability to concentrate and participate	Schools in Afar, Amhara, Oromia, Southern Nations, Nationalities, and Peoples (SNNP), Tigray, and Somali	Primary schools (grades one to eight) chosen using the chronic vulnerability index	555,000 in 2010
Treatment of severe acute malnutrition (health center–based institutional approach)	Government of Ethiopia	2000	Provides traditional government-implemented treatment, consisting of inpatient care at a stabilization center (with some recent shift toward outpatient care); provides special milk during the inpatient treatment	387 *woredas* covered in Addis Ababa, Dire Dawa, and all regions except Benshangul-Gumuz	Children under five years of age with moderate to severe malnutrition	137,997 in 2009 (including 43.2% reporting rate)
Managing Environmental Resources to Enable Transitions to More Sustainable Livelihoods (MERET)	Government of Ethiopia, World Food Programme	2002	Provides food for asset creation: three kilograms of wheat per day of labor on a locally identified project (for example, maintaining small roads, checking dams, making compost)	72 *woredas* in six regions	Households chosen by local committees within *woredas*; chosen using the chronic vulnerability index	600,000 in 2010

Source: Authors, based on program data.
Note: EOS = Enhanced Outreach Strategy for Child Survival.

Building Program, which is part of the Productive Safety Net Program (also described below).

The objectives of the Food Security Project were to (a) support chronically poor rural households, (b) increase employment and income, (c) reduce food costs, and (d) improve nutrition in children less than two years of age and in pregnant and lactating women. The project's components included the following:

- Funds to *kebeles* (communities)
- Community-based child growth promotion
- Capacity-building funds to *woredas*, regions, and federal ministries for specific project-related activities
- Investments in communications, financial administration, and monitoring and evaluation

EMERGENCY FOOD AID

Broad national estimates of emergency food aid needs, used for planning and resource mobilization, are based on the results of the *meher* and *belg*[1] assessments conducted annually in November–December and June, respectively. In 2010, 620,000 metric tons of food aid were provided in Ethiopia. Food aid is distributed in all regions, with the exception of Addis Ababa and Harari. The challenges of targeting food aid are discussed at length in chapter 5.

PROTRACTED RELIEF AND RECOVERY OPERATION IN ETHIOPIA

Protracted Relief and Recovery Operation in Ethiopia, which began in 2000, is a program designed and supported by the World Food Programme. It provides food assistance to refugees hosted in camps or communities. Refugees receive monthly general food rations, and malnourished children and pregnant and lactating women receive supplementary food. Refugee children benefit from on-site or take-home school-feeding rations. Recipients also benefit from income-generating activities, environmental rehabilitation, and the receipt of nonfood items to improve livelihood opportunities in selected camps.

TARGETED SUPPLEMENTARY FOOD PROGRAM

The Targeted Supplementary Food Program (TSFP) is a key component of the Enhanced Outreach Strategy for Child Survival (EOS) Program, which began in March 2004. It is a partnership between the Disaster Risk Management and Food Security Sector,[2] the former disaster prevention and preparedness bureau,[3] the Ministry of Health, regional health bureaus, the World Food Programme, and the United Nations Children's Fund (UNICEF). The TSFP aims to rehabilitate moderately malnourished children under five years of age and pregnant and lactating women identified during EOS biannual screenings held in food-insecure *woredas*; it also aims to enhance basic nutrition knowledge of mothers and other women in communities targeted by the program.

Beneficiaries of the TSFP include children less than five years of age with a mid-upper arm circumference (MUAC) of between 11 and 12 centimeters or bilateral edema (or both) and pregnant and lactating women with a MUAC less than 17 centimeters or with a MUAC less than 18 centimeters together with recent weight loss or an underlying chronic illness. These beneficiaries are identified during the EOS biannual screenings. They receive a food ration every three months, consisting of 25 kilograms of blended food, such as Famix or corn soya blend, and three liters of vegetable oil. Currently, 163 *woredas* are in the program.

The program is not intended to treat severe malnutrition; rather, it provides treatment for moderate malnutrition. In each *woreda*, 10 to 12 food distribution sites are established and run by local women called food distribution agents. In addition to distributing food, the agents teach proper nutrition and feeding techniques and deliver specific health messages to aid recipients. To reinforce these messages, the program also distributes posters to each site, which are written in Amharic, Oromifa, Somali, and Afaric. The posters convey messages about proper food preparation techniques, ration sizes, exclusive breast-feeding, and complementary feeding.

PRODUCTIVE SAFETY NET PROGRAM

The Productive Safety Net Program was introduced in 2005. Aimed at the country's chronically food-insecure population, it marked a shift from a policy of emergency relief to programming oriented toward sustainable development for this population. Families selected for the program are provided an opportunity to create assets to stabilize their livelihoods and strengthen their ability to cope with shocks. The program consists of a labor-intensive public works component for households with able-bodied members who work constructing roads, health clinics, and schools. A direct support component assists more vulnerable, labor-poor households that are chronically food insecure but lack productive labor and have no other means of support. Some beneficiaries receive cash transfers, while others receive in-kind transfers. The community selects the public works based on its needs for environmental rehabilitation.

The program employs a combination of geographic, administrative, and community-based targeting to identify consistently vulnerable households. These households include orphans; pregnant and lactating women; households headed by an elderly person; other labor-poor, high-risk households with sick individuals, such as people living with human immunodeficiency virus (HIV)/acquired immune deficiency syndrome (AIDS); and female-headed households with young children. The Productive Safety Net Program is currently active in Tigray, Amhara, Oromia, SNNP, rural Harari, Dire Dawa, Afar, and Somali.

TREATMENT OF SEVERE ACUTE MALNUTRITION (HEALTH CENTER–BASED INSTITUTIONAL APPROACH)

In Ethiopia, the traditional approach to treating severe acute malnutrition has been to treat patients in therapeutic feeding centers. In 2007, the national protocol for managing severe acute malnutrition was revised to include community-based management of acute malnutrition—previously known as community-based therapeutic care. The new protocol focuses on outpatient management with the support of community volunteers. Since then, the Ministry of Health, with support from UNICEF and various nongovernmental organizations (NGOs), has introduced outpatient treatment programs for severe acute malnutrition at select health centers. Although this is a significant advance, health centers remain inaccessible to many Ethiopians, particularly individuals needing treatment for severe acute malnutrition. To bridge this gap, the Ministry of Health, with its nutrition partners, is establishing outpatient treatment programs at health posts (which are generally more accessible to households than health centers)[4] and training health post–based health extension workers in community-based management of acute malnutrition. But data for outpatient treatment programs at health posts are not readily available, and so the analysis of the health center–based institutional approach in this book focuses on interventions at the health center level.

The outpatient treatment programs based at health centers—which still form a significant element of the institutional approach—treat individuals with severe acute malnutrition who present with no medical complications and good appetite. These individuals are given routine medicines and a take-home nutritional supplement that is a highly fortified peanut butter paste.[5] The caretakers bring patients to the health center each week to assess their progress, replenish their ration, and attend health education sessions. Where resources permit, families are also given a ration of corn soya blend to decrease leakage of the nutritional supplement to other family members, as well as to treat the relapse of moderate malnutrition at home. Individuals with severe malnutrition and additional medical complications or poor appetite are referred to the inpatient program called the stabilization center. There, patients are fed therapeutic milk and given medical treatment. When their complications resolve or their appetite returns, individuals are released to the outpatient program and continue their recovery at home.

The institutional approach to treating severe acute malnutrition is classified in this chapter as a program providing food. In fact, the approach also provides medical treatment and trains health workers, in addition to providing rations of the peanut-based nutritional supplement or special milk described above.

In areas where there is a sudden rise in the prevalence of severe acute malnutrition due to an emergency situation, certain NGOs often implement community-based management of acute malnutrition on a temporary basis. The institutional approach and the NGO approach to treating severe acute malnutrition are compared at the end of this chapter.

CHILDREN IN LOCAL DEVELOPMENT (SCHOOL FEEDING PROGRAM)

In 1994, the Ethiopian government and the World Food Programme began a school feeding program. In 2004, a community planning component—Children in Local Development—was added to strengthen the development of the learning environment. This program targets schools in Afar, Amhara, Oromia, SNNP, Tigray, and Somali regions. It provides primary schoolchildren with meals of Famix or corn soya blend (blended foods fortified with vitamin A, iron, and zinc), fortified vegetable oil, and iodized salt. The key objectives are to increase attendance as well as to improve the children's ability to concentrate and participate at school. Schools are chosen according to, among other criteria, gender ratio and measures of vulnerability and accessibility. The program focuses on schools with grades one through eight.

MANAGING ENVIRONMENTAL RESOURCES TO ENABLE TRANSITIONS TO MORE SUSTAINABLE LIVELIHOODS

Managing Environmental Resources to Enable Transitions to More Sustainable Livelihoods (MERET) has been active in Ethiopia in some form since the 1980s. Run jointly by the government of Ethiopia and the World Food Programme, as of December 2010, MERET operates in 72 *woredas* in six regions (Tigray, Amhara, Oromia, SNNP, Somali, and Dire Dawa).

The program provides workers with three kilograms of wheat per day of labor. Participating households are chosen by local committees within *woredas* identified by the chronic vulnerability index.[6] Public works projects are identified by local committees and include building small roads, making compost, and doing whatever the community identifies as a need.

PROGRAMS THAT DO NOT GIVE FOOD OR CASH, OTHER THAN THOSE FOCUSING ON COMMUNITY VOLUNTEERS

Two important programs that fall into this category—the Enhanced Outreach Strategy for Child Survival and the Health Extension Program—are not discussed in this section. Instead, they are discussed at length at the end of this chapter. See table 3.2 for a summary of these two programs as well as the others discussed in this section.

WATER SUPPLY, SANITATION, AND HYGIENE

The Water, Sanitation, and Hygiene (WASH) Program is a collaborative effort of the Ministry of Water Resources, the Ministry of Health, the World Bank, the African Development Bank, UNICEF, the United Kingdom's Department for International Development, and other donors. The objective is to increase sustainable water supply and sanitation services for both rural and urban areas and to improve capacity at all levels. WASH committees are formed at the community level; in addition, volunteers are trained and work with health extension workers. *Woreda*, zone, and regional levels all have WASH committees with specific tasks.

EXPANDED PROGRAM ON IMMUNIZATION

The Expanded Program on Immunization was initiated in Ethiopia in 1980 and targets all children who need immunizations. Currently, the program provides vaccines for eight preventable diseases: measles; a pentavalent formulation of diphtheria, pertussis, tetanus, hepatitis B, and haemophilus influenza type B; polio; and Bacille Calmette-Guerin for tuberculosis. The pentavalent formulation was introduced in Ethiopia in the first quarter of 2007 (Ethiopia, Federal Ministry of Health 2007).

EMERGENCY NONFOOD AID PROGRAM

The Emergency Nonfood Aid Program is managed by the Early Warning and Response Directorate (EWRD) of the Disaster Risk Management and

Table 3.2 Programs That Do Not Give Food or Cash in Lieu of Food, Other Than Those Focusing on Community Volunteers

Program or intervention	Managing agencies	Year began	Brief description	*Woredas* covered (at time of writing)	Target beneficiaries	Estimated number of beneficiaries (at time of writing)
Enhanced Outreach Strategy for Child Survival (EOS) and Extended EOS	Government of Ethiopia, United Nations Children's Fund (UNICEF)	March 2004	Features mass mobilizations twice a year. Provides vitamin A, measles vaccinations, deworming, screening for malnutrition and referral to the Targeted Supplementary Food Program or a therapeutic feeding center, insecticide-treated bed nets, iodated oil capsules, and information on or communication of key messages	773 *woredas*	Children 6–59 months of age and pregnant and lactating women	11.1 million children and 900,000 women in 2010
Health Extension Program	Government of Ethiopia	2004	Provides extensive public health program aimed at bringing health care to rural areas. Goals are prevention, promotion, and basic treatment. Health extension workers implement 16 packages and are essential to the program.	All rural and urban *woredas*	The community in which individuals live and work	Entire population of 74 million (2007 census figure)
Water Supply, Sanitation, and Hygiene Program	Government of Ethiopia	2004	Aims to increase sustainable water supply and sanitation services for both rural and urban areas	349 rural and urban *woredas*	Members of communities who do not have access to adequate water supply and sanitation services	About 18 million

(continued)

Table 3.2 *(continued)*

Program or intervention	Managing agencies	Year began	Brief description	*Woredas* covered (at time of writing)	Target beneficiaries	Estimated number of beneficiaries (at time of writing)
Expanded Program on Immunization	Government of Ethiopia, World Health Organization, UNICEF	1980	Features immunization program with goal of 90% or more coverage. Provides immunizations for measles, diphtheria, pertussis, tetanus, hepatitis B, haemophilus influenza type B, polio, and tuberculosis	All *woredas*	All nonimmunized children, specifically under age five	1.7 million in 2010
Emergency Nonfood Aid Program	Government of Ethiopia, UNICEF	1973	Provides shelter, water, health, nutrition services, and first aid following fast-onset disasters. What is delivered depends on the crisis and the needs of the population.	40 *woredas* in total (covering all regions, except Harari) in 2010	Households and communities facing a shock	Typically exceeds 5 million each year[a]
Household Asset Building Program	Government of Ethiopia	2010	Aims to diversify the income sources and productive assets of food-insecure households by increasing (a) the ability of rural savings and credit cooperatives and microfinance institutions to extend lending capacity in chronically food-insecure *woredas* and (b) awareness among chronically food-insecure households about how to generate off-farm income	Chronically food-insecure *woredas* in all regions	All members of chronically and transitory food-insecure households	Plans to reach 80% of Productive Safety Net Program beneficiaries by 2014. As of January 2011, the number reached is not certain

Source: Authors, based on program data.
a. Precise estimation is difficult due to nature of interventions.

60

Food Security Sector. The directorate provides shelter and other nonfood items following fast-onset disasters, such as floods and displacement caused by conflict. The regional governments send requests for aid to EWRD. Following an initial disbursement, further aid is dependent on the results of a more thorough needs assessment, including the specific number of beneficiaries and the estimated duration of assistance needed. The EWRD conducts this assessment.

HOUSEHOLD ASSET BUILDING PROGRAM

The Household Asset Building Program was introduced into the Government Food Security Program in 2010. It aims to diversify the income sources and productive assets of food-insecure households in chronically food-insecure *woredas*. To do this, it works with microfinance institutions, the Small and Medium Enterprise Agency (in the Ministry of Trade and Industry), and the Ministry of Women's Affairs to improve (a) the ability of rural savings and credit cooperatives and microfinance institutions to extend lending capacity in chronically food-insecure *woredas* and (b) awareness among chronically food-insecure households about how to generate off-farm income. The program aims to achieve six specific outputs:

- An increase in access to viable on- and off-farm income-generating opportunities
- An increase in access to sustainable financial services
- The creation of sustainable systems of input sourcing, production, and delivery
- An increase in access to effective product and labor markets
- An ability to manage and implement the program at local levels
- An increase in knowledge, skills, and confidence among food-insecure households

PROGRAMS WITH A STRONG COMMUNITY VOLUNTEER FOCUS

An important program that falls into this category—Essential Services for Health in Ethiopia—is not discussed in this section. Instead, it is discussed at length at the end of this chapter. See table 3.3 for a summary of this program as well as the others discussed in this section.

COMMUNITY-BASED REPRODUCTIVE HEALTH AGENTS

Pathfinder International's Community-Based Reproductive Health Agents Program began in 1995 and merged with the Essential Services for Health

Table 3.3 Programs with a Strong Community Volunteer Focus

Program or intervention	Year began	Brief description	Volunteer incentives	Number of volunteers (at time of writing)	Woredas covered (at time of writing)	Target beneficiaries
Essential Services for Health in Ethiopia (ESHE)	2003	Community health promoters (trained volunteers) sensitized their communities to various health messages and encouraged small, doable actions to empower the community. A key task was to act as role models. In 2008, the ESHE and Community-Based Reproductive Health Agent (CBRHA) programs were merged to form the Integrated Family Health Program.	Community health promoters were not required to change their routine and were only expected to work two hours a week. They were not paid for their time.	About 18,000 community health promoters were trained.	64 woredas in Amhara, Oromia, and Southern Nations, Nationalities, and Peoples (SNNP) regions in 2007	Communities where the community health promoters live
Community-Based Reproductive Health Agents Program	1995	Community-chosen volunteers counsel women house-to-house on contraceptives, sanitation, and nutrition. Plan was to phase out when awareness and demand had been created. In 2008, ESHE and CBRHA were merged to form the Integrated Family Health Program.	Community-based reproductive health agents worked several days a week and received a substantial incentive package of training with per diem, transport allowance, shoes, and uniforms.	More than 10,000 community-based reproductive health agents in 2007	More than 250 woredas in 2007 in Amhara, Oromia, and SNNP; to a lesser extent in Tigray, Benshangul-Gumuz, and Addis Ababa	Communities where they live, specifically women and religious leaders
Integrated Family Health Program (IFHP)	2008	The IFHP merged the activities of ESHE and CBRHA and focuses on family planning and maternal, neonatal, and child health packages. Volunteer community health workers from the community implement the health packages and are supervised by health extension workers.	Volunteer community health workers do not receive financial incentives for their work, but they do not incur personal expenses to attend meetings.	Health extension workers are responsible for training volunteers in the communities, and they train as many as is feasible and practical.	286 woredas mainly in Amhara, Oromia, SNNP, and Tigray regions. The majority of woredas formerly covered under ESHE and CBRHA are included.	Communities where volunteer community health workers live

Program	Year	Description	Incentives	Number	Coverage	Target population
Community-Based Nutrition Program	2008	Aims to develop and strengthen the capacity of communities to assess and analyze the causes of malnutrition and to make better use of family, community, and external resources to improve the nutrition status of women and children	Volunteer community health workers receive a per diem for their time in pre-service and in-service training, but do not receive other incentives.	57,636	228 *woredas* covered in Tigray, SNNP, Oromia, and Amhara	Children under five years of age and pregnant and lactating women
Child Growth Promotion component, Food Security Project	2005	Focused on monitoring growth and providing nutrition education for children under two years of age. The project was phased out in 2010 and replaced by the Community-Based Nutrition Program.	In-service training quarterly and skills building through on-the-job training are provided.	Between five and eight volunteers per *kebele* in 2009	751 *kebeles* in 50 *woredas* in Amhara, Oromia, SNNP, and Tigray in 2009	Children under two years of age in chosen *kebeles*
Community-based therapeutic care implemented by nongovernmental organizations (NGOs)[a]	2002	Early detection, assessment, and home-based management of cases with severe malnutrition, using volunteers in the community	Incentives vary among NGOs, but volunteers typically receive incentives for their work.	Difficult to measure with precision because of constant changes	Covered *kebeles* in about 150–200 *woredas* (usually one or a small number of *kebeles* within each *woreda* covered at any one time, and the number of *woredas* fluctuates a lot over time)	Children 6–59 months of age who are severely malnourished and their mothers

Source: Authors, based on program data.
a. International Medical Corps, Cooperative for Assistance and Relief Everywhere, Concern/Valid, Action Against Hunger, GOAL, Save the Children United States, Samaritan's Purse, World Vision, and Islamic Relief.

in Ethiopia (ESHE) Program in 2008 to form the Integrated Family Health Program (IFHP). Before the merger, community-based reproductive health agents, working with the regional health bureaus, the Ministry of Justice, and local NGOs (specifically faith-based organizations), conducted home visits to disseminate information on reproductive health, family planning, and contraceptive methods and also attended religious and social community gatherings to spread health messages. They worked in collaboration with health extension workers and often overlapped with ESHE *woredas* before the two programs merged. Most of the activities undertaken as part of the CBRHA Program, and by the reproductive health agents themselves, are now part of the IFHP, specifically the volunteer community health workers component.

INTEGRATED FAMILY HEALTH PROGRAM

The Integrated Family Health Program resulted from the merger of Pathfinder International's CBRHA Program and the ESHE Program. Launched in late 2008, the IFHP aims to (a) expand community access to family planning, integrate family planning in HIV/AIDS prevention, and increase adolescent interventions for improved sexual and reproductive health; (b) improve antenatal and intrapartum care and strengthen referral for skilled delivery and obstetric and newborn care; (c) promote the integrated management of neonatal and childhood illness; (d) integrate prevention, bed net use, and artemisinin-based combination therapy for the treatment of malaria; and (e) expand nutrition counseling.

Building on experiences with community-based reproductive health agents and community health promoters, the IFHP mobilizes and trains volunteer community health workers, who carry out family planning and maternal, neonatal, and child health interventions. Volunteer community health workers with reproductive training provide family planning and reproductive health services to the community and promote interventions that address maternal, neonatal, and child health. As the IFHP evolves, it is envisioned that all volunteer community health workers will have a common core of essential knowledge and communication skills in family planning and maternal, neonatal, and child health interventions and that some will have specialized skills.

Volunteer community health workers are supervised and mobilized by health extension workers, and regional managers are responsible for ensuring that they are trained to respond to the needs of each *woreda*.

The program targets approximately 32.7 million beneficiaries in 286 *woredas*, mainly in the Amhara, Oromia, SNNP, and Tigray regions and, to a lesser extent, in Benshangul-Gumuz and Somali regions. Pathfinder International and John Snow, Incorporated, are the main partners for this program, with the Academy for Educational Development and the Consortium of Reproductive Health Associations providing additional support. In total, 11 NGOs support the program through individual grant agreements.

COMMUNITY-BASED NUTRITION

The Community-Based Nutrition (CBN) Program was launched in 39 *woredas* in 2008, funded initially by UNICEF. It is now a joint undertaking of the government of Ethiopia, UNICEF, and the World Bank that hopes to scale up to 300 *woredas* by the end of 2011. At the time of writing, 228 *woredas* were covered. The objective of CBN is to develop and strengthen the capacity of communities to assess and analyze the causes of malnutrition in their community and to take action by making better use of family, community, and external resources to improve the nutrition status of women and children.

To meet its objective, the CBN Program trains volunteer community health workers who, with the support of the existing health extension workers, raise nutritional awareness and perform basic nutritional activities. They, as well as health extension worker supervisors, are trained in community-based nutrition, essential nutrition actions, growth promotion techniques, referrals to and linkages with other programs, community mobilization skills, and monitoring and reporting. Specifically, these workers perform a household inventory and community mapping, which serves as a basis for understanding the initial nutrition situation in their community. On a monthly basis, they then conduct Community Growth Promotion sessions for all children under two years of age and conduct community conversations to promote essential nutrition actions. Volunteer community health workers have the authority to refer severely underweight children to health facilities. Health extension workers also conduct maternal nutrition and child care promotion activities for pregnant and lactating women.

CHILD GROWTH PROMOTION COMPONENT OF THE FOOD SECURITY PROJECT

As noted, the Food Security Project, which ended in 2010, included a CGP component that aimed to increase beneficiaries' income and access to food, while improving the nutrition status of vulnerable children, pregnant women, and lactating mothers. CGP targeted 751 *kebeles* in 50 *woredas* in four regions: Amhara, Oromia, SNNP, and Tigray. It relied on trained community volunteers to implement two models: (a) in Amhara, Oromia, and Tigray, health volunteers trained for 30 days on the weighing of children and counseling of mothers and (b) in the SNNP, health extension agents—with support from health promoters trained for two days in about five sessions at one- to two-month intervals—weighed children and counseled mothers. In both models, during monthly weighing and counseling sessions, the volunteer worked with the mother to record the child's weight on a growth chart and to jointly evaluate the weight gain or loss by comparing the child's current weight to his or her previous weight and to the growth curve of the reference population.

Volunteers also made home visits, discussed child growth trends with community leaders and members, and prepared reports for monitoring, evaluation, and supervision purposes. The CGP also provided community grants to *kebeles* for community-developed and -approved proposals to reduce community-level causes of malnutrition. The CGP component was phased out in 2010 and replaced by CBN, which is part of the National Nutrition Program.

COMMUNITY-BASED THERAPEUTIC CARE IMPLEMENTED BY NGOS

The institutional approach to treating severe acute malnutrition focuses on inpatient care in health centers. In areas where there is a sudden rise in the prevalence of severe acute malnutrition due to an emergency situation, certain NGOs implement community-based management of acute malnutrition, also known as community-based therapeutic care, on a temporary basis. NGOs specializing in community-based therapeutic care in Ethiopia include International Medical Corps, Cooperative for Assistance Everywhere, Concern/Valid, Action Against Hunger, GOAL, Save the Children United States, Save the Children United Kingdom, Samaritan's Purse, World Vision, and Islamic Relief.

Community-based therapeutic care implemented by the NGOs focuses on outpatient home-based treatment, with significant involvement by community volunteers, unlike the health center–based institutional approach. It stresses early detection and assessment of severely malnourished cases in the community and home-based management of uncomplicated cases. Community volunteers work with the health post–based health extension workers. Caretakers go to health posts each week to collect their take-home peanut-based nutritional supplement rations, which are a mainstay of the treatment of severe acute malnutrition in Ethiopia, and to attend health education sessions. Approximately 5–10 percent of individuals with severe acute malnutrition have poor appetite or medical complications. These individuals must first be treated on an inpatient basis at a stabilization center until their appetite returns or the complications resolve. If a stabilization center does not exist, the NGOs generally establish one at a health center to treat these individuals.

A CLOSER LOOK AT FOUR PROGRAMS AFFECTING NUTRITION IN ETHIOPIA

This section takes a closer look at four programs that are among the most widespread and the most critical for nutrition in Ethiopia. First, it examines in detail the Health Extension Program and the Enhanced Outreach Strategy for Child Survival, both of which are classified above as programs that do not give food or cash, other than those focusing on community volunteers. Next, the section discusses the Essential Services for Health in Ethiopia, which is categorized above as a program with a strong community volunteer focus. Finally, a detailed discussion is provided on treatment of severe acute malnutrition in Ethiopia.

HEALTH EXTENSION PROGRAM

The Health Extension Program is a landmark Ethiopian initiative that has been a key factor in the accelerated improvements in basic health indicators since it was launched in 2004 (see table 3.4).

The Health Extension Program gives priority to the prevention and control of communicable diseases through active community participation, with the goal of providing equitable access to health services. The program seeks to expand the health care infrastructure by building health

Table 3.4 Basic Health Indicators in Ethiopia, 2003–09

Rate	2003	2004	2005	2006	2007	2008	2009
Immunization rate							
Measles (%)	50	61	70	77	77	85	82
DPT3[a] (%)	43	52	61	67	68	76	77
Contraceptive acceptor rate (%)	21.5	23	25.2	37.9	34.8	53.9	56.2
Bed nets, purchased and distributed (millions, cumulative)	1.28	1.86	5.13	9.5	18.2	20.49	22.18

Source: Health Management and Information System, Federal Ministry of Health, Ethiopia. Various health management and information reports of the Federal Ministry of Health, 2003–09.
a. Diphtheria, pertussis, and tetanus.

posts in rural areas and developing a cadre of health extension workers to provide basic curative and preventive health services in every community.[7] To support health extension workers, the program aims to train 50 community volunteers per health extension worker in the *kebeles*.

The Health Extension Program places two government-salaried female health extension workers and one health post in every *kebele* to shift the emphasis of the country's health care system to prevention and improving the distribution of resources. Health extension workers receive extensive training in four health areas as well as in personal development. As shown in table 3.5, the program was established in all rural *kebeles* in less than six years. By March 2009, a total of 30,193 health extension workers (out of the planned 31,523) had been trained and deployed. By June 2009, the remaining health extension workers had completed their training. By June 2009, 15,478 health posts, or one in every rural *kebele*, had been established.

Table 3.6 describes the 16 health packages that health extension workers are asked to focus on in their communities: the program addresses all

Table 3.5　Implementation of the Health Extension Program in Ethiopia, 2004–09
number

Program component	2004 (inception)	2006	2008	2009
Health posts	0	5,000	11,446	15,478
Health extension workers	0	9,612	24,571	31,523
Health centers	412	673	721	3,153

Source: Ethiopia, Ministry of Health.

Table 3.6　Focus of Health Extension Workers

Area of focus	Percentage of training time[a]	Health packages
Hygiene and environmental sanitation	22.1	Building and maintaining of a healthy home; control of insects, rodents, and other biting species; food hygiene and safety measures; personal hygiene; construction, use, and maintenance of a sanitary latrine; management of solid and liquid waste; water supply safety measures
Family health services	24.4	Adolescent reproductive health; family planning; maternal and child health; nutrition; vaccination services
Disease prevention and control	14.7	First aid; HIV/AIDS and tuberculosis prevention and control; malaria prevention
Health education and communication	2.2	Health education

Source: Ethiopia, Ministry of Health.
a. The remainder of the training time is devoted to common courses (23.7 percent), others (8.6 percent), and community documentation (4.3 percent).

except the first of the four components of nutrition security (to provide secure access to food, a sanitary environment, adequate health services, and knowledgeable care).

A key role played by the health extension workers is to provide education to communities on optimal practices affecting health, nutrition, and food hygiene. A report by Lloyd and others (2007) funded by the World Food Programme discusses how certain child care practices in some parts of rural Ethiopia are underlying causes of child malnutrition. For example, some Ethiopians visit a traditional healer when they or their children are ill before consulting a health extension worker. Some cultural practices can prove harmful and even fatal to children and pregnant and lactating women. The Health Extension Program addresses these issues by encouraging community members to connect with health extension workers.

The large scale of the program and its rapid scaling up have inevitably resulted in growing pains. For example, there are often insufficient numbers of trained community volunteers to support the health extension workers, a constraint that is expected to endure for some time because of the considerable time required to find and adequately train community volunteers. In *kebeles* with NGO and regional health bureau projects, community volunteers identified and trained as part of these projects can often provide support to health extension workers operating in those areas. But these community volunteers often focus only on the specific activities funded by their project and not on others that are a part of the full 16 health packages.

Inadequate supervision is another constraint. Medical staff members at the *woreda* level, and at health clinics to a lesser extent, were originally designated to supervise health extension workers, but they are already overextended by their duties. As a result, the government created a new cadre of staff: health extension worker supervisors (about 3,200 in total). These supervisors are responsible for monitoring the performance of health extension workers, providing them with technical support to implement the 16 health packages, gathering data on the program, and regularly evaluating their performance.

The extensive demands on the time of health extension workers and their strained capacity to implement all 16 packages are growing concerns. Each package requires extensive time and outreach. Other programs and projects, such as the Expanded Program on Immunization, have called on the health extension workers for assistance, even though they generally are not yet fully supported by the community volunteer system. As a result, since the health extension workers' debut, their workload has burgeoned without additional compensation.

Because of their success, the Ministry of Health is also interested in transferring Enhanced Outreach Strategy for Child Survival and Extended EOS program activities to the health extension workers. Before such an action is undertaken, appropriate preparatory activities are required to ensure that the system is ready to assume such a large-scale activity. As previously mentioned, the community volunteer program designed to support the health extension workers is not yet firmly established. Once it is, the community volunteers will need time to master their duties at a reasonable pace. Without the support of adequately trained and motivated community volunteers, it is premature to transfer EOS and Extended EOS (EEOS) activities to health extension workers. A thorough program review is necessary and many questions must be answered, such as how health extension workers handle their current workload and the demands of being involved as *kebele* coordinators for one or more programs other than the Health Extension Program. Before expanding their duties, a better understanding is needed of how their time is allocated to specific activities, their relationships with community members and volunteers, and their ability to assume responsibility for the EOS/EEOS activities.

THE ENHANCED OUTREACH STRATEGY FOR CHILD SURVIVAL

EOS began in March 2004 as a pilot program to stem the need for yearly emergency action in chronically vulnerable *woredas*. The EOS (with the Targeted Supplementary Food Program) is a partnership between the government of Ethiopia, the Ministry of Health, regional health bureaus, the Disaster Risk Management and Food Security Sector, UNICEF, the World Food Programme, and various NGOs. As of 2010, the TSFP was providing benefits to about 625,000 children under five years of age and 294,000 pregnant and lactating women living in the 163[8] most food-insecure *woredas*.

EOS is a large-scale program, with mass mobilizations occurring twice a year in all target *woredas*. The goal is to reduce morbidity and mortality among children less than five years of age and among pregnant and lactating women by promoting preventive health care at the community and household levels. The EOS provides the following:

- Vitamin A supplementation to children between six months and five years of age
- Deworming for children between two and five years of age
- Screening and the referral of malnourished children and pregnant and lactating women to the TSFP or to a therapeutic feeding center[9]
- Catch-up measles vaccination of children 9–23 months of age

- Distribution of long-lasting insecticide-treated bed nets in *kebeles* with at least three months of exposure to malaria annually
- Iodine capsules to children and pregnant and lactating women in some *woredas* (especially those identified as having iodine deficiency disorder, as a bridging strategy until iodized salt is widely available)
- Information, education, and communication, with messages focusing on the proper feeding of infants and young children; promotion of hand washing; HIV/AIDS prevention; and demonstrations of the construction, use, and maintenance of household latrines

An abridged and lower-cost version of EOS—the Extended EOS—is implemented in most *woredas* that do not have the full program. EEOS includes all the EOS interventions listed above except nutritional screening, and there is no link to the TSFP. The target population for interventions such as vitamin A and deworming—which are provided under the EEOS as well as the full EOS—is about 12 million.

The performance of EOS/EEOS has garnered both rave reviews and criticisms. Despite the criticism, strong evidence indicates that mass vitamin A and measles campaigns have saved large numbers of lives in the *woredas* receiving services. And the vitamin A supplementation and deworming interventions successfully reach more than 90 percent of the target population of approximately 12 million. The vitamin A supplementation coverage by region is shown in table 3.7.

Table 3.7 Vitamin A Supplementation Coverage of EOS/EEOS, by Region, 2010

Region	Vitamin A coverage (% of children under five years of age)
SNNP	99.0
Oromia	97.2
Amhara	103.4
Tigray	90.7
Benshangul-Gumuz	93.3
Afar	103.1
Gambela	107.8
Harari	84.8
Dire Dawa	71.2
Somali	88.8
Total	92.8

Source: Data from UNICEF.
Note: Calculated as percentages of estimates of the population of children less than five years of age in each region.

Because of a lack of data, it is not possible to assess the impact of many of the EOS/EEOS interventions. But the program outcomes demonstrate that it is a cost-effective intervention—with or without TSFP—even if vitamin A supplementation and measles vaccinations were the only interventions with any impact. The economic benefits of the interventions (from increased total lifetime earnings)[10] are about four times the costs, if (a) the interventions other than vitamin A supplementation and measles vaccinations are assumed for the sake of illustration to have no benefit and (b) the costs of these other interventions (including the TSFP) are still included in the computation of total costs.[11]

The EOS/EEOS was independently assessed in November and December 2006 (Hall and Khara 2006). The evaluation provided concrete evidence of the program's strengths and weaknesses. Table 3.8 summarizes some of the findings of the evaluation. Steps have been taken to address some of the flaws listed. For example, tetanus toxoid injections are being administered to pregnant and lactating women as part of the Expanded Program on Immunization, and efforts have been undertaken to reduce the time between EOS screenings and the delivery of TSFP rations.

The key findings of the evaluation match this book's conclusions and recommendations. Because the EOS/EEOS program was born of necessity during an acute crisis, it is less a development program than a transitional program bridging the gap between chronic emergencies and development. And because of their urgency and nature, emergency programs commonly do not conduct thorough baseline studies or implement monitoring

Table 3.8 Select Findings of the 2006 EOS/EEOS Independent Assessment

Positive	Negative
EOS/EEOS is the largest program of its kind, targeting more than 11 million children and 900,000 pregnant and lactating women.	Data regarding EOS/EEOS implementation and impact are lacking.
Children are now dewormed on a regular basis.	Due to practical and administrative reasons, the TSFP ration may not be provided for up to three months after the screening.
TSFP is now in place and provides food to malnourished children and women every three months (versus only during emergencies).	Coverage rates are flawed. The denominator is the number of children 6–59 months of age, whereas the entry criterion is children with a MUAC of between 11 and 12 centimeters.
Malnourished children are identified regularly, and the severely malnourished are referred for treatment.	A key opportunity to target pregnant and lactating women with tetanus toxoid, iron and folate supplements, and so forth is missed.
Vitamin A coverage rates have substantially increased.	EOS data have limitations and cannot be used for nutrition surveillance.

Source: Hall and Khara 2006.

systems, even though monitoring is essential for program implementation. To improve the EOS/EEOS programs, more information must be consistently gathered, with appropriate attention paid to quality. An effective monitoring and evaluation system requires an effective nutrition information and surveillance system (see chapter 5).

ESSENTIAL SERVICES FOR HEALTH IN ETHIOPIA

In November 2003, John Snow, Incorporated; the Academy for Educational Development; and the government of Ethiopia began the Essential Services for Health in Ethiopia. In September 2008, the program merged with Pathfinder International's Community-Based Reproductive Health Agents Program to form the Integrated Family Health Program. The bulk of ESHE's program activities are now part of the IFHP; details on the merger are provided above. This section describes ESHE both because it was a major success and because some of the analysis in chapter 4 uses data from the period when it was operational.

Essential Services for Health in Ethiopia focused on strengthening health workers' skills, improving community and household health-related practices, and assisting in health sector reform. It also worked with regional health bureaus to develop standards of care for child health services and made these standards accessible to all health workers. ESHE operated in 64 *woredas* in the three most populous regions of Ethiopia: Amhara, Oromia, and SNNP, which together are home to approximately 59.4 million people.

A key component was the Community Health Promoter Initiative. ESHE worked with regional and *woreda* health offices to enable community volunteers to improve community and household health-related practices and support health extension workers. Community health promoters, as they were called, mobilized communities for immunization outreach and promoted optimal nutrition practices, including optimal breast-feeding and improved hygiene and sanitation practices. They also encouraged caretakers to seek medical care for sick children when danger signs were apparent. (Most of these activities are now the responsibility of the volunteer community health workers of the IFHP.[12])

Data from the ESHE mid-term report suggest that the program had a significant impact in increasing the practice of optimal breast-feeding practices (ESHE 2006; table 3.9 and figure 3.1). The proportion of mothers exclusively breast-feeding until the age of six months increased, and the prevalence of breast-feeding within one hour of delivery substantially increased. The percentage of infants who were bottle-fed decreased from 13 percent in 2004 to 8 percent in 2006.

Table 3.9 Percentage of Under-One Children Whose Mothers Initiated Breast-Feeding within One Hour of Delivery in ESHE Project Areas, 2004 and 2006

Region	Baseline (2004)	Mid-line (2006)	P value
Amhara	23	60	<0.001
Oromia	43	77	<0.001
SNNP	45	50	Not significant

Source: ESHE 2006.

Figure 3.1 Percentage of Infants Less than Six Months of Age Who Were Bottle-Fed in ESHE Project Areas, 2004 and 2006

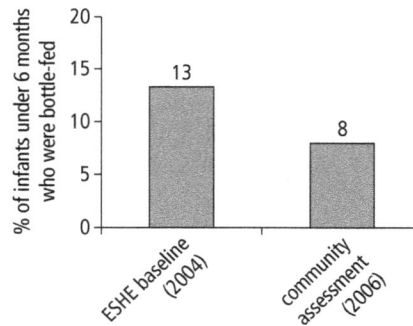

Source: ESHE 2006.

ESHE programs also had an impact on an infant's intake of colostrum, which is critical because of its immunization properties. The percentage of newborns given colostrum rose from 49 to 56 percent in ESHE regions (table 3.10; figure 3.2). In Oromia, for example, the percentage of newborns given colostrum increased from 62 percent in 2004 to 71 percent two years later. In 2006, the percentage of newborns given colostrum in Oromia was also higher relative to the regional baseline and the baseline of the 2005 Demographic and Health Survey.

The appropriate introduction of complementary foods also improved significantly in the ESHE *woredas* over the course of two years (see figure 3.3). This evidence highlights a key message of this book: *Improved breast-feeding practices result in improved child mortality and nutrition indicators, and optimal breast-feeding practices can be significantly improved by programs that educate mothers in appropriate breast-feeding practices.* The positive results show that community volunteer programs can have a substantial positive impact on promoting optimal breast-feeding behavior and that proper breast-feeding behavior can strongly affect child mortality and child nutrition. Chapter 4 illustrates the high cost-effectiveness of interventions promoting optimal breast-feeding practices, such as the ESHE.

Table 3.10 Percentage of Newborns Who Were Given Colostrum in ESHE Project Areas, 2004 and 2006

Region	Baseline (2004)	Mid-line (2006)	P value
Amhara	57	50	Not significant
Oromia	62	71	<0.01
SNNP	35	45	<0.001

Source: ESHE 2006.

Figure 3.2 Percentage of Newborns Who Were Given Colostrum in ESHE Project Areas, 2004 and 2006

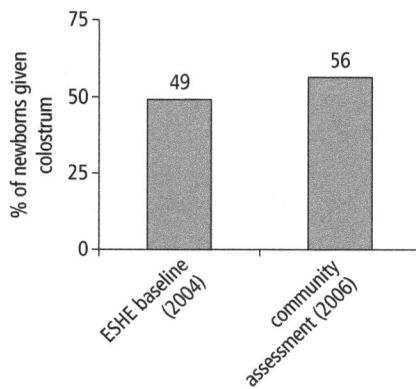

Source: ESHE 2006.

Figure 3.3 Percentage of Children 6–9 Months of Age Who Received Appropriate Complementary Feeding in ESHE Project Areas, 2004 and 2006

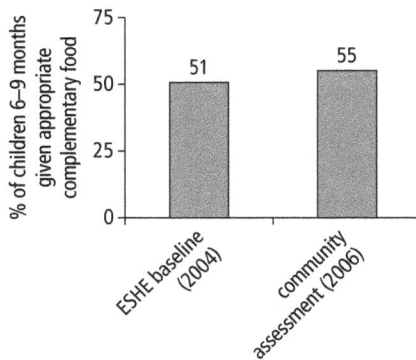

Source: ESHE 2006.

TREATMENT OF SEVERE ACUTE MALNUTRITION: A FURTHER FOCUS

This chapter has discussed two approaches used to treat severe acute malnutrition in Ethiopia: the health center–based institutional approach and the community therapeutic care approach, which some NGOs have used temporarily in certain "hot spots." This section compares and analyzes these two approaches. The community therapeutic care approach involves community volunteers and outpatient treatment, whereas the institutional approach is oriented toward inpatient treatment. Both programs provide limited access to the Ethiopian population, for different reasons.

The institutional approach to treating severe acute malnutrition was traditionally based in health centers, which are inaccessible to many Ethiopians. Recently, there has been a move toward a system of outpatient therapy at health posts where patients are better able to access health care. Health posts are more readily accessible than health centers; there are about five times as many health posts as health centers in the country and one health post in every rural *kebele*. Access to community therapeutic care can be limited due to the limited number of *kebeles* or hot spot areas covered by NGOs at any one time (although treatment does center around health posts and communities in the "hot spot" areas).

Institutionalization of the NGO approach to treating severe acute malnutrition—that is, relocating the institutional approach to health posts and focusing on outpatient treatment and community volunteers— is already in place at a number of health posts. Scaled up nationally, this approach would lead to a significant increase in access to treatment for severe acute malnutrition and an appreciable reduction in the unit costs of treatment. Patient access would increase because of the widespread use of health posts, and a larger number of patients could be treated with the same amount of resources because of the lower unit cost of treatment.

Implementing outpatient therapeutic programs at health posts on a large scale would imply relatively low unit costs of treatment for severe acute malnutrition, even when compared to the costs currently incurred by NGO community therapeutic care programs. The temporary community therapeutic care programs in hot spot areas[13] can be costly due to, for example, the relatively high start-up costs resulting from the need to train community volunteers each time an intervention is started in a new hot spot area. Institutionalizing the NGO approach would result in widely available outpatient, community-oriented treatment through health posts on a continuous basis without constant start-up costs. NGOs would be involved in some, but probably not all, cases. Links between inpatient and outpatient treatment would be strong, which is not always the case in areas with NGO-run community therapeutic care programs because these programs tend to focus exclusively on outpatient treatment.

NOTES

1. The two main crop seasons in Ethiopia are the *meher* and *belg*, which receive rainfall from June to October and from February to June, respectively.

2. The Disaster Risk Management and Food Security Sector was formerly called the Disaster Prevention and Preparedness Agency.

3. The disaster prevention and preparedness bureaus have changed name in the regions to the Food Security Coordination and Disaster Prevention Bureau in Amhara; the Disaster Prevention, Preparedness, and Food Security Sector in Tigray and SNNP; the Disaster Prevention and Food Security Bureau in Harari, Afar, and Dire Dawa; the Disaster Prevention and Preparedness Bureau in Somali and Gambela; the Food Security, Disaster Prevention, and Preparedness Commission in Oromia; and the Food Security and Resettlement and Disaster Prevention and Preparedness Office in Benshangul-Gumuz.

4. There are about 15,000 health posts in the country or one for every rural *kebele*. By contrast, there are about 3,200 health centers, and these are less common in the more rural areas.

5. The most common brand name is Plumpy'nut.

6. The chronic vulnerability index, the product of a multiagency initiative to develop a baseline of *woredas* needing assistance, began in 1999. Nine variables were chosen and used to develop a list of the most vulnerable *woredas*. This list was used when implementing MERET and the school feeding program. Due to a lack of data, however, some regions were not represented in developing the index, including Afar and Somali.

7. Even though the key focus is on health posts, health extension workers, and associated activities, the Health Extension Program is actually a four-tier system. The lowest level is a primary health care unit composed of a health center with five satellite health posts. Each health post has two extension workers.

8. The 163 areas are defined by UNICEF.

9. Although the EOS screens persons into the TSFP, the TSFP is otherwise independent of the EOS.

10. Increased earnings are due to reduced child and maternal mortality.

11. These calculations use the same techniques and data and are based on similar assumptions as the calculations in chapter 4.

12. The IFHP recruits former community health promoters and community-based reproductive health agents to assist health extension workers in promoting family planning, reproductive health, child health, and nutrition.

13. However, some initiatives involving NGOs carry out interventions on a continuous basis in certain areas, rather than only on a temporary basis in hot spots. These include a pilot project conducted by the regional bureaus of health together with the NGO Concern, funded by a Japanese social development grant.

CHAPTER 4

Assessing the Costs and Benefits of Nutrition-Related Programs

Cost-effectiveness as well as benefit-cost analysis is useful for guiding decision making regarding a range of existing and potential interventions affecting nutrition in Ethiopia. This chapter draws together Ethiopia-specific data on the costs of government, donor, and nongovernmental organization (NGO) programs affecting nutrition security in a unique attempt to apply cost-effectiveness and benefit-cost analysis to a broad range of nutrition-related interventions in Ethiopia.

METHODS AND LIMITATIONS OF COST-EFFECTIVENESS AND BENEFIT-COST ANALYSIS OF NUTRITION INTERVENTIONS IN ETHIOPIA

Cost-effectiveness analysis compares the costs of different interventions to achieve a goal, such as averting a child's death. The lower the cost of a particular intervention to achieve the goal, the more cost-effective it is compared to other interventions. Benefit-cost analysis quantifies the benefits of each intervention in monetary terms. The ratio of the benefits to the costs (the benefit-cost ratio) is assessed, and, if it is more than 1, the intervention is potentially desirable because its benefits are larger than the costs, although other factors should also be considered.

Ideally, cost-effectiveness analysis should be conducted for each outcome. If the goal is to reduce child deaths, it is useful to compare the cost per child death averted for a range of interventions. If several outcomes are of interest, such as reducing child stunting or enhancing cognitive development in children, then it is also useful to compare the cost per unit (or percentage) decrease in stunting or the cost per unit (or percentage) increase in cognitive development for each intervention in the spectrum of possible interventions.

Conducting these analyses is hampered by the lack of quantitative data with which to compute the cost-effectiveness of all relevant interventions. The analysis conducted for this book calculates quantitative estimates of the cost per child death averted for a range of interventions, but the necessary data were not available to compute other cost-effectiveness measures for most of the interventions—such as the cost per unit (or percentage) reduction in stunting or the cost per unit (or percentage) increase in cognitive development in children.

This problem was resolved to some extent as follows. The cost per beneficiary and the cost per capita were computed for a range of interventions on the basis of the best available data. In addition, *qualitative* measures of each intervention's impact were identified along different dimensions. For each intervention—based on the literature—the chapter indicates whether the intervention has a high, medium, or negligible impact on each of several "good" outcomes, for example, reducing maternal mortality, reducing childhood illness, increasing child cognitive development, and so on.

When quantitative estimates of cost-effectiveness could be calculated, estimates of the benefit-cost ratio were derived, focusing each time on different types of benefits. For example, when it was possible to compute quantitative estimates of the cost per child death averted for an intervention, the benefit-cost ratio for this intervention was also computed, with benefits calculated solely from valuing the child lives saved—referred to as the benefit-cost ratio from reducing child mortality. The value of a child life saved, or of a child death averted, was assumed in these cases to be equal to the discounted value of the child's lifetime earnings. Similar comments apply to cases where quantitative estimates could be computed for the cost per maternal death averted.

When other types of cost-effectiveness measures could be calculated, it was possible to compute measures for other types of benefits. More precisely, for more limited subsets of interventions, it was possible to estimate the benefit-cost ratio from increasing economic productivity, or the benefit-cost ratio from enhancing child ability, or both. For these interventions, the total benefit-cost ratio was also computed, that is, the sum of the benefit-cost ratios from reducing child and maternal mortality, from increasing economic productivity (where available), and from enhancing child ability (where available).

Nevertheless, there were some interventions for which no type of cost-effectiveness estimate or benefit-cost ratio could be calculated due to a dearth of relevant data. For example, no estimates could be derived for more generalized programs affecting health and nutrition, such as the

World Food Program's School Feeding Program and Pathfinder International's Community-Based Reproductive Health Agents (CBRHA) Program. These programs might have (or have had) an impact on nutritional outcomes, but they are not classified as nutrition interventions per se.

In other instances, the benefit-cost ratios are only partial. For example, while it was possible to calculate the benefits due to reduced child mortality and reduced prevalence of low birthweight resulting from distribution of bed nets, it was not possible to calculate the benefits due to increased agricultural productivity resulting from a decrease in the number of days agricultural laborers are sick. When benefits that were not included in the computed benefit-cost ratios are well known, they are mentioned in the text.

The estimates presented in this chapter are based on data from just before the recent food price crisis, specifically early 2007. Since then, prices in general, particularly food prices, have spiked upward and then fallen, but not to previous levels (see figure 4.6 below). Given these fluctuations in prices, developing precise estimates of costs and benefits at any one point in time is difficult. Therefore, the estimates in this chapter should be considered indicative.

Many factors other than cost-effectiveness or benefit-cost ratios must be considered in selecting interventions. The interventions examined offer a range of benefits, which are captured only partially in the analysis, and this book does not advocate that policy makers choose *only* interventions with the highest benefit-cost ratios. Ideally, if resources were completely unconstrained, *all* interventions with ratios greater than 1 would be funded. But the reality is that resources for nutrition-related interventions are limited relative to Ethiopia's vast need. Although in some circumstances a case could be made for discontinuing interventions with lower benefit-cost ratios, these ratios are, in practice, only one criterion to use when considering which interventions to prioritize. For example, some executing agencies with specific funding sources may be limited to implementing certain interventions even if they do not have the highest benefit-cost ratios. In this case, the better course may be to continue the intervention rather than to withdraw it and lose all benefits.

Programmatic, managerial, and other on-the-ground constraints, which are not included in the analysis, should also be taken into account in deciding which interventions to prioritize. For example, the managerial capacity to implement some programs may be low, even for programs with high benefit-cost ratios. Political and other constraints need to be considered as well.

The analysis in this chapter focuses on calculating cost-effectiveness and benefit-cost estimates for four categories of programs: those giving food or cash in lieu of food, those not giving food or cash in lieu of food, those with a strong community volunteer focus, and micronutrient interventions (involving supplementation as well as fortification of food with micronutrients). A range of assumptions was necessary, and these underlie the estimates presented. The detailed assumptions are included in appendix B.

Finally, it was not possible to compute benefit-cost ratios or cost-effectiveness figures for multiple interventions that were simultaneously implemented. No information is available on this despite its importance. Certain benefits accrue to a significant degree *only* when several nutrition-related interventions are implemented jointly, according to evidence in the literature. Additional follow-up research is recommended on multiple interventions that are implemented simultaneously.

COSTING OF INTERVENTIONS AND EFFECT ON MORTALITY

This section estimates the costs and benefits of reducing mortality for several nutrition interventions in Ethiopia. It focuses first on existing interventions—interventions that are currently or were recently being implemented in the country—and then on other "potential" interventions that are proposed as possible candidates for introduction into national programming at some point. Finally, the existing and potential interventions are compared along several dimensions, taking into account their effectiveness for lowering mortality.

EXISTING INTERVENTIONS

Estimates of the costs per beneficiary, per capita, and per death averted for several current programs in Ethiopia are shown in table 4.1. "Current" programs or interventions refer to those active in Ethiopia now or until very recently.[1] When a program includes more than one intervention, its component interventions are disaggregated and costed separately. Most of the programs listed in chapter 3 or separate interventions within those programs are costed.[2] For the Enhanced Outreach Strategy for Child Survival (EOS) and Extended EOS (EEOS) programs, estimates are prepared with and without distribution costs. When distribution costs are excluded, only the costs of the supplement and its transport to Ethiopia are factored into the calculations. The with-distribution costs for the EOS/EEOS interventions include the costs associated with internal distribution and administration of the supplements to the beneficiaries.

Table 4.1 Costing of Current Programs

Program or intervention	Coverage in active *woredas*	Cost per beneficiary (US$)	Cost per capita (US$)	Cost per death averted (US$)	Benefit-cost ratio from reducing child and maternal mortality	Mode of delivery
Programs giving out food (or cash in lieu of food)						
Productive Safety Net Program	High	34.94	7.611	—	—	Community work programs
MERET	High	39.60	1.598	—	—	Community work programs
School feeding	High	18.82	0.830	—	—	Schools
Treatment of severe acute malnutrition (health center–based institutional)	Low	131.78	0.314	767.92	2.04	Health centers
Targeted supplementary food	High	46.30	1.123	1,097.19	1.43	Distribution sites
Emergency food aid	High	53.11	2.964	908.77	9.38	Distribution sites
Programs not giving food (or cash in lieu of food), excluding programs with strong community volunteer focus						
EOS/EEOS (with distribution costs)						
Vitamin A	High	0.29	0.042	124.90	12.57	Community mobilization
Deworming	High	0.32	0.251	—	—	Community mobilization
Measles	High	0.50	0.072	847.77	1.85	Community mobilization
EOS/EEOS (without distribution costs)						
Vitamin A	High	0.04	0.006	17.38	90.33	Community mobilization
Deworming	High	0.05	0.041	—	—	Community mobilization
Measles	High	0.13	0.016	221.69	2.36	Community mobilization

(continued)

Table 4.1 *(continued)*

Program or intervention	Coverage in active *woredas*	Cost per beneficiary (US$)	Cost per capita (US$)	Cost per death averted (US$)	Benefit-cost ratio from reducing child and maternal mortality	Mode of delivery
Bed nets	High	0.54	0.499	551.30	13.98	Community mobilization
Expanded Program on Immunization	High	4.33	0.069	—	—	Community mobilization
Health extension workers	Low	6.77	6.771	—	—	Community mobilization
Iron and folate: pregnant women	Medium	0.96	0.021	321.82	4.43	Health facility
Iodated oil: pregnant women	High	0.36	0.008	28.85	49.37	Community mobilization
Iodated oil: pregnant women, children 6–24 months of age	High	0.36	0.035	127.90	11.14	Community mobilization
Salt fortified with iodine	High	0.05	0.050	170.64	8.35	Fortification
Programs with strong community volunteer focus						
Community-Based Nutrition Program	High	0.83	0.162	—	—	Community mobilization
Community health promoters (ESHE)						
Promotion of optimal breast-feeding	High	0.55	0.034	57.89	27.12	Community mobilization
Promotion of hand washing	High	0.36	0.023	224.21	7.00	Community mobilization
Promotion of construction and use of latrines	High	0.03	0.023	—	—	Community mobilization
Community-based reproductive health agents (CBRHA, Pathfinder International)	High	0.93	0.765	—	—	Community mobilization

Source: Authors' calculations based on program data.

Note: These are estimates for various interventions in existence in Ethiopia now or until very recently (2008 or later). Coverage in active *woredas* is assessed qualitatively as high, medium, or low. — = the effect on mortality could not be determined. Per capita coverage is determined by using the population of *woredas* in which each program is (or was until recently) active. The figures for the treatment of severe acute malnutrition using the health center–based institutional approach only include data from in-patient treatment at health centers because data on outpatient treatment are scarce.

EOS = Enhanced Outreach Strategy for Child Survival, EEOS = Extended EOS, ESHE = Essential Services for Health in Ethiopia, MERET = Managing Environmental Resources to Enable Transitions to More Sustainable Livelihoods.

The defined "beneficiary" for each program is included in appendix B. For a program targeting a specific geographic area, cost estimates cannot be calculated in per capita terms simply by dividing the program costs by the entire national population. Instead, the per capita cost is calculated using the program cost divided by the population of the *woredas* (districts) in which the program is active. The result is an estimate of the program's costs if it were to be scaled up. The estimates do not account for the possibility that per unit costs may change to some extent if programs are scaled up. Managing large-scale programs presents challenges relatively unknown to small-scale ones, although the former can sometimes benefit from economies of scale. Nonetheless, a rough measure of per capita cost is preferable to none.

To calculate the benefits of reducing child and maternal mortality, the discounted value of the lost lifetime earnings of each child and each mother is estimated. Calculating the economic value of a life is a complex process, and this analysis uses a conservatively high discount rate of 5 percent and values each year of productive life as the real per capita gross domestic product (GDP, assumed to be US$174 in 2007), remaining constant throughout the benefit accrual period. The productive lifespan is defined as lasting from 15 until 53 years of age. With this formula, a child's life saved at two years of age is valued at US$1,570, and a mother's life saved at 25 years of age is valued at $2,635 (see appendix B for details).[3]

The results of this analysis are not surprising. Programs with a strong community volunteer focus have some of the lowest costs per beneficiary.[4] Essential Services for Health in Ethiopia (ESHE), which promoted proper breast-feeding techniques and other optimal behavioral practices (see chapter 3), aimed for a ratio of one volunteer per 50 households. Given that the target audience was the entire community, the beneficiary population was quite large. With an average rural household size of 5.2 persons, there would be one volunteer for 260 individuals. Pathfinder International trained about 10,000 community-based reproductive health agents overall and reached almost 7 million people. In late 2008, both programs were discontinued and merged into the new Integrated Family Health Program (see chapter 3). The calculations in this section are based on data gathered on these two programs before they merged.

Another key program with a community volunteer focus is the Community-Based Nutrition (CBN) Program, which trained more than 24,000 community health workers and more than 2,200 health extension workers in its first phase. Focusing on intensively improving nutrition awareness, the program covered 39 *woredas*, with a total beneficiary population of about 1.23 million (children under five years of age and pregnant and lactating women), in its first phase. The cost for this intervention is low, at US$0.83 per beneficiary and just US$0.162 per capita. Additional *woredas* have since been phased into the program, and a total of 228 *woredas* were covered at the time of writing.

In addition to community-based volunteer-focused programs, other interventions with low costs per beneficiary include those of the EOS/EEOS campaign,[5] salt iodization (fortification of salt with iodine), provision of iodated oil capsules to young children and pregnant women, distribution of bed nets, and the Expanded Program on Immunization.

According to the figures used here, supplying vitamin A is the cheapest way to save a life, at a cost of around US$17 per death averted (excluding distribution). Another of the programs with the lowest cost per death averted was the ESHE (with its community health promoters). With this program, the cost of saving an under-five life through the promotion of breast-feeding is estimated at just US$50–US$60. The benefit-cost rankings for reducing mortality have a close inverse relationship with the rankings for cost per death averted, as can be expected. Vitamin A supplementation (without distribution costs) and breast-feeding promotion are two of the interventions with the highest benefit-cost ratios.

Programs distributing food have higher costs per beneficiary, ranging from US$18.82 to US$131.78, with an average of US$54.09 (see table 4.1). Beneficiaries of the Managing Environment Resources to Enable Transitions to More Sustainable Livelihoods (MERET) Program receive only grain, while the beneficiaries of emergency food aid typically receive a combination of grain, supplementary food, and oil. The higher costs of these programs are to be anticipated because the costs of the product and its transport to and through the country are high relative to those of other programs. However, they play an indispensable role in maintaining community health, especially during periods of emergency. Three programs disbursing food—the Productive Safety Net Program, MERET, and the School Feeding Program—do not have documented quantitative effects on mortality; thus, they could not be included in the calculations of benefits and costs for this chapter.[6]

COSTING OF POTENTIAL INTERVENTIONS

Costing estimates were also prepared for several interventions (mostly micronutrient) that are not currently being implemented in Ethiopia (see table 4.2). Micronutrient deficiencies are prevalent in Ethiopia (see chapters 1 and 2), and interventions to counter their adverse effects are

Table 4.2 Costing of Potential Programs

Program or intervention	Possible or likely coverage in active *woredas*	Cost per beneficiary (US$)	Cost per capita (US$)	Cost per death averted (US$)	Benefit-cost ratio from reducing child and maternal mortality	Mode of delivery
Micronutrient or antihelmintic (deworming) supplementation						
Iron and folate: children 6–24 months of age	Medium	0.50	0.037	—	—	Health facility
Zinc: children 6–24 months of age	Medium	1.26	0.095	550.08	2.85	Health facility
Deworming: pregnant women	High	0.06	0.001	1.10	648.41	Community mobilization
Food fortification						
Iodized salt fortified with iron	High	0.45	0.450	6,922.55	0.38	Fortification
Sugar fortified with vitamin A	Medium	0.10	0.041	102.48	15.32	Fortification

Source: Authors' calculations based on program data.

Note: These are estimates for potential programs that do not currently exist in Ethiopia. Possible coverage in active *woredas* is assessed qualitatively as high, medium, or low. — = no effect on mortality. The costs per death averted for fortifying iodized salt with iron represent only the costs from averted maternal mortality. Per capita coverage is determined using the population of *woredas* in which each program would be active.

extremely cost-effective. Costing estimates were also prepared for providing deworming to pregnant women. Although deworming is provided to children under five years of age as part of EOS/EEOS, pregnant women are not currently included in this intervention.[7] The cost per beneficiary for deworming and for every other intervention listed in table 4.2 is less than US$1 (except for supplying zinc supplements to sick children). The target groups for each supplementation intervention are defined in table 4.2. To maintain consistency with the EOS/EEOS cost data—where beneficiaries are defined as those receiving treatment regardless of their deficiency status—the beneficiaries for the fortification programs are assumed to be everyone who will consume the fortified product.

The supplementation costs per beneficiary are calculated by interviewing procurement specialists at the United Nations Children's Fund (UNICEF) and elsewhere as well as by consulting the international drug price calculator.[8] The costs used in the calculations are included in appendix B. When more than one price is quoted for a particular supplement, the lowest or second-lowest price is used.

When a program's estimated efficacy suggests a high impact in terms of reducing malnutrition or mortality among children or mothers who are able to access the program, the potential coverage of the program must also be considered. For example, treating children with zinc during bouts of diarrhea has a high efficacy in reducing under-five mortality due to diarrhea. But when zinc treatment is delivered through health facilities (whether health centers or posts), which are not always easily accessible, or if parents are unaware of the treatment's importance, many sick children will not receive this life-saving intervention. Possible coverage in active *woredas* is assessed qualitatively as high, medium, or low. It is assumed that supplementation interventions delivered through health facilities will result in a medium level of coverage. In contrast, child survival interventions delivered through mechanisms such as the mass mobilizations of EOS/EEOS have high coverage within the targeted *woredas*, resulting in a higher impact on reducing overall child mortality in those areas.

It is important to note some caveats regarding two interventions: iron and folate supplementation and zinc supplementation for children 6–24 months of age. A recent study showed that iron supplementation to young children in malaria-endemic areas may increase their risk of contracting malaria (Sazawal and others 2006). In the case of both iron and folate as well as zinc, the tablets need to be taken once a day or once every few days, rather than just once or twice a year, like iodated oil capsules or deworming for pregnant women. Distribution through the biannual EOS/EEOS mass mobilizations may be problematic due to difficulties ensuring compliance; improper compliance may be dangerous. Instead, distribution would probably have to be done through health centers and health posts, as is now the case for dispensing iron and folate supplements to pregnant women. This would require mothers or caregivers to visit health posts or heath centers regularly to obtain the supplements for their young children, which is not always likely to happen, especially if these individuals live far from the facilities. (That is why these interventions are listed as having "medium" coverage.) Furthermore, there is still some risk of improper compliance (for example, improper administration of the tablets, leading to choking), although this risk can be minimized by teaching the mothers or caregivers, during visits to health facilities, how to administer the tablets correctly.

However, as the reach of health facilities and services expands, and as knowledge increases regarding proper compliance and the benefits of iron and folate as well as zinc supplementation, some of these constraints may be reduced over time. In addition, community volunteers could potentially distribute iron and folate as well as zinc tablets to young children (as well as to mothers in the case of iron and folate) as part of nutrition programs (such as the CBN Program), although the feasibility of this needs to be examined carefully.

COMPARING THE COST-EFFECTIVENESS OF DIFFERENT EXISTING AND POTENTIAL INTERVENTIONS, WITH MORTALITY AS A YARDSTICK

Among the interventions listed in tables 4.1 and 4.2, there is a large variation in the cost per death averted. Correspondingly, the benefit-cost ratios for these interventions also vary greatly, with deworming for pregnant women ranking the highest. But it is important to note that these benefit-cost ratios are calculated by measuring benefits only due to reductions in child and maternal mortality. Below, benefit-cost ratios are calculated by measuring benefits along other dimensions, such as productivity and ability. But even considering only the benefit-cost ratios from reducing child and maternal mortality, as in tables 4.1 and 4.2, most of these ratios exceed 1, and thus the majority of the listed interventions should be considered cost-effective along this dimension alone.

It is nevertheless useful to determine which are the *most* cost-effective interventions among the ones under consideration (and still only taking into account the benefits from reduced child and maternal mortality). The Macroeconomic Commission on Health argues that an intervention is especially cost-effective if its cost per death averted is less than three times per capita GDP (WHO 2001). Figure 4.1 goes further and depicts the cost per death averted for the interventions where this indicator is less than one times per capita GDP. It includes all of the interventions considered in the analysis—both current and potential programs—and shows that several interventions not currently being implemented are very cost-effective. Micronutrient interventions are among the most cost-effective interventions. Deworming pregnant women is the cheapest way to save the lives of children under five years of age; its implementation cost is low, and it has a high efficacy in reducing mortality.

Figure 4.2 shows the cost per death averted for the relatively less cost-effective interventions. Out of all the interventions considered, iodized salt fortified with iron is the most expensive way to save a life. Targeted

Figure 4.1   Cost per Death Averted for the Most Cost-Effective Current and Potential Interventions

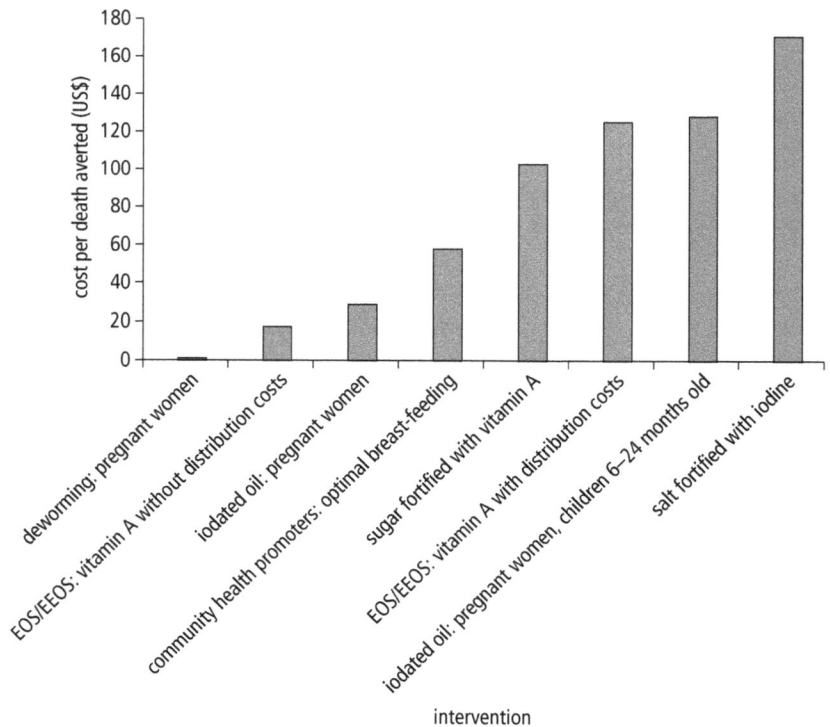

Source: Authors' calculations based on program data.

Figure 4.2   Cost per Death Averted for the Relatively Less Cost-Effective Current and Potential Interventions

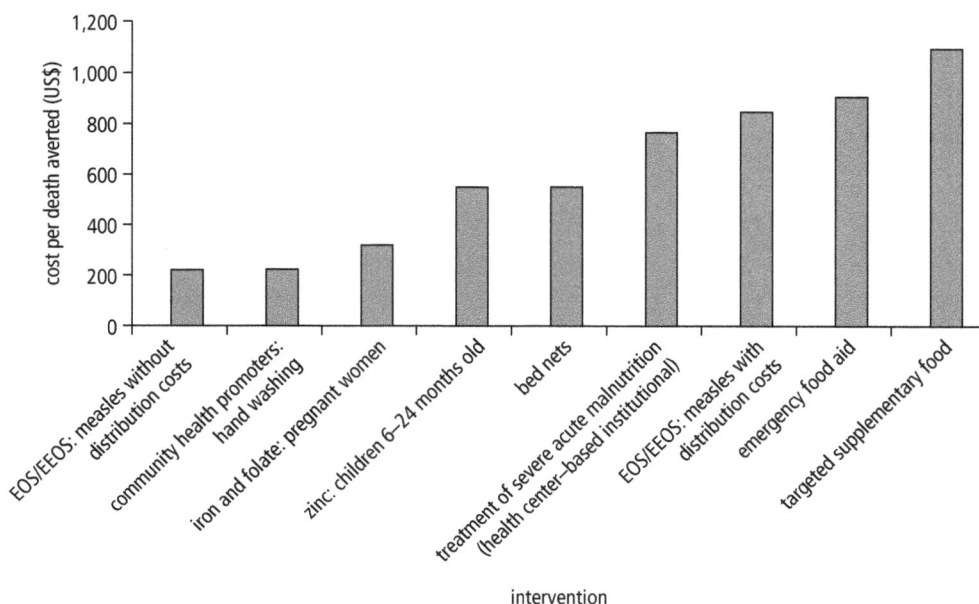

intervention

Source: Authors' calculations based on program data.
Note: Iodized salt fortified with iron, which costs US$6,922 to save a life, was excluded from the figure to show more detail for the other interventions.

supplementary food is the most expensive way to avert a death. However, in some cases, no other alternative exists. The Target Supplementary Food Program (TSFP) saves large numbers of lives despite its cost. The interventions depicted in figure 4.2 are less cost-effective than those depicted in figure 4.1, by this analysis, but they can still be considered cost-effective as long as their benefits exceed their costs, that is, if their benefit-cost ratio exceeds 1. As shown below, *all* of the interventions listed in both figures 4.1 and 4.2 have benefit-cost ratios exceeding 1, in many cases by large margins, if benefits are considered along several dimensions.

Figure 4.3 compares the per capita cost of an intervention with the number of under-five lives saved if the intervention were scaled up nationwide. The figure shows that among the interventions with the largest potential to save under-five lives, there are relatively expensive and inexpensive options. Among the interventions with relatively low cost per capita and the potential to save large numbers of lives are deworming for pregnant women and the provision of bed nets. In contrast, emergency

Figure 4.3 Number of Under-Five Deaths Averted and Cost per Capita for Various Interventions

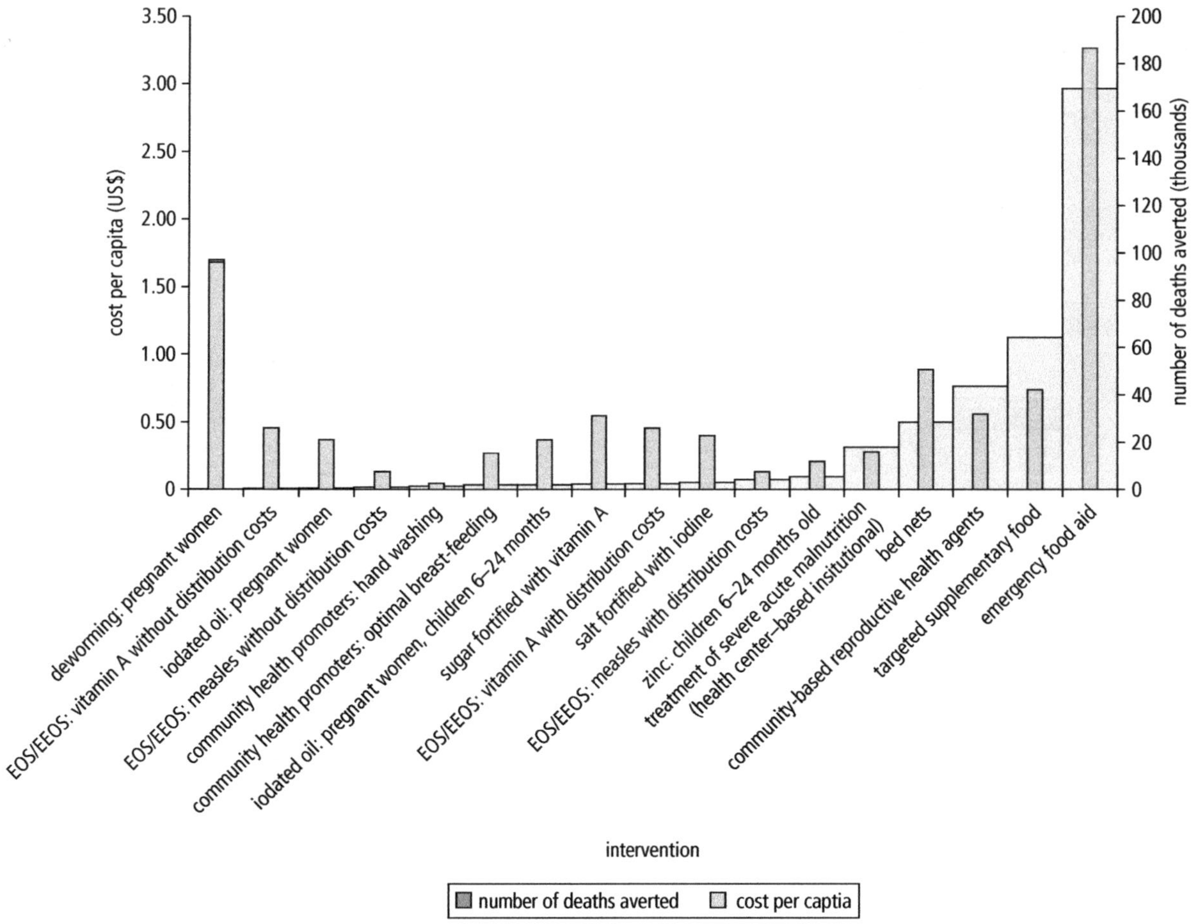

Source: Authors' calculations based on program data.

Note: The baseline for under-five deaths is the number for 2005. For each program, the number of deaths averted is calculated under a scenario where the program is scaled up nation-wide. EOS = Enhanced Outreach Strategy for Child Survival; EEOS = Extended EOS.

food aid and targeted supplementary food have relatively high costs per capita, largely because they entail the provision of food. Nevertheless, they all have the potential to save the lives of large numbers of children under the age of five.

NONQUANTITATIVE ASSESSMENT OF AN INTERVENTION'S IMPACTS

Many interventions have an impact on society or a person's lifetime earnings or welfare through means other than reduced mortality. Table 4.3 consolidates information on the efficacies of different interventions along dimensions other than mortality—childhood illness, childhood growth, cognitive development, and labor productivity. The information in the table is derived from Jamison and others (2006) and a literature review.

IMPACT ON ECONOMIC PRODUCTIVITY

Several of the analyzed interventions improve labor productivity and education outcomes, as shown in table 4.3. These improvements are largely due to the interventions' impact on reducing stunting and low birthweight (which in turn leads to stunting), both of which lead to significant individual economic losses throughout life and reduced national economic productivity (Alderman, Behrman, and Hoddinott 2005).

Table 4.4 presents benefit-cost ratios in which the benefits are calculated solely from reductions in stunting or low birthweight for interventions with demonstrable effects on these outcomes. The underlying assumptions regarding the impact of low birthweight and stunting on yearly earnings are given in appendix B.

The calculations do not capture all of the benefits from the various interventions. The Targeted Supplementary Food Program, for example, almost certainly has an effect on the adult height of a malnourished individual, but its affect on stunting has not been quantitatively studied. Therefore, TSFP and several other interventions are not included in the table because of a lack of information. Furthermore, the analysis does not take into account the fact that providing targeted supplementary food significantly decreases wasting in children. If the benefits due to decreased wasting were included, the benefit-cost ratio calculated for the TSFP in this study would be higher. Also, there is reportedly significant sharing of food with individuals who are not program beneficiaries, and the benefits accruing to this group are not included in the calculations.

Table 4.3 Nonquantitative Assessment of Impacts

Program or intervention and target beneficiaries	Maternal mortality	Low birthweight	Neonatal mortality	Under-five mortality rate	Childhood illness[a]	Childhood growth[b]	Cognitive development and function	Labor productivity and education outcomes
Current								
Vitamin A supplementation: neonates and infants	...	...	Low	High	High	Low	...	...
Deworming: children	...	...	...	Low	High	High	High	High
Breast-feeding: children	...	...	High	High	High	High	High	High
Iodine supplementation								
Pregnant and lactating women	High	High	High	...	...	...	...	High
Infants	...	...	...	Low	Low	Low	High	High
Children	...	...	...	Low	Low	Low	High	High
Iodine fortification: universal	Low	High	High	High	High	High	High	High
Iron and folic acid supplementation: pregnant and lactating women	High	High	Low	High	High	...	Low	Low
Potential								
Iron and folic acid supplementation								
Infants	...	...	...	...	Low	Low	High	High

School-age children	Low	Low	Low	Low	High	...	Low	Low
Vitamin A supplementation: pregnant and lactating women	High	Low	Low	Low	Low	...	...	...
Zinc supplementation								
Infants	...	...	...	High	High	High	High	High
Children with diarrhea	...	...	...	High	High	Low	Low	Low
Iron fortification: universal	High	High	High	...	...	...	High	High
Vitamin A fortification: universal	High	Low	Low	Low	Low	Low	Low	Low
Deworming: pregnant and lactating women	High	High	High	...	...	...	Low	High
Community Volunteer Program with Child Growth Promotion: pregnant and lactating women and children under two	High	High	High	High	High	High	High	High

Source: Authors, based on Jamison and others (2006) and a literature review.

Note: ... = none or negligible (for interventions with a demonstrated lack of impact on a particular outcome).

a. Childhood illness is a qualitative measure indicating occurrence and severity of illness from birth until five years of age.

b. Childhood growth is a qualitative measure of the height of a child; stunting is the result of especially low childhood growth.

Table 4.4   Impacts on Stunting and Low Birthweight and Economic Productivity

Program or intervention	Cost per beneficiary (US$)	Cost per capita (US$)	Impact on stunting or low birthweight	Benefit-cost ratio
Emergency food aid	53.11	2.96	Height increase of 1.75 centimeter	0.12
Bed nets	0.54	0.50	28% reduction of low birthweight	124.39
Salt fortified with iodine	0.05	0.05	Increase of birthweight by 50 grams	4.27
Iron and folate: pregnant women	0.96	0.02	13% reduction in low birthweight	3.68
Iodized salt fortified with iron	0.45	0.45	13% reduction in low birthweight	0.17

Source: Authors' calculations based on program data.
Note: Costs for bed nets and for iron and folate are only for pregnant women (and the benefits are from a reduction in low birthweight when these women give birth). Costs for emergency food aid are only for children under two years of age (and the benefits are from a reduction in stunting among these children). The benefit-cost ratio for all interventions is from increasing economic productivity due to decreasing stunting or low birthweight.

IMPACT ON MENTAL ABILITY

The positive effects of micronutrients on a child's mental ability can be dramatic. Micronutrient interventions can be extremely cost-effective and have high benefit-cost ratios from the standpoint of enhancing mental ability. Table 4.5 lists several current and potential interventions with benefit-cost ratios calculated solely from the benefits due to normalizing an individual's mental ability to function. A change of one standard deviation in IQ (intelligence quotient, 15 points) is assumed to change yearly earnings by about 10 percent (Alderman, Behrman, and Sabot 1996).

Iodine deficiency substantially decreases individuals' IQ, impairing their ability to perform mentally as they grow older. Supplementing pregnant women with iodated oil capsules can recoup these lost earnings, resulting in an extraordinarily high benefit-cost ratio of 437 for enhancing mental ability. When iodated oil capsules are given to pregnant women as well as children 6–24 months of age, the benefits are still about 99 times higher than the costs. Providing deworming to under-five children as part of the EOS/EEOS mechanism also has a very high benefit-cost ratio, either of 62 (if distribution costs are included) or 378 (if distribution costs are not included). And decreasing anemia by supplementing young children with iron and folate is another advantageous intervention, producing economic benefits that are 24 times the

Table 4.5 Impacts on Mental Ability and Economic Productivity

Program or intervention	Cost per beneficiary (US$)	Cost per capita (US$)	Impact on ability	Benefit-cost ratio
Iron and folate: children 6–24 months of age	0.50	0.037	Increases IQ in 30% of anemic children by 7.5 points	23.79
Iodized salt fortified with iron	0.45	0.450	Increases IQ in 30% of anemic children by 7.5 points	1.97
Iodated oil: pregnant women	0.36	0.008	Increases IQ in deficient children by 13.5 points	436.89
Iodated oil: pregnant women, children 6–24 months of age	0.36	0.035	Increases IQ in deficient children by 13.5 points	98.54
Salt fortified with iodine	0.05	0.050	Increases IQ in deficient children by 13.5 points	68.39
EOS/EEOS: deworming with distribution costs	0.32	0.251	Increases IQ in 50% of anemic children by 7.5 points	61.85
EOS/EEOS: deworming without distribution costs	0.05	0.041	Increases IQ in 50% of anemic children by 7.5 points	378.19

Source: Authors' calculations based on program data.

costs. However, there are several caveats regarding the supplementation of iron and folate to young children, mentioned above.

TOTAL IMPACTS ON MORTALITY, ECONOMIC PRODUCTIVITY, AND MENTAL ABILITY

Figure 4.4 shows the total benefit-cost ratios for both current and potential interventions when one takes into account the effect of each intervention on mortality, economic growth, and mental ability (see also table 4.6). The benefit-cost ratios range from 1.43 for targeted supplementary food to more than 648 for providing pregnant women with deworming medication. The mean value is 95, and the median is 15.3. When the high value for deworming pregnant women is removed from the calculations, the mean becomes 67 and the median becomes 14. Every intervention examined here has a benefit-cost ratio greater than 1, indicating that it produces more economic gains than the cost of its inputs.

The difference between the costs of EOS/EEOS interventions with and without distribution is dramatic. If the sole purpose of the EOS/EEOS were to distribute vitamin A, the cost of vitamin A supplementation

Figure 4.4 Benefit-Cost Ratio of Current and Potential Interventions

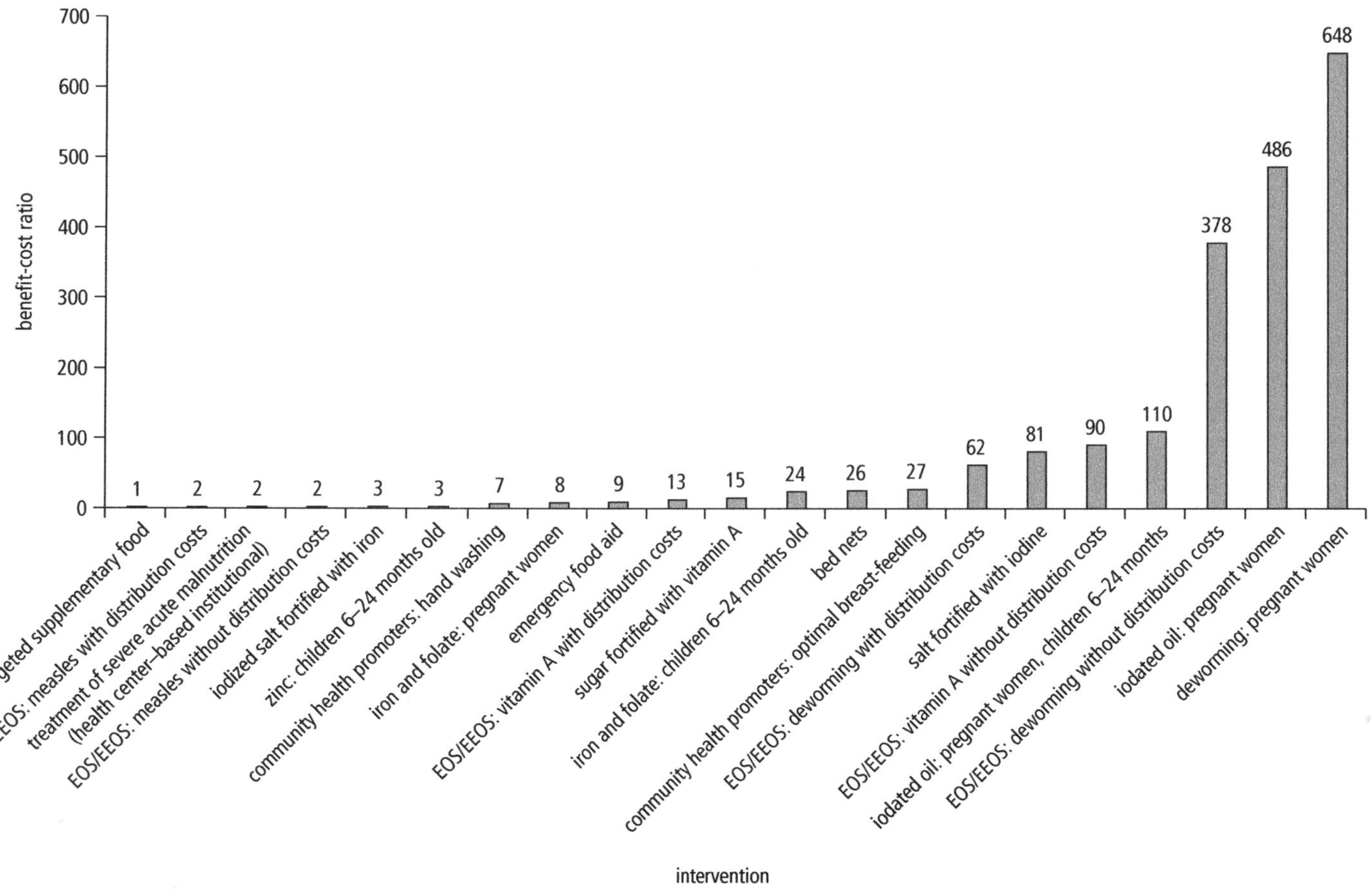

Source: Authors' calculations based on program data.

Note: Graph shows total benefit-cost ratios for current and potential interventions from reducing child and maternal mortality, increasing economic productivity, and enhancing child ability.

Table 4.6 Total Benefit-Cost Ratio from Reduced Mortality, Increased Economic Productivity, and Increased Child Ability in Ethiopia

Program or intervention	Benefit-cost ratio from reducing child and maternal mortality	Benefit-cost ratio from increasing economic productivity	Benefit-cost ratio from enhancing child ability	Total benefit-cost ratio
Programs giving out food (or cash in lieu of food)				
Treatment of severe acute malnutrition (health center–based institutional approach)	2.04	—	—	2.04
Targeted supplementary food	1.43	—	—	1.43
Emergency food aid	9.38	0.12	—	9.43
Programs not giving out food (or cash in lieu of food), excluding programs with strong community volunteer focus				
EOS/EEOS (with distribution costs)				
Vitamin A	12.57	—	—	12.57
Deworming	—	—	61.85	61.85
Measles	1.85	—	—	1.85
EOS/EEOS (without distribution costs)				
Vitamin A	90.33	—	—	90.33
Deworming	—	—	378.19	378.19
Measles	2.36	—	—	2.36
Bed nets	13.98	124.39	—	25.63
Iron and folate: pregnant women	4.43	3.68	—	8.10
Iron and folate: children 6–24 months of age	—	—	23.79	23.79
Iodated oil: pregnant women	49.37	—	436.89	486.26
Iodated oil: pregnant women, children 6–24 months of age	11.14	—	98.54	109.68
Salt fortified with iodine	8.35	4.27	68.39	81.00
Iodized salt fortified with iron	0.38	0.17	1.97	2.53
Sugar fortified with vitamin A	15.32	—	—	15.32
Zinc: children 6–24 months of age	2.85	—	—	2.85
Deworming: pregnant women	648.41	—	—	648.41
Programs with strong community volunteer focus				
Community health promoters (ESHE)				
Promotion of optimal breast-feeding	27.12	—	—	27.12
Promotion of hand washing	7.00	—	—	7.00

Source: Authors' calculations based on program data.
Note: — = no effect or lack of data demonstrating an effect on the outcome. The benefit-cost ratios of emergency food aid and bed nets are not additive, as the different categories of benefits accrue to different target groups, which have different costs. The total benefit-cost ratios are therefore the sum of the benefits divided by the sum of the costs.

would include the full cost of mass mobilizations necessary to provide the vitamin A supplementation. This full cost would be the distribution cost. But if deworming (for children two to five years of age) and measles vaccinations were implemented as part of the EOS/EEOS and "tagged on" to the vitamin A supplementation, one methodological approach would be to exclude the costs of mass mobilization (the distribution costs) from the costs of the deworming and measles interventions. This would make the benefit-cost ratios for deworming and measles vaccinations, respectively, 378 and 2.4 instead of 62 and 1.9.

The extremely high benefit-cost ratio for providing deworming supplementation to pregnant women can be explained by this intervention's significant benefits relative to the low cost of supplying only pregnant women in rural areas with one capsule that costs US$0.05 plus distribution costs. Unlike the three EOS/EEOS interventions listed in table 4.6, whose benefit-cost ratios are calculated both with and without distribution costs, providing deworming supplementation to pregnant women is treated as a stand-alone intervention (outside of EOS/EEOS), factoring in distribution costs. If this activity were "piggybacked" onto the existing EOS/EEOS architecture, its distribution costs could be considered zero, resulting in an even higher benefit-cost ratio.

On the whole, the most cost-effective interventions consist of fortification and supplementation programs as well as the EOS/EEOS components without distribution costs. The provision of bed nets and the promotion of optimal breast-feeding also have two of the highest benefit-cost ratios of all the interventions analyzed.

The cost-effectiveness estimates and the benefit-cost ratios should be interpreted with caution, however. Interventions with lower estimated costs per death averted or higher benefit-cost ratios should not be advocated over programs with higher estimated costs per death averted or lower benefit-cost ratios without factoring in other considerations. Using other indicators—including the number of lives that could potentially be saved—is critical when evaluating and comparing programs. For example, programs providing food are generally expensive, in terms of the cost per death averted, because of the relatively high cost of food. However, these interventions are necessary and have the potential to save the lives of large numbers of children (figure 4.3). Often, there are no low-cost substitutes to providing food. The Targeted Supplementary Food Program is necessary to treat moderate malnutrition; no readily available program can substitute for it. Treating severe malnutrition by using the institutional approach has among the lowest benefit-cost ratios in our analysis, but it has the potential to have substantially lower costs and higher benefit-cost ratios, as discussed in chapter 3.[9] Each intervention included in this analysis has a benefit-cost ratio above 1, usually well above 1, and each intervention serves an important purpose.

COMMUNITY VOLUNTEER PROGRAMS

Community volunteer programs play a large role in providing health and nutrition services in Ethiopia. Table 4.7 describes the community-based volunteer programs examined in this study. Major dimensions of interest include the number of days of pre-service and in-service training, the level of per diems for training, and other incentives that might

Table 4.7   Community Volunteer Programs in Ethiopia

Program	Description	Per diem (US$ equivalent a day)	Pre-service training	In-service training
Community health promoters (ESHE)	Supported the child survival strategy across the Expanded Program on Nutrition and the Integrated Management of Childhood Illness based on the essential nutrition actions through community volunteers trained to be role models and to transfer knowledge and practice to the community	5.68 preservice; 4.55 in-service	3–6 days	One day per quarter
Community-based reproductive health agents (CBRHA, Pathfinder International)	Improved the knowledge of family planning methods by having community volunteers provide counseling and distribute free contraception	6.82 pre-service; 6.82 in-service	5–6 days	One day per quarter
Community-Based Nutrition	Uses community volunteers (called volunteer community health workers) to counsel pregnant and lactating women and families with young children in the essential nutrition actions; weighs and monitors or promotes growth of children under two years of age; provides vitamin A supplementation and mid-upper arm circumference screening for children 6–59 months and deworming for children 24–59 months of age	Health extension workers and supervisors: 11.36 pre-service and yearly in-service; volunteer community health workers: 3.98 pre-service and yearly in-service	Health extension workers and supervisors: 12 days; volunteer community health workers: six days	Health extension workers and supervisors: six days a year; volunteer community health workers: two days a year

Source: Program data.
Note: The figures for the per diems were converted from Ethiopian birr to U.S. dollars using the prevailing official exchange rate. The EHSE and Pathfinder International programs were merged to form the Integrated Family Health Program in 2008.

influence performance. Pre-service training is initial training provided to a volunteer at the time of enrollment in a program. In-service training occurs on a regular basis once the volunteer is fully engaged in on-the-ground activities.

Table 4.8 outlines the specific costs per beneficiary for community volunteer programs. The beneficiaries include everyone in the target group who lived for at least one year in the *kebeles* (communities) covered by the program. As the data show, all of the programs have a very low cost per beneficiary. The costs of the CBN Program are dominated by per diems for the large number of trainees it supports. Supervisors and health extension workers receive a per diem of Br 100 (US$6.00), while volunteer community health workers receive Br 35 (US$2.10). These can be large incentives in rural Ethiopia, where the monthly salary for a health extension worker is about Br 800 (US$48.02).[10] Unlike some other community volunteer programs in Ethiopia, the CBN Program purchases few supplies, and most of these, including weighing scales for monitoring child growth, have a relatively long life span (for example, about five years for scales).

The CBN Program has the potential to have a substantial impact on the nutrition status in its beneficiary *woredas*. The program was modeled on others elsewhere that, according to the literature, have had a large impact in their first year or two, followed by years with more moderate

Table 4.8 Component Cost per Beneficiary for Community Volunteer Programs
US$

Program	Training	Transport	Supplies	Personnel	Overhead	Total	Beneficiaries
Community health promoters (ESHE)							
Optimal breast-feeding	0.12	0.12	0.02	0.24	0.04	0.55	Pregnant women
Hand washing	0.08	0.08	0.01	0.16	0.03	0.36	Pregnant women
Latrines	0.01	0.01	0.00	0.01	0.00	0.03	80% of the population
Community-based reproductive health agents (CBRHA, Pathfinder International)	0.04	0.06	0.63	0.18	0.02	0.93	Entire population
Community-Based Nutrition	0.67	0.02	0.09	0.05	0.00	0.83	Pregnant and lactating women and children under five years of age

Source: Authors' calculations based on program data.
Note: The table depicts annualized costs per beneficiary by program, taking into account costs over the life of each program and using this to produce annual averages.

improvements (Mason and others 2006). Well-designed and adequately resourced programs of this nature have typically produced an additional reduction in moderate malnutrition (as defined by underweight prevalence)—on top of any trend reduction that would have occurred anyway, without the programs—of around 1 to 2 percentage points a year after the initial reduction in the first year or two, which could be up to several percentage points.

The initial outcome data from the CBN Program in Ethiopia are encouraging. Figure 4.5 shows the trends in underweight prevalence among under-two children in the 39 *woredas* that were included in the first phase of the CBN Program in late 2008, based on data collected from the CBN monthly weighing sessions. Over the initial two years of the program, there was a reduction in underweight prevalence of around several percentage points as a whole in these *woredas*. The bulk of this reduction occurred starting around mid-2009, during a period of more or less stable food prices (see figure 4.6), so the sharp fall in underweight prevalence cannot be attributed to factors such as falling food prices or favorable changes in weather conditions, which would likely have shown up in falling food prices. More analysis is needed on the possible reasons for the large fall in underweight prevalence. But as a starting hypothesis, it appears likely that much or most of the improvements may indeed be due to implementation of the CBN Program in the *woredas* from which the data were collected.

This last statement needs to be rigorously tested in the 39 first-phase CBN *woredas* as well as others that more recently have been included in the program. An impact evaluation is currently under way, with control as well as intervention *woredas* included, to obtain a rigorous assessment of the effectiveness of the program.

THE HEALTH EXTENSION PROGRAM: HEALTH EXTENSION WORKERS

The Health Extension Program reflects a government commitment to expand access to health care. This section presents a brief description of the program's costs. A more extensive study might examine the impacts as well as the costs for each of the 16 packages that health extension workers are supposed to implement (see table 4.9).

Table 4.9 presents all costs for each component of the Health Extension Program, including construction, personnel, training, and supply and transport, annualized when necessary. The most expensive of the three focus areas is family health services at US$3.44 per beneficiary,

Figure 4.5   Prevalence of Underweight in the First-Phase CBN *Woredas*, by Region, 2008–10

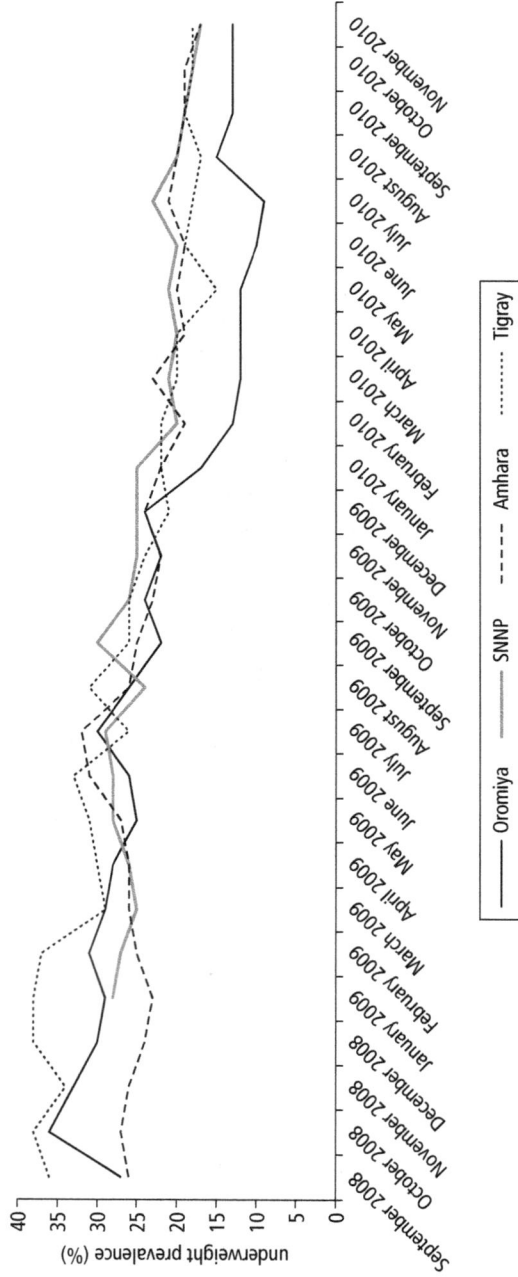

Source: Program data.

Note: The figure depicts the prevalence of underweight among under-two children, based on data from the monthly weighing sessions in the 39 *woredas* included in the first phase of the CBN Program.

Figure 4.6   Food Consumer Price Index for Ethiopia, 2007–10

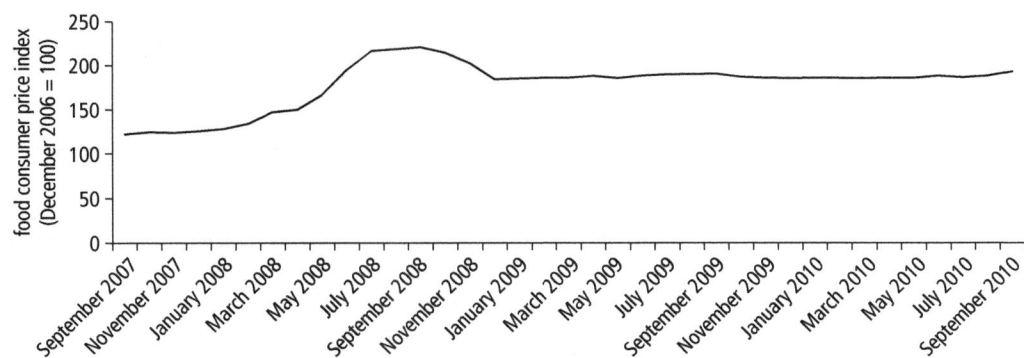

Source: Ethiopia Central Statistical Agency.

Table 4.9   Cost per Beneficiary for Each of the 16 Packages of the Health Extension Program

Package	Cost per beneficiary (US$)
Family health services	3.435
Maternal and child health	1.655
Immunization	0.618
Family planning	0.881
Adolescent and reproductive health	0.060
Nutrition	0.221
Disease prevention and control	2.825
HIV (human immunodeficiency virus)/AIDS (acquired immunodeficiency syndrome) and other sexually transmitted infections	0.576
Tuberculosis	0.047
Malaria	2.033
First aid	0.170
Environmental health	0.510
Safe excreta disposal	0.060
Solid and liquid waste disposal	0.057
Water supply and safety	0.143
Food hygiene and safety	0.083
Healthy home environment	0.067

(continued)

Table 4.9 *(continued)*

Package	Cost per beneficiary (US$)
Insect and rodent control	0.050
Personal hygiene	0.050
Total cost	6.771

Source: Calculations by the Center for National Health Development in Ethiopia.
Note: These annual total costs include medicine, wages, and training, where training costs are annualized, with an assumed average tenure per health extension worker of 10 years. Each rural *kebele* (community) is supposed to be covered by two health extension workers, and everyone in the *kebele* is considered a beneficiary.

while the cheapest is environmental health (see figure 4.7). Furthermore, a program review found that health extension workers learned the environmental health components well and that this component was more likely to be implemented than the other components. All of the program components were designed to improve Ethiopians' nutrition security. In general, the costs are low given the scope of the program.

MAJOR FINDINGS AND IMPLICATIONS

Each intervention considered in this study has high levels of benefits relative to costs. If resources were not constrained, all of these interventions would be funded, but, since resources are limited, benefit-cost ratios are useful as a criterion when one considers which interventions to prioritize. But other factors should also be considered, including the potential for large-scale impact and other factors discussed at the end of this section.

The analysis shows that micronutrient interventions are extremely cost-effective and have very high benefit-cost ratios. Five of the 10 interventions above the median benefit-cost ratio are micronutrient interventions, mostly targeting pregnant women or children under five years of age (figure 4.4). The recommended micronutrients increase economic gains in three ways: by reducing mortality, increasing productivity, and increasing child ability. Iodine supplementation benefits a population in all three ways. Salt iodization has a very high benefit-cost ratio of 81, and supplementing pregnant women with iodated oil has an even higher benefit-cost ratio of 486. Providing iron and folate supplementation to children 6–24 months of age has a high impact on their future productivity, and the benefits of supplementation exceed costs by 24 times. Vitamin A supplementation through the EOS/EEOS programs has a benefit-cost ratio of 13 when distribution costs are included or 90 when they are excluded.

Figure 4.7 Cost per Beneficiary for the Three Focus Areas of Health Extension Workers

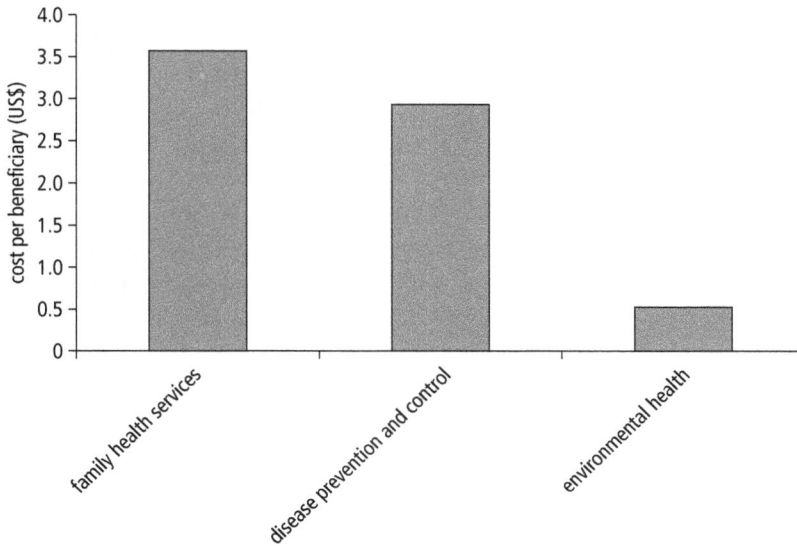

Source: Calculations by the Center for National Health Development in Ethiopia.

Although the provision of deworming medicine and the distribution of bed nets are not micronutrient interventions, their economic benefits are very high. Providing bed nets and deworming medicine to pregnant women will return economic gains that are, respectively, 26 and 648 times higher than their costs. When scaled up, these interventions will potentially also save large numbers of lives.

The analysis also finds exceptional gains from community volunteer programs with a focus on promoting nutrition activities. The promotion of optimal breast-feeding is a high-ranking intervention with a benefit-cost ratio of 27. Overall, the community volunteer programs studied have benefits exceeding costs by seven to 27 times. Quantifying all of the benefits from health and nutrition promotion programs is difficult, and therefore many benefits are not captured in the estimates presented here. For example, several diverse volunteer health messages are typically conveyed as part of these programs, and their impacts can be diffused throughout the population rather than just among targeted beneficiaries. In this way, the program gains are substantially greater than calculated here.

There are high levels of benefits relative to costs for all the interventions considered. For each intervention, the benefit-cost ratio is greater than 1. For many, it is much greater. Largely because of the costs of food provision, interventions such as emergency food aid, targeted supplementary food, and treatment for severe acute malnutrition (using the health center–based institutional approach) have a relatively high cost per beneficiary compared to the other interventions. But they are still quite cost-effective and have the potential to save the lives of many under-five children. Significant scope remains to increase the benefit-cost ratio for the treatment of severe acute malnutrition through the institutional approach (see chapter 3).

Several potential interventions reviewed should be implemented in Ethiopia, including providing deworming medicine to pregnant women,[11] which would prevent 40 percent of infant deaths for a cost of about US$0.05 per rural pregnant woman—the lowest cost per beneficiary of any program. The EOS/EEOS currently provides deworming medicine to children under five years of age, but not to pregnant women. Until recently, Ethiopian children 6–23 months of age and pregnant women were not beneficiaries of salt iodization or supplementation of iodated oil capsules, despite the very high benefit-cost ratios of these interventions. In April and May 2008, as part of the EOS/EEOS, a program providing iodated oil capsules to young children as well as pregnant and lactating women was started in some regions. This program was meant as a temporary measure until large-scale salt iodization commenced in Ethiopia, an effort that is now under way (see chapter 2). Until such a program is in place on a large enough scale, supplementation of iodated oil capsules is expected to continue.[12]

Deworming of pregnant women would reach a large proportion of the affected population without significant additional cost, an advantage it shares with several other types of micronutrient interventions. The existing structure of the EOS/EEOS would easily facilitate incorporating the provision of deworming medicine to pregnant and lactating women. Distribution for this intervention could "piggyback" on the existing distribution structure for interventions that are already part of the EOS/EEOS, as was done for iodated oil capsules.

Distributing iron and folate to young children would greatly improve their cognitive abilities. This intervention is not currently being implemented in Ethiopia, but Ethiopian society would benefit by 24 times more than the costs of the intervention, if it were introduced. However, there are some caveats with this intervention, including issues with compliance, limits to coverage of the population, and the possibility of an increased risk of contracting malaria in malaria-endemic areas.

Salt iodization and the provision of iodated oil capsules to pregnant women are both highly cost-effective interventions. But salt iodization is more sustainable in the longer run and is the much preferred option. Supplementation of iodated oil capsules requires sustained funding from the public sector or donors. Universal salt iodization requires the private sector to produce and sell only adequately iodized salt, passing the low cost of iodization to the consumer.

Community volunteer programs have great potential to reduce malnutrition through community-based nutrition. When implemented countrywide and in an appropriate manner, as in Bangladesh and Thailand, such programs have dramatically reduced the percentage of underweight and stunted children, which has substantially improved the associated outcomes, such as economic productivity and cognitive ability. The Community-Based Nutrition Program is modeled on the experience in countries such as Bangladesh and Thailand, and initial results have been encouraging (figure 4.5). The CBN Program covered 228 *woredas* at the time of writing, and the program is expected to cover 300 *woredas* by the end of 2011. If the initial success observed in a subset of CBN *woredas* is continued and replicated in other CBN *woredas*, the results would indicate that the approach should be implemented countrywide in Ethiopia.

Finally, several other interventions were not included in the analysis, but have been shown elsewhere to have high impacts relative to their costs. These include, for example, home fortification of complementary foods with micronutrient powder. This intervention is not currently being implemented in Ethiopia, but there is a strong case for doing so, perhaps initially on a pilot basis.

These recommendations are based on an examination of various quantitative measures to assess different nutrition interventions, including benefit-cost ratios, indicators of cost-effectiveness, and estimates of the potential number of lives saved when scaled up nationwide. But other important factors should also be considered when determining whether and which nutrition interventions to implement, including the availability of human resources to deliver and monitor the intervention at the local level, the existence of sufficient supplies and delivery structures, the political environment, the short- and long-term funding situation, and various programmatic, feasibility, and sustainability considerations.

NOTES

1. The Essential Services for Health in Ethiopia and Pathfinder International programs are included under "current" programs even though they were discontinued in late 2008 and merged to form the Integrated Family Health Program.

Additionally, iodated oil capsules are being provided to beneficiaries through the Enhanced Outreach Strategy for Child Survival (EOS)/Extended EOS programs as a bridging strategy until iodized salt is produced on a large scale and is widely available.

2. One intervention listed in chapter 3 that has not been costed is community-based therapeutic care implemented by NGOs because of the high variability in costs between the different NGO programs and the high variability even within each program (for example, the same organization may find unit costs to be substantially different when implementing community-based therapeutic care in different *woredas* with different emergency situations).

3. The mother's value is much higher because of the high discount rate and the fact that a child whose life is saved will see his or her stream of earnings start to accrue many years into the future when his or her working life begins (assumed to be at age 15). By contrast, a mother whose life is saved will see her earnings continue to accrue annually starting from the time her life is saved. The child's future stream of earnings is significantly reduced when converted to present value terms, due to the high discount rate.

4. Of course, it is necessary to consider the differences between services delivered for each program. For example, community-based reproductive health agents were paid a higher per diem, but they were expected to donate more of their time than the community health promoters of ESHE.

5. The EOS/EEOS costs are for Amhara and Oromia only and are based on detailed costing done for these two regions (see Fiedler and Chuko 2008). If the program were costed for all the regions participating in EOS/EEOS, these costs would probably change to some extent.

6. The estimated impact for the two other food distribution programs—the Targeted Supplementary Food Program and emergency food aid—are based on estimates from other studies and reasonable assumptions.

7. Deworming calculations are based on the assumption that deworming pregnant women reduces the mortality of children six months of age or younger by 40 percent. Lactating women and children 6–12 months of age are not included in these calculations; however, providing deworming to lactating women has benefits on the same order of magnitude (and similar unit costs) as providing deworming to pregnant women.

8. Manager's Electronic Resource Center, Management Sciences for Health; see http://erc.msh.org/.

9. As mentioned in the note to table 4.1, the calculations for the treatment of severe acute malnutrition using the health center–based institutional approach are based only on in-patient treatment. But as explained in chapter 3, there is now a shift toward using outpatient treatment, which is much more cost-effective and would potentially have a substantially higher benefit-cost ratio.

10. These dollar figures were converted from Ethiopian birr using the prevailing official exchange rate at the time of writing.

11. As mentioned, the very high benefit-cost ratios shown in this chapter for the provision of deworming to pregnant women suggest that there are also high benefit-cost ratios for the provision of deworming to lactating women. Deworming should thus be provided to pregnant as well as lactating women.

12. In November and December 2009, iodated oil capsules were distributed in all *woredas* in Amhara, Tigray, Benshangul-Gumuz, and SNNP regions. In June 2010, supplementation was provided in all *woredas* in Oromia. Since then, no more distributions have taken place, but further distributions are planned for the near future.

CHAPTER 5

A Targeted, Multisectoral Approach to Combating Malnutrition in Ethiopia

In addition to the larger nutrition-related programs discussed in earlier chapters, a range of other programs are being implemented in Ethiopia. These interventions can save lives, improve the well-being of individuals and families, and increase economic productivity. The ones analyzed earlier were found to be extremely cost-effective, among the best in value for money of all development interventions.

But maximizing these programs' effectiveness requires work on three fronts: coordination among the many actors, sectors, and programs involved; timely and accurate data and effective nutritional surveillance; and well-targeted programs. The government of Ethiopia recognizes the importance of all three and has made strides to address these issues, but much more can and must be done. This chapter examines these three areas in turn and offers practical recommendations for moving forward.

THE NATIONAL NUTRITION PROGRAM: A HARMONIZED, PROGRAMMATIC APPROACH

Many factors other than food affect the prevalence of malnutrition in Ethiopia. As shown in this chapter, even in many food-secure areas of Ethiopia, the prevalence of wasting and especially stunting is high. Improving nutrition therefore requires interventions targeting a range of sectors—health, water, agriculture, and education, among others. The most effective approach to reducing malnutrition and achieving nutrition security in Ethiopia is a national nutrition program encompassing all sectors, that is, a "programmatic approach" providing agencies the opportunity to harmonize their programs and maximize the efficiency of program inputs. It is crucial to have communication and collaboration on nutrition-related issues and programs among the government agencies responsible for health, agriculture, water and sanitation, education, food security, and emergency response, as well as among the multilateral and bilateral agencies, nongovernmental agencies (NGOs), and other actors working in these sectors.

Ethiopia formulated and approved its first National Nutrition Strategy in February 2008. Approved in a high-profile ceremony presided over by the deputy prime minister and minister for agriculture and rural development, as well as the minister for health, the strategy stresses the critical need for a multisectoral approach with committed involvement from all relevant sectors. The five-year National Nutrition Program was subsequently designed and approved in December 2008, once again in a high-profile ceremony with high-level participation, reflecting the commitment of the government of Ethiopia to addressing the problem of malnutrition (Ethiopia, Federal Ministry of Health 2008).

The Ministry of Health is taking the lead in overseeing and implementing key aspects of the National Nutrition Program, but other ministries and sectors are also involved. Table 5.1 outlines the program's two main components and eight subcomponents, and table 5.2 lists the key linkages planned with other programs.

Table 5.1 Outline of the National Nutrition Program in Ethiopia

Component and subcomponent	Description
Component 1. Strengthening nutrition services delivery	
Subcomponent 1(a). Sustaining the Enhanced Outreach Strategy for Child Survival (EOS) with targeted supplementary food and transitioning of EOS into the Health Extension Program (HEP)	The EOS program with targeted supplementary food (EOS/TSFP) is an interim or "bridging" strategy focused on enhancing child survival by reducing mortality and morbidity in children less than five years of age and in pregnant and lactating women. It will transition into the Health Extension Program in the longer term (see chapter 3 for more details). Health extension workers, an integral part of the HEP, are already actively taking part in the program. The National Nutrition Program seeks to maintain the high coverage rates of EOS/TSFP as it transitions into HEP and to include community health days and community-based nutrition—the principle being to keep high service coverage with three-month or six-month events organized at the *kebele* (community) level.
Subcomponent 1(b). Management of severe malnutrition	The overall objective is to continue and modify as needed the existing modalities for treating severe acute malnutrition so that access and coverage can be increased and treatment success rates can be maintained or improved.
Subcomponent 1(c). Community-based nutrition	This subcomponent seeks to provide community-based nutrition and health services, fully using existing HEP outreach and model household service provision and building on these with additional community-based resources and activities. The activities can be broadly classified as (a) those relevant to health extension workers and their supervisors (based at health centers) and (b) those relevant to volunteer community health workers and model households.

(continued)

Table 5.1   *(continued)*

Component and subcomponent	Description
Subcomponent 1(d). Micronutrient interventions and high-impact commodities	The four main micronutrients of concern are iodine, vitamin A, iron, and zinc. Key goals include establishing universal salt iodization, maintaining high coverage of vitamin A supplementation for children under five years of age, improving the supply of iron and folate tablets for pregnant and lactating women, and establishing zinc supplementation for the treatment of diarrhea.
Component 2. Institutional and knowledge base strengthening	
Subcomponent 2(a). Strengthening human resources and capacity building	This subcomponent supports (a) nutrition coordination mechanisms at different levels, (b) institutional capacity building for implementing units and activities at different levels of government (including human resource strengthening), and (c) training and capacity building for research and training institutions.
Subcomponent 2(b). Advocacy, social mobilization, and program communication	This subcomponent focuses on developing an effective communications strategy (a) to raise consciousness of the importance of malnutrition-related problems and the efforts under way to address them and (b) to identify priority behavioral change messages and systematically incorporate them into communications systems in the health and other sectors.
Subcomponent 2(c). Strengthening nutrition information, surveillance, monitoring and evaluation, and operations research	With the goal of strengthening information systems to effectively support nutrition programming, this subcomponent redefines the information needed and the indicators and mechanisms for data collection, analysis, and use by strengthening the existing health management information system, integrated disease surveillance and response, and demographic surveillance sites, as well as the functions undertaken by the regional Emergency Nutrition Coordination Units (ENCUs), which are part of the Early Warning System. It also strengthens the ability of the existing system to provide appropriate data for proper nutritional surveillance, to undertake overall monitoring and evaluation of the National Nutrition Program, and to cover relevant operational research.
Subcomponent 2(d). Strengthening multisectoral nutrition linkages	This subcomponent strengthens the linkages to other relevant programs and sectors to enhance the impact of programs and to galvanize nutrition efforts through a multisectoral approach. While many valuable linkages are possible, the National Nutrition Program decided to concentrate initially on its links with five other categories of programs or projects, as shown in table 5.2.

Source: Authors.

STRENGTHENING COORDINATION BETWEEN PROGRAMS AND WITH THE PRIVATE SECTOR

The linkages between the different nutrition-related sectors and programs need urgent strengthening—particularly the weaker links. Typically, the programs affecting nutrition operate independently of one another. A key goal of the National Nutrition Program is to harmonize nutrition efforts through a coordinated approach that enhances the linkages between programs. This section discusses how to resolve problems caused by inadequate linkages and program coordination.

Table 5.2   Key Linkages Planned with the National Nutrition Program

Type of linkage	Description
Productive Safety Net Program and Food Security Project	Ensure that young children and pregnant and lactating women in families receiving aid are being nutritionally monitored; use contact points as opportunities to provide counseling about changing nutrition behaviors (for example, regarding breast-feeding and complementary feeding practices, optimal pregnancy practices, and use of iodized salt) and to distribute iron and folate tablets to pregnant and lactating women; include nutritional status (nutritional anthropometry) and food security score in the evaluation of the Productive Safety Net Program and the Food Security Project
Water, Sanitation, and Hygiene (WASH) Program	Ensure that young children and pregnant and lactating women in families receiving WASH assistance are targeted for nutritional services; enable WASH volunteers, health extension workers, and volunteer community health workers to interact closely to encourage mutually supportive extension services; ensure that training manuals for each category of worker contain consistent messages emphasizing the linkages among hygiene, nutrition, and health
Other Ministry of Agriculture and Rural Development programs and interventions	Use agricultural extension workers (development agents) and, where available, model farmers as change agents to disseminate information on the importance of adequate food intake for young children and women of reproductive age, particularly pregnant and lactating women; provide funds to intensify research efforts (a) to improve the production possibilities for crops disproportionately produced and consumed by low-income households, (b) to promote nutrient-rich varieties, such as quality protein maize and micronutrient-rich varieties of cereals, and (c) to promote the consumption of orange-flesh sweet potatoes; facilitate the retraining of agricultural extension workers (development agents) and model farmers to promote the production and consumption of the above-mentioned crops; encourage research and extension efforts to introduce improved cassava processing (to reduce the food's goitrogenic properties)
Ministry of Education programs and interventions	Promote the inclusion of nutrition information (consistent with the priority messages of the National Nutrition Program) in relevant primary- and middle-school classes, giving particular attention to key "take-home" messages; provide school health and nutrition inputs (deworming, iodized salt, and iron and folate tablets, in addition to school meals presently provided in some areas) to optimize active learning capacity; include non-school-going children in weekly nutrition counseling, deworming, and micronutrient provision; engage schoolchildren in making soap (given the strong association between the use of soap by child caretakers and morbidity and malnutrition) and in testing iodized salt by using salt testing kits
HIV (human immunodeficiency virus)/AIDS (acquired immunodeficiency syndrome) programs and interventions	Coordinate HIV-related counseling and service delivery by health extension workers and volunteer community health workers with nutrition-related services and counseling, emphasizing the value of good nutrition in improving immune response and, among HIV-positive individuals, in delaying the onset of AIDS and improving the efficacy of antiretrovirals and reducing their side effects (an estimated 50 percent of individuals using antiretrovirals drop out of treatment partly because of these side effects); conduct a study of food intake and other behaviors of AIDS-infected individuals who have benefited from extended longevity

Source: Authors.

IMPROVING COORDINATION BETWEEN PROGRAMS OPERATING IN THE SAME *WOREDAS* (DISTRICTS)

Each nutrition-related program often independently chooses a focus *woreda*(s) without consulting other programs. When two or more programs overlap in the same *woreda*, typically no harmonized mechanism exists for selecting or distinguishing between beneficiary households of other programs. Setting up a harmonized procedure for choosing beneficiary households—including a common database of beneficiaries or a similar tool—would greatly assist the effective targeting of resources. Linking existing databases or lists of beneficiaries would help to determine where duplicate efforts are wasting resources and ensure that programs are targeting resources to the households where they can have the greatest impact.

Other methods exist to increase harmonization among nutrition-related programs, especially where they coexist in the same *woredas* or *kebeles*. Many programs share the same goals and could achieve greater results by linking their efforts. For example, many programs use community volunteers to implement interventions. While the content and duration of training vary greatly among organizations, the objectives are often similar (see the program descriptions in chapter 3). Although these volunteer cadres may serve in the same *woredas* or *kebeles*, two parallel systems may be operating. By coordinating the programs, the same volunteers could have more intense, but harmonized, training and incentives to accomplish the same tasks. The volunteers' level of understanding and ability to serve their communities would improve as the program inputs are shared and channeled to fewer volunteers with greater expertise.

Implementing two or more programs affecting nutrition in the same *woredas* or *kebeles* can be complementary. But if not harmonized, the results may produce diminishing returns. For example, adding more programs can stretch existing local capacity and can reduce—rather than increase—the impact of each program. This may be especially true for health extension workers, who are asked to play a coordinating role on the ground and are often tasked with supervising the community volunteers of one or more programs other than the Health Extension Program. Yet the health extension workers are already overworked, implementing their own "packages" of the Health Extension Program.

Involving workers in community volunteer programs in addition to the HEP indeed has the potential to enhance the programs' effectiveness, under the right circumstances. But in practice, involving the health extension workers in two or more community volunteer programs (other than the HEP) in the same *woreda*, each with different mechanisms of operation and different types of training and roles for community volunteers, may reduce rather than increase the impact of each program. Such a scenario risks overburdening both the health extension workers and the *woreda* and *kebele* officials.

Linkages between and the coexistence of different programs need to be considered more fully and explicitly when monitoring and evaluation are conducted. Currently, program administrators often conduct monitoring and evaluation without considering the impact of coexisting programs (see box 5.1).

IMPROVING INTERSECTORAL COORDINATION

The government and donors need to strengthen linkages between different programs and sectors, and collaboration by the Ministry of Health and the Ministry of Agriculture is particularly important to reduce malnutrition. As in many countries, the government structure is not amenable to different agencies, especially from different ministries, working together in a harmonized fashion. And donor agencies administering different programs often operate independently of each other, which complicates cooperative efforts.

Some of these coordinating difficulties were resolved by creation of the Emergency Nutrition Coordination Unit (ENCU) at the federal level. The ENCU is a unit in the government's Disaster Risk Management and Food Security Sector and is mandated to monitor nutrition surveys and emergency interventions (generally implemented by NGOs) mainly in "hot spot" areas experiencing an emergency or crisis situation. A regional ENCU was also created and is fully functional and staffed in Amhara, Oromia, Southern Nations, Nationalities and Peoples (SNNP), Somali, and Tigray. The regional ENCUs have helped to increase harmonization of the various nutrition-related programs.

The ENCUs play a key role in producing and disseminating information about the emergency nutrition and health needs of vulnerable people. But they operate with limited resources and a somewhat limited mandate. Therefore, their role in increasing coordination between nutrition-related programs is limited, and their focus is generally only on the *woredas* where emergency situations are occurring or have occurred. The ENCUs' coordinating role is limited to a number of *woredas* and in each *woreda* is limited to collaboration between the relevant disaster prevention and preparedness bureau, desk, or department;[1] the relevant regional health bureau; and the implementing NGO. The Ministry of Education

BOX 5.1   PROGRAM COORDINATION AND LINKAGES IN SNNP

The Southern Nations, Nationalities, and Peoples (SNNP) region is at the forefront of much research about nutrition indicators and programs. Many documents and stakeholders concerned with nutrition security laud SNNP for its successes in programming, targeting, and coordination, as demonstrated by the EOS results and increased coverage with each round. During implementation, SNNP officials often take the time to critique and adapt methods specifically for their own population. For example, the region uses the HEP standards for their health extension workers, but requires them to spend 75 percent of their time in the field. Various key stakeholders were asked about SNNP and how they accomplish such a high level of collaboration. Some of the reasons they shared are listed below.

- SNNP was one of the first regions in the country to have a fully functioning regional Emergency Nutrition Coordination Unit (ENCU) office. The key personnel at this office meet every month with the head of the regional bureau of health and the child survival team. This meeting is attended by all NGOs and United Nations staff active in the region. Hot spots are discussed, recent assessments and surveys are presented, and programming is coordinated between the *woredas*.
- All of the government offices in Awassa seem to be very well organized. If information is needed, they generally provide it quickly and are aware of what is happening in their sector.
- All surveys and emergency interventions are overseen by the regional ENCU office; a member of the office is often present during assessments.
- The regional capital of Awassa is well placed for access and communication by NGOs, United Nations offices, and donor agencies.
- Administrative boundaries in SNNP are drawn along ethnic boundaries; this has decreased infighting and improved working relationships in government offices.
- During the green famine in the 1990s, substantial amounts of resources were poured into the SNNP region to build capacity at all levels.
- During the 1960s and 1970s, there was a massive missionary campaign in parts of the SNNP. This led to high education levels in rural areas where many schools were built; these schools are still maintained in many areas.

Ethiopia would be well served to investigate the SNNP's methods further to ascertain which methods truly helped to develop the system, how the system is run, and which methods are transferable to other parts of the country. Many may not be transferable, but those that are should be investigated and possibly implemented in other areas after thorough research.

and the Ministry of Water Resources generally are not involved in ENCU work.

A key goal of the National Nutrition Program is to resolve coordination issues to substantially improve linkages among different programs and agencies. As called for by the National Nutrition Strategy and in line with the program, the National Nutrition Coordination Committee was established in late 1998. This high-level cross-sectoral coordinating body is tasked with ensuring that different agencies work together to reduce malnutrition. The establishment of the committee was mandated by the Plan for Accelerated and Sustained Development to End Poverty, the government's overall poverty strategy document covering all sectors. The committee members include (a) the ministers or state ministers[2] of the following ministries: health, agriculture and rural development, water resources, education, finance and economic development, and women's affairs as well as (b) representatives of academia, the private sector, and donor agencies. The committee meets once every three months and focuses particularly on cross-sectoral issues, such as linkages between the various nutrition-related programs administered by the ministries.

The National Nutrition Program provides a framework for increased government and donor harmonization and coordination among different sectors and programs on issues such as choosing target *woredas* and beneficiaries, training community volunteers, and conducting monitoring and evaluation. Specific complementarities between programs are being highlighted and strengthened, for example, between core nutrition interventions and the Productive Safety Net Program.

PILOT PROJECT ENHANCING COORDINATION BETWEEN SECTORS AND PROGRAMS

A small pilot project is currently taking place with a specific focus on strengthening community-level linkages between core nutrition interventions under the National Nutrition Program (implemented by the health sector) and the activities of the Productive Safety Net Program (implemented by the agriculture sector). Both programs expect to contribute to Ethiopia's achievement of the first Millennium Development Goal by reducing the number of Ethiopians suffering from extreme hunger, malnutrition, and poverty. The shared objectives and the geographic overlap in implementing the two programs are expected to provide opportunities for synergy, but currently (outside of the pilot) there are no linkages and only limited coordination between them. The Ministry of Health assumes the most direct responsibility for nutrition but has no influence over the supply and availability of food, which fall under the Ministry of Agriculture.

The pilot has identified community-based opportunities for intersectoral collaboration over specific issues that relate supply to demand and production to consumption. These opportunities will constitute a promising focus of exchange between sectors. They are expected to lead gradually to government line ministries coordinating certain policies around select issues as part of a scaling-up process. The pilot was initiated in late 2009 in one *woreda* in each of the following regions: Amhara, Oromia, Tigray, and SNNP.

The efforts at creating linkages are still small, relative to what needs to be done, but they nevertheless need to be sustained and increased. Similar pilot projects involving other sectors need to be initiated, and successful pilots should be scaled up in the future after careful evaluation. Linkages must be formed and strengthened, not just with the sectors typically linked with nutrition, such as health and agriculture, but also with other sectors such as water and sanitation, education, infrastructure, and microlending.

PUBLIC-PRIVATE PARTNERSHIPS

Public-private partnerships need to be explored and developed in the face of the current nutritional problems. Many nutrition interventions can be strengthened with the help of the private sector and those working in industry. These interventions include fortifying foods with micronutrients such as iodine and vitamin A. The Afar regional government, the federal government, salt producers, and large salt distributors are now working together to establish a structure for continued large-scale iodization of salt in the Afar region (see chapter 3). Other potential cooperative efforts with private companies to fortify food are being sought.

Public-private partnerships can also be effective in producing food and food products to treat moderate and severe malnutrition, such as ready-to-use therapeutic food and ready-to-use supplementary food. International organizations such as the United Nations Children's Fund (UNICEF) and the World Food Program wish to purchase these nutrition-related commodities from local suppliers. But because the supply is very limited relative to the demand, large quantities of these products are imported to fill the gap.[3] Importing ready-to-use therapeutic food and ready-to-use supplementary food is expensive and delays prompt emergency responses. Promoting the production of food and food products through local groups is crucial to improving the coverage and timeliness of nutritional interventions. Several experts have been hired to identify industry constraints and to explore potential interventions and innovative partnerships. For example, because access to finance throughout the value chain is a major problem hampering increased local production, one useful intervention that is being explored is the provision of financial support for the entire value chain of relevant products.

Developing complementary foods with locally available inputs is also important to improve the population's daily dietary intake. Compared to the production of ready-to-use therapeutic and supplementary food, this effort would be a smaller-scale public-private partnership project, but it would contribute to strengthening nutritional status and help to prevent malnourishment, particularly during emergency situations. A working group of various stakeholders including public and private research institutes, private companies, NGOs, and international organizations is examining feasible interventions and working to establish potential pilot projects in Ethiopia.

NUTRITION INFORMATION AND SURVEILLANCE

Planning, coordination, and harmonization among players across the nutrition landscape, as well as accurate and effective targeting, are impossible without accurate and timely information. But regularly tracking trends in Ethiopian nutrition nationally, regionally, or even locally, such as for *woredas* or *kebeles*, is currently impossible. Although national and regional representative surveys are conducted with broad geographic coverage, such as the Welfare Monitoring Surveys and the Demographic and Health Surveys, they are undertaken only once every three to five years. To establish a baseline, the National Nutrition Program conducted a survey to assess the national nutrition situation in 2009; a final survey is planned for 2013. The health management information system collects facility-based data on a limited number of nutrition indicators, including the percentage of children under three years of age who are moderately underweight. Data are collected monthly at the zonal and regional levels and reported quarterly as part of regional and national reports. However, the data are not representative of the community level because information is collected only from children brought to health facilities. The community-level nutrition information collected in some *woredas* is not currently reported as part of the 108 indicators flowing through the health management information system.

The ENCU directs and oversees NGOs conducting ad hoc rapid assessments and nutrition surveys in selected *woredas* where an emergency situation appears to be developing. But these surveys are conducted on an emergency basis and are not regularly carried out in any *woredas*. Demographic surveillance sites have been set up in select areas of the country, with universities conducting localized surveys, but they currently collect demographic data without nutrition indicators.

Strengthening the country's nutrition information and surveillance system is a key goal of the National Nutrition Program to better track nutritional trends in different parts of the country and within population subgroups as well as to facilitate a better understanding of the impacts of different interventions and programs. A more robust nutrition information and surveillance system would feature, among others, (a) strengthened flow of data collected under the EOS and the Community-Based Nutrition (CBN) programs from the *kebele* to the regional level and enhanced use and interpretation of these data; (b) linkage of these data to agro-economic data to support the Early Warning System; (c) regular nationally representative nutrition surveys and inclusion of additional indicators on priority nutrition areas (such as infant and young child feeding and food insecurity) in the Welfare Monitoring Survey and the Demographic and Health Survey; (d) increased use of secondary analyses of national surveys to improve understanding of Ethiopia's nutrition situation; (e) use of the facility-level underweight data obtained through the health management information system and under the EOS and CBN programs to examine trends in underweight by "triangulating" different sources of data;[4] and (f) possible inclusion of nutrition indicators in demographic surveillance sites around the country.

OPTIMAL TARGETING OF NUTRITION-RELATED PROGRAMS

Many programs that seek to reduce malnutrition in Ethiopia target areas that regularly receive food aid and are designated as food insecure. This approach is problematic. First, food aid targeting is often based on out-of-date designations about which areas are food insecure and lacks the flexibility to adapt to new realities and respond to shocks. Second, and more fundamentally, even if food aid targeting were perfect, basing the targeting of nutrition programs on the targeting of food aid would still be problematic because the correlation between food insecurity and malnutrition is only partial and is especially weak if the latter is measured by looking at stunting rates.

The latter point is clearly illustrated in the analysis of food security status and malnutrition in chapter 2 and is particularly relevant for the analysis that follows. The analysis in chapter 2, which is based on data from the 2004 Welfare Monitoring Survey, found that while child wasting is higher in households with a higher degree of self-reported food insecurity (or food shortages), the overall rate of child wasting is still high (almost 8 percent for total wasting) in households with *no* self-reported food insecurity. And no clear relationship was found between stunting rates and the extent of self-reported household food insecurity.

Nonetheless, the targeting of nutrition-related interventions continues to be inextricably linked to the targeting of food aid. This section discusses the problems with how food aid is targeted and then describes the implications for nutrition programming based on such targeting.

TARGETING OF FOOD AID

This section draws preliminary conclusions about the impact and targeting of food aid based on the available information, with a few caveats. Malnutrition in Ethiopia is caused by a range of factors; food insecurity is only one of them. Emergency food aid is a vital intervention, but *food aid can address only the component of malnutrition resulting from food insecurity.* Emergency food is a topic that requires more in-depth analysis, and additional research is needed on this important issue.

Overall, the emergency food aid system in Ethiopia has performed well by international standards. In the 1980s, Ethiopia developed a reputation for regularly having famines, leading in 1985 to a large-scale international effort to raise funds for aid and to the famous Live Aid concert featuring Bob Geldof and others.[5] Since then, there has been little change in the frequency and intensity of weather shocks, and this—together with rapid population growth and environmental degradation—has led to the continued high prevalence of food insecurity. But in recent times, this high degree of food insecurity has not translated into large-scale famines. This is due in large part to the performance of the emergency food aid system over the last 20 years or so.

As in many other countries, however, the targeting of food aid can be improved. The needs for emergency food aid are determined with the help of the Early Warning System *meher* and *belg* (crop season) assessments that are conducted in November-December as well as in June, respectively, every year. This process has several drawbacks, including relatively poor coverage in some parts of the country, such as certain areas with pastoral, nonfamine-prone, nomadic, historically marginalized, and urban populations.

Notwithstanding the annual *meher* and *belg* assessments, food aid targeting ultimately remains inflexible in many ways. The pattern of food aid provision in Ethiopia appears to be determined largely by factors other than shocks. Many communities experiencing shocks do not receive food aid. Certain *woredas* were labeled food insecure in the past according to targeting or selection mechanisms that were applied years ago. These *woredas* tend to retain the food-insecure label even now, and they appear to receive food aid consistently, sometimes even in years when weather conditions are not especially bad. Conversely, the so-called food-secure *woredas* are much less likely to receive food aid. A flexible system would channel food to *woredas* that suffer negative shocks in any particular year rather than to *woredas* categorized as food insecure many years in the past.

The inflexibility of the food aid targeting system in Ethiopia has been highlighted in several reports. Reasons given for this inflexibility include a build-up of investments in the food-insecure *woredas* over time, including investments in personnel, contacts, infrastructure, and institutional reputation, which create a system prone to inertia.[6]

An analysis of the data shows that there are large proportions of food-insecure households living in the *woredas* designated as food secure, and these households should be considered in targeting food aid. A snapshot of the extent of food insecurity in different groups of *woredas* is shown in table 5.3 as well as in figures 5.1 and 5.2, based on calculations using 2004 Welfare Monitoring Survey data. The data are based on household responses to survey questions asking (a) whether or not the household

Table 5.3 Extent of Self-Reported Household Food Insecurity in *Woredas*, by Food Security Designation, 2004

Designation	Number of *woredas*	Number of households in sample	Percentage of households reporting food shortage within previous 12 months	Average number of months of food shortage within previous 12 months
Woredas designated as fully food secure	182	2,818	24.7	0.85
Woredas designated as partially food secure	161	4,209	32.0	1.24
Woredas designated as food insecure	213	4,150	35.8	1.30

Source: Authors' calculations using data from the 2004 Welfare Monitoring Survey (CSA 2004) and food aid data from the Disaster Risk Management and Food Security Sector.
Note: Woredas here are defined according to 2004 boundaries. The figures for the average number of months of food shortage incorporate households reporting no food shortage; these households were taken to have zero months of food shortage within the previous 12 months.

Figure 5.1 Percentage of Households Reporting Food Shortage within Previous 12 Months in *Woredas*, by Food Security Designation

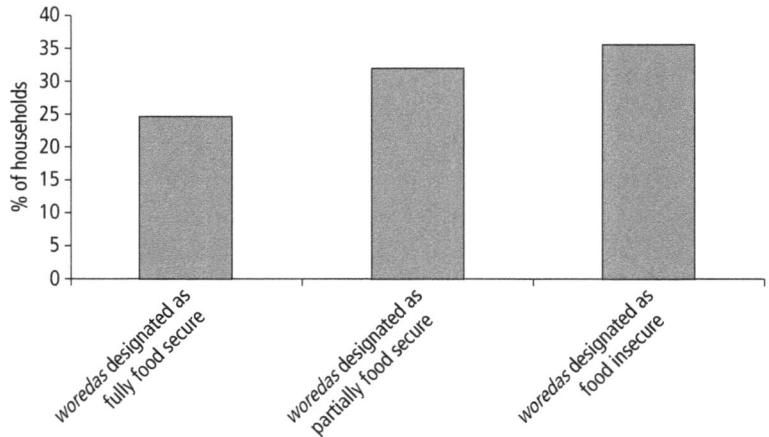

Source: Authors' calculations using data from the 2004 Welfare Monitoring Survey (CSA 2004) and food aid data from Disaster Risk Management and Food Security Sector.
Note: Woredas here are defined according to 2004 boundaries.

Figure 5.2 Average Number of Months of Food Shortage within the Previous 12 Months as Reported by Households in *Woredas*, by Food Security Designation

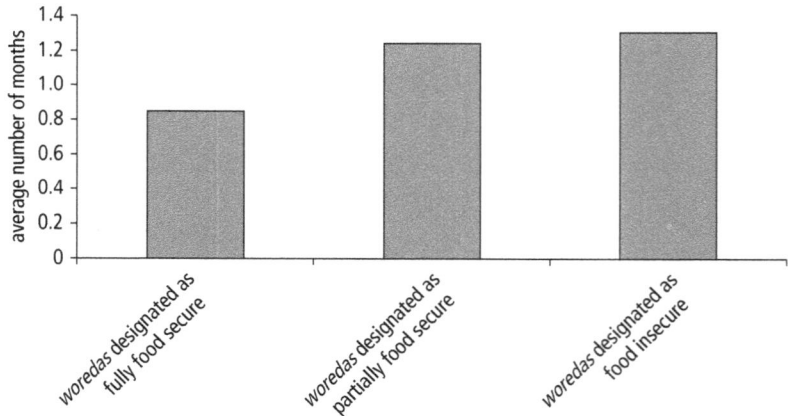

Source: Authors' calculations using data from the 2004 Welfare Monitoring Survey (CSA 2004) and food aid data from the Disaster Risk Management and Food Security Sector.
Note: Woredas here are defined according to 2004 boundaries. The graph incorporates households reporting no food shortage; these households were taken to have zero months of food shortage within the previous 12 months.

experienced food shortage in the previous 12 months, and (b) if the answer given was yes, how many months of food shortage were experienced (see chapter 2). For this section's analysis, *woredas* are categorized as those designated as food insecure, those designated as partially food secure, or those designated as fully food secure, according to the frequency with which they received food aid from 2000 to 2004, before the Productive Safety Net Program was introduced. *Woredas* identified as needing food aid for all five years of the period are labeled as food insecure (by designation). *Woredas* identified as not requiring food aid in any of the five years are labeled as fully food secure (by designation); the remaining *woredas* are labeled as partially food secure (by designation). Note that this classification is based on the outcomes of the process used to designate *woredas* as food insecure or food secure in each year; flaws in this process would translate to errors in the designation of some *woredas*. Note also that not all of the *woredas* identified as needing food aid in any one year actually obtained it.

According to the information in table 5.3 and figures 5.1 and 5.2, the difference in the extent of food insecurity between the *woredas* designated as food secure and those designated as food insecure is less than might be expected. The small difference can be attributed in part to the equalizing effect of emergency food aid, which tends to be distributed almost exclusively in the so-called food-insecure *woredas* and is clearly having a positive impact in them. But the data suggest that large numbers of food-insecure people in the *woredas* designated as food secure are not being reached. About 25 percent of households in the *woredas* designated as fully food secure reported food shortages within the previous 12 months, according to the 2004 Welfare Monitoring Survey (see figure 5.1). The corresponding percentage of households in the *woredas* designated as food insecure is about 36 percent. The average number of months of self-reported food shortage within the previous 12 months for the different categories of *woredas* again varies surprisingly little (figure 5.2).

An analysis of stunting and wasting rates based on the 2004 Welfare Monitoring Survey data for the different categories of *woredas* also produces startling results. There appears to be little difference in stunting and wasting rates between the *woredas* classified as food insecure, partially food insecure, and fully food secure (see table 5.4). The classification of *woredas* here is the same one used throughout this section and is based on the frequency with which the various *woredas* received food aid over the five-year period from 2000 to 2004. The results show that the so-called food-insecure *woredas* had a slightly higher stunting rate in 2004 than the other *woredas*, but the difference is not very large. In addition, they did not have higher wasting rates in 2004 than the other *woredas*, according to the analysis. In fact, the *woredas* designated as food insecure had somewhat *lower* wasting rates than those designated as fully food secure.

This finding should be interpreted alongside (a) the findings regarding self-reported household food insecurity in the different categories of

Table 5.4 Malnutrition Rates in *Woredas*, by Food Security Designation, 2004

Designation	Number of *woredas*	Stunting rate (%)		Wasting rate (%)	
		Total	Severe	Total	Severe
Woredas designated as fully food secure	213	47.2	24.5	10.0	2.0
Woredas designated as partially food secure	161	46.8	24.3	7.5	1.4
Woredas designated as food insecure	182	48.6	24.0	9.0	1.8

Source: Authors' calculations using data from the 2004 Welfare Monitoring Survey (CSA 2004) and food aid data from the Disaster Risk Management and Food Security Sector.
Note: Woredas here are defined according to 2004 boundaries. Total stunting refers to moderate as well as severe stunting, while total wasting refers to moderate as well as severe wasting.

woredas (table 5.3; figures 5.1 and 5.2) and (b) the analysis regarding the links between child malnutrition and the extent of self-reported household food insecurity in chapter 2 (table 2.2; figures 2.8 and 2.9). The analysis in chapter 2 finds a partial correlation between child wasting rates and the extent of household food insecurity in 2004, but also finds that a very large component of wasting cannot be explained by food shortage alone. No clear relationship is found between child stunting rates and the extent of household food insecurity.

Together, these three sets of findings give rise to some insights. First, one reason for the results shown in table 5.4 and figures 5.3 and 5.4—that there is little, if any, difference in stunting and wasting rates between the *woredas* designated as food insecure, partially food insecure, and fully food secure—is that emergency food aid appears to have an equalizing effect across the three sets of *woredas*. Food aid is distributed mainly to the *woredas* designated as food insecure (and to some extent those designated as partially food insecure), despite the large proportions of food-insecure households in the so-called food-secure *woredas*, and this brings the food insecurity levels of the three sets of *woredas* closer than they otherwise would be.

Second, the findings could also be partly attributed to the fact that a substantial component of both wasting and stunting is due to factors other than household food shortages. These include poor health status, inadequate safe water and sanitation, and inappropriate child care and child-feeding practices. These factors may, on average, be more prevalent in the *woredas* designated as food secure than in those designated as food insecure. This may be a reason that the *woredas* designated as food secure and food insecure have similar stunting and wasting rates, even though

Figure 5.3   Wasting Rates in *Woredas,* by Food Security Designation, 2004

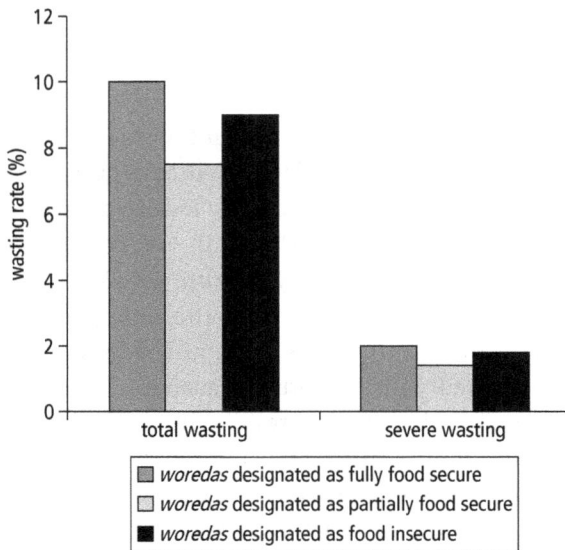

Source: Authors' calculations using data from the 2004 Welfare Monitoring Survey (CSA 2004) and food aid data from the Disaster Risk Management and Food Security Sector.
Note: Total wasting refers to moderate as well as severe wasting.

Figure 5.4   Stunting Rates in *Woredas,* by Food Security Designation, 2004

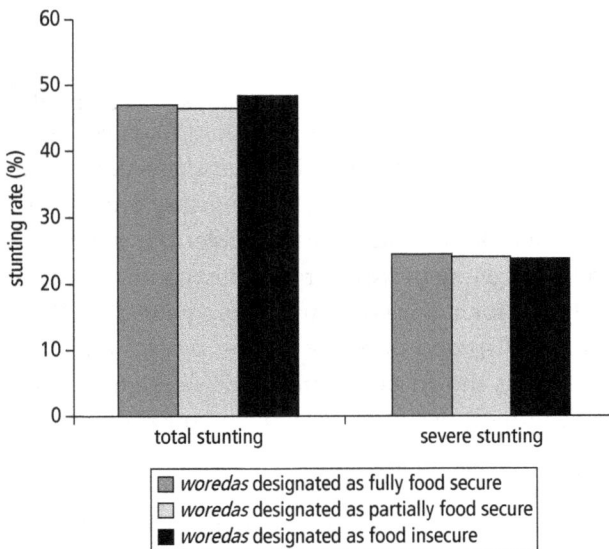

Source: Authors' calculations using data from the 2004 Welfare Monitoring Survey (CSA 2004) and food aid data from the Disaster Risk Management and Food Security Sector.
Note: Total stunting refers to moderate as well as severe stunting.

there is more food insecurity, on average, in the *woredas* designated as food insecure.

TARGETING OF PROGRAMS AFFECTING NUTRITION

The overall targeting of nutrition programs needs to be improved. A major problem to begin with is the lack of a proper nutrition information system, as discussed earlier. Because of this, localized data on nutritional indicators are limited, making it very difficult or even impossible for programs to target the most nutritionally insecure *woredas*.

Effective targeting is also hampered by the widespread but mistaken notion that nutrition security is the same as food security. This misinformation—combined with a dearth of available representative local data about nutrition insecurity—results in programs targeted and designed to reduce malnutrition by using measures of food insecurity or other types of vulnerability, such as the chronic vulnerability index.[7] These measures generally do not correlate strongly with nutrition insecurity. As mentioned throughout this report, and as shown using 2004 Welfare Monitoring Survey data in chapter 2, the correlation between food and nutrition insecurity is only partial. Many factors other than food provision have a strong and large impact on malnutrition indicators, especially stunting rates.

To compound the problem, targeting food insecurity is a difficult process in and of itself, even if one explicitly aims to ignore the other factors that contribute to malnutrition. The approach taken by many programs aiming to combat malnutrition is to focus largely on the *woredas* designated as "food insecure"; these are also the *woredas* that have been regularly receiving emergency food aid since a targeting process. But this chapter has discussed ways in which the targeting process for food insecurity in Ethiopia is flawed and quite inflexible, as it is in many countries. Problems in the targeting process for food insecurity thus compound the targeting problems for a range of nutrition programs as well, since the latter tend to focus disproportionately on the *woredas* designated as food insecure. And yet, as shown earlier, the *woredas* designated as food secure also have large proportions of food-insecure households.

As noted, many programs aiming to combat malnutrition focus largely on the *woredas* designated as food insecure, while often ignoring those designated as food secure, as shown in table 5.5 (which lists by food security designation the *woredas* included in 2007 in several major programs that affect nutrition[8]). The *woredas* are categorized by the frequency with which they received food aid from 2000 to 2004.

Table 5.5 Percentage of *Woredas* Included in Each Major Program Affecting Nutrition, by Food Security Designation, 2007

Program	*Woredas* designated as fully food secure	*Woredas* designated as partially food secure	*Woredas* designated as food insecure
Full EOS	8.1	68.7	88.6
TSFP[a]	4.1	48.8	78.4
Productive Safety Net Program[a]	0.0	46.9	94.6
MERET[a]	2.0	6.2	28.6
School Feeding Program[a]	2.7	21.8	37.8
ESHE	5.4	9.0	18.9
Child Growth Promotion	0.0	3.3	13.5
Pathfinder International	35.1	34.6	31.4
WASH	49.3	50.2	48.6

Source: Authors' calculations using program data and food aid data from the Disaster Risk Management and Food Security Sector.
Note: EOS = Enhanced Outreach Strategy for Child Survival; TSFP = Targeted Supplementary Food Program; MERET = Managing Environmental Resources to Enable Transitions to More Sustainable Livelihoods; ESHE = Essential Services for Health in Ethiopia; WASH = Water, Sanitation, and Hygiene.
a. The program aims to reduce malnutrition only or largely through food provision.

In analyzing the data, one must distinguish between programs that aim to reduce malnutrition solely or largely by providing food and programs that do not provide food. In table 5.5, and in the tables with program statistics that come after it, an asterisk denotes programs that provide food. For all the other programs listed in the tables (except Pathfinder International and the Water, Sanitation, and Hygiene (WASH) Program), improving nutritional indicators through pathways other than food provision is a key goal.

Most of the analyzed programs include a high—sometimes very high—percentage of *woredas* designated as food insecure relative to the percentage of those designated as partially food secure or fully food secure. This is true even for some of the programs that do not provide food. The only programs that do not include much higher percentages of *woredas* designated as food insecure than *woredas* designated as food secure are the Pathfinder International and WASH programs, whose objectives do not explicitly address nutrition insecurity.

Next, the programs listed in table 5.5 are analyzed by looking at the degree of targeting of each of the major programs affecting nutrition. For each program, all *woredas* in the country are subdivided into two groups: *woredas* included in the program in 2007 and those not included. In each case, nutritional indicators based on data from the 2004 Welfare Monitoring Survey (collected before most of the programs had started) are compared for the two groups. The results, presented in table 5.6, show that these programs are generally poorly targeted toward the most nutritionally vulnerable *woredas*. There is little difference between the stunting and wasting rates for *woredas* included in each program versus those excluded, although there are some exceptions.

As a result of the targeting practices described above, the favored food-insecure (by designation) *woredas* tend to be the beneficiaries of several major nutrition-related programs, which are generally not coordinated well with each other and which sometimes overburden health extension workers. In contrast, the less favored food-secure (by designation) *woredas* tend to have disproportionately fewer programs or no programs at all.

This situation can be illustrated by further analysis: (a) classifying all *woredas* into groups based on the number of major programs active in them in 2007 and (b) comparing the overall stunting and wasting rates in these different groups of *woredas* in 2004, according to data from the 2004 Welfare Monitoring Survey, which was conducted before most of the analyzed programs began. Table 5.7 presents the results of this analysis for all

Table 5.6 Stunting and Wasting Rates in 2004 in *Woredas* Targeted by Specific Programs in 2007
percent

Program	Stunting rate		Severe stunting rate		Wasting rate		Severe wasting rate	
	In	Out	In	Out	In	Out	In	Out
Full EOS	47.2	45.4	23.7	22.3	8.2	8.8	1.7	1.5
TSFP[a]	46.6	48.3	22.5	27.4	8.6	7.2	1.8	1.3
Productive Safety Net Program[a]	50.6	44.5	27.1	21.1	8.0	8.5	1.7	1.7
MERET[a]	42.8	47.4	18.3	24.1	7.3	8.4	1.5	1.7
School Feeding Program[a]	47.4	46.2	24.5	22.0	8.9	7.3	1.8	1.5
ESHE	48.7	46.6	23.6	23.5	10.1	7.9	2.3	1.6
Child Growth Promotion	50.4	46.2	23.8	23.4	9.0	8.1	1.8	1.6
Pathfinder International	48.3	46.6	24.0	22.9	8.0	8.7	1.8	1.6
WASH	52.5	45.4	27.3	22.4	9.5	8.0	2.1	1.6

Source: Authors' calculations using program data and data from the 2004 Welfare Monitoring Survey (CSA 2004).
Note: EOS = Enhanced Outreach Strategy for Child Survival; TSFP = Targeted Supplementary Food Program; MERET = Managing Environmental Resources to Enable Transitions to More Sustainable Livelihoods; ESHE = Essential Services for Health in Ethiopia; WASH = Water, Sanitation, and Hygiene. Addis Ababa was excluded from the calculations.
a. The program aims to reduce malnutrition only or largely through food provision.

Table 5.7 Stunting and Wasting Rates in 2004 in *Woredas* Grouped by Number of Active Major Programs in 2007

Number of active programs	Number of *woredas*	Stunting rate (%)		Wasting rate (%)	
		Total	Severe	Total	Severe
Four or more	91	52.5	27.3	9.5	2.1
Three	91	45.5	23.7	6.5	1.1
Two	90	42.7	19.8	7.2	2.0
One	149	50.2	26.2	7.8	1.7
None	135	42.9	19.5	9.8	1.6

Source: Authors' calculations using program data and data from the 2004 Welfare Monitoring Survey (CSA 2004).
Note: Woredas here are defined according to 2004 boundaries. The programs considered exclude WASH and emergency food aid. Total stunting refers to moderate as well as severe stunting, while total wasting refers to moderate as well as severe wasting.

Figure 5.5 Stunting Rates in 2004 in *Woredas* Grouped by Number of Major Programs Affecting Nutrition in 2007

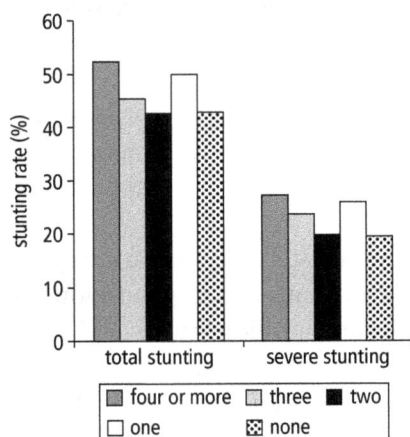

Source: Authors' calculations using program data and data from the 2004 Welfare Monitoring Survey (CSA 2004).
Note: WASH and emergency food aid are not considered. Total stunting refers to moderate as well as severe stunting.

the major programs listed in table 5.6 except for WASH. These results are also depicted in figures 5.5 and 5.6.

Table 5.7 and figure 5.5 show that *woredas* benefiting from one or more major nutrition-related programs in 2007 had, overall, higher stunting rates in 2004 (before most of the programs started) than *woredas* with no major programs. The difference in stunting rates is not very large, however. The 2004 wasting rates for the *woredas* with one or more major programs in 2007 are not higher than the *woredas* with no

Figure 5.6 Wasting Rates in 2004 in *Woredas* Grouped by Number of Major Programs Affecting Nutrition in 2007

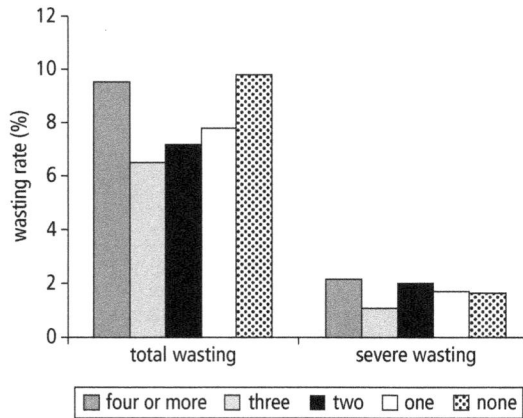

Source: Authors' calculations using program data and data from the 2004 Welfare Monitoring Survey (CSA 2004).
Note: WASH and emergency food aid are not considered. Total wasting refers to moderate as well as severe wasting.

such programs (table 5.7; see figure 5.6). In short, large numbers of *woredas* with two to four major active programs did not have a much higher prevalence of malnutrition in 2004 than the *woredas* with no major programs.

These results demonstrate that the targeting process for selecting *woredas* for the major programs affecting nutrition could be substantially improved. Ethiopia's malnutrition rate could likely be substantially reduced by shifting some of the programs from the *woredas* with a high concentration of major programs into those with high malnutrition rates but no major programs.

Others may disagree and may counter that overlapping but different programs create strong complementarities. To examine this possibility, imagine a hypothetical scenario where (a) two *woredas* have similarly high malnutrition rates and no program to reduce malnutrition and (b) two program managers are deciding which of the two *woredas* to select for their two different programs. Because of limited resources, each manager can chose one only *woreda*. If the two programs have strong complementarities and each program has little effectiveness without the other, it is best for the two managers to choose one *woreda* for both programs and to invest all their resources into that *woreda*, leaving the other without a program. But if the two programs are more substitutes than complements, it is best to assign one program to each *woreda*, so that both have nutrition program coverage.

Hypothetical scenarios aside, there are no apparent complementarities between the different programs that are strong enough to justify the large number of *woredas* with no major program at all (table 5.7). To obtain further insights, the programs included in the analysis of table 5.7 are disaggregated into two groups. The analysis is then conducted for each group separately and depicted in tables 5.8 and 5.9. Table 5.8 classifies *woredas* by the number of major programs providing food, excluding emergency food aid (TSFP, Productive Safety Net Program, Managing Environmental Resources to Enable Transitions to More Sustainable Livelihoods, and School Feeding/Children in Local Development). Table 5.9 classifies *woredas* by number of major programs with a strong community volunteer focus (Child Growth Promotion, Essential Services for Health in Ethiopia, and Pathfinder International).[9]

Table 5.8   Moderate and Severe Stunting and Wasting Rates in 2004 in *Woredas* Grouped by Number of Major Active Food-Providing Programs in 2007

Number of major programs	Number of *woredas*	Stunting rate (%)		Wasting rate (%)	
		Total	Severe	Total	Severe
Three or more	115	49.6	23.6	9.9	2.2
Two	142	46.6	24.9	6.6	1.4
One	72	45.9	23.8	7.2	1.9
None	227	46.9	23.1	8.8	1.6

Source: Authors' calculations using program data and data from the 2004 Welfare Monitoring Survey (CSA 2004).
Note: Woredas here are defined according to 2004 boundaries. WASH and emergency food aid are not considered. Total stunting refers to moderate as well as severe stunting, while total wasting refers to moderate as well as severe wasting.

Table 5.9   Moderate and Severe Stunting and Wasting Rates in 2004 in *Woredas* Grouped by Number of Major Active Community Volunteer Programs in 2007

Number of major programs	Number of *woredas*	Stunting rate (%)		Wasting rate (%)	
		Total	Severe	Total	Severe
Two or more	44	49.6	27.2	8.2	1.4
One	186	51.7	27.6	7.9	1.7
None	326	42.9	19.2	8.9	1.8

Source: Authors' calculations using program data and data from the 2004 Welfare Monitoring Survey (CSA 2004).
Note: Woredas here are defined according to 2004 boundaries. Total stunting refers to moderate as well as severe stunting, while total wasting refers to moderate as well as severe wasting.

The major programs providing food demonstrate little relationship between malnutrition rates and the presence of a major program, especially for stunting (see table 5.8). Large numbers of *woredas* have no major food-providing program at all, while others have high concentrations of overlapping programs. These findings imply poor targeting by these food-providing programs from a nutritional standpoint.

However, the major programs with a strong community volunteer focus generally seem to be targeted to the *woredas* with higher stunting rates (see table 5.9). The *woredas* in which these programs are located had stunting rates in 2004 that were significantly higher than the *woredas* in which there were no community volunteer programs. Furthermore, relatively few *woredas*—about 8 percent of the total (44 *woredas*)—had two or more overlapping community volunteer programs, which supports the finding of relatively superior targeting and coordination among the community volunteer programs.

Further insights can be obtained from a geographic analysis of the data used to generate tables 5.7, 5.8, and 5.9. Map 5.1 was produced using the same classification of *woredas* that was used to generate table 5.7. The map shows a high degree of overlap between the *woredas* where the major programs affecting nutrition (except food aid and WASH) are located and the *woredas* regularly receiving food aid. It also shows that the major programs affecting nutrition are particularly concentrated in a vertical belt starting roughly a bit south of mid-country, continuing upward, and then finishing in the north of the country, where the programs are especially heavily concentrated.

Map 5.2 was produced using the same classification of *woredas* as was used to generate table 5.8 and table 5.9. The map shows that the major food-providing programs (excluding food aid) are concentrated in a vertical belt running through the middle of the country, similar to what is depicted in map 5.1. But a comparison of the two maps shows that the programs focused on community volunteers tend to be spread more evenly and that the *woredas* where they are active overlap much less with the *woredas* regularly receiving food aid than do the focus *woredas* of the major food-providing programs.

Maps 5.3, 5.4, and 5.5 depict the wasting, stunting, and underweight prevalence in 2004, respectively, based on Welfare Monitoring Survey data. Most of the programs analyzed in this section had not yet started operations in 2004. Note that the depictions in the maps are somewhat incomplete because the requisite data are not available for many *woredas*, unlike for maps 5.1 and 5.2.

Map 5.1 Concentration of Major Programs in Ethiopia Affecting Nutrition (Excluding Food Aid and WASH) and Location of *Woredas* Regularly Receiving Food Aid, 2007

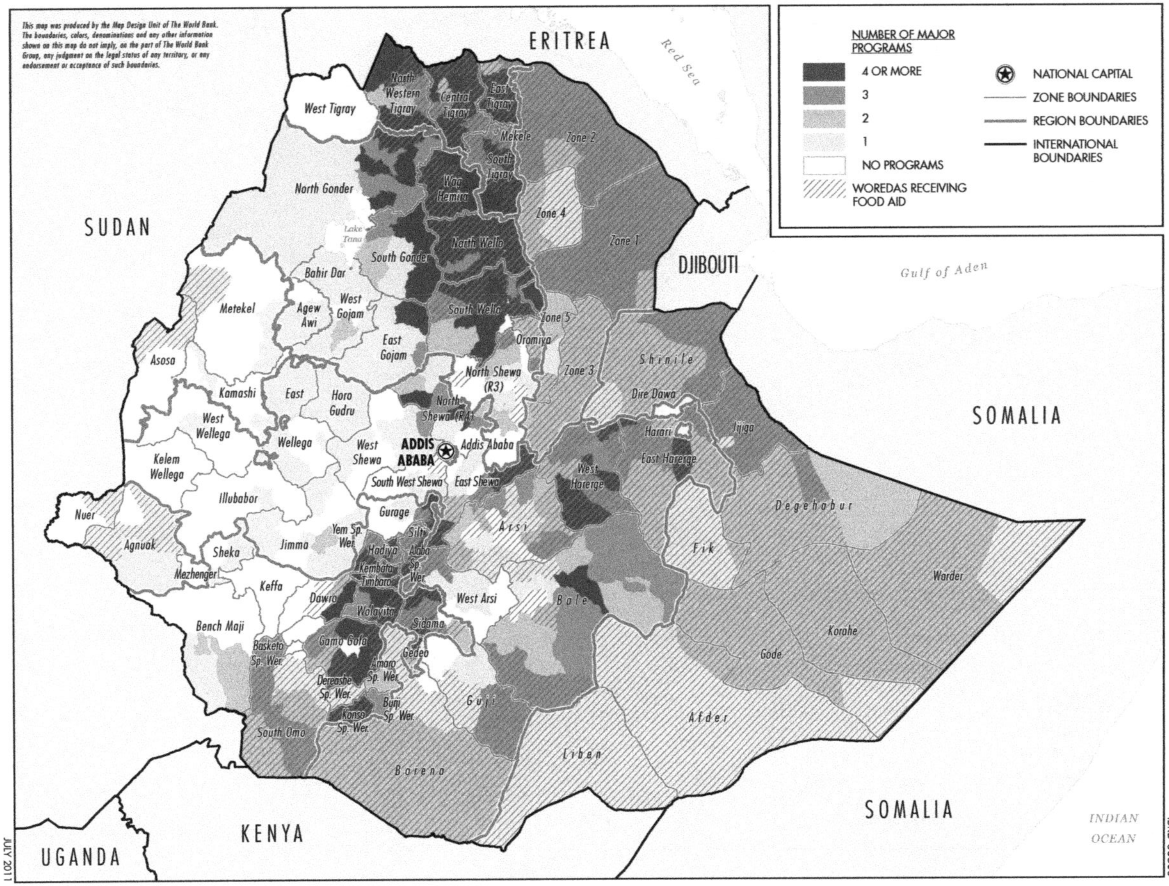

Source: Generated from program data and food aid data from the Disaster Risk Management and Food Security Sector (DRMFSS).

Map 5.2 Concentration of Major Programs in Ethiopia Providing Food (Excluding Food Aid) and Location of *Woredas* with at Least One Major Nutrition-Related Program with a Strong Community Volunteer Focus, 2007

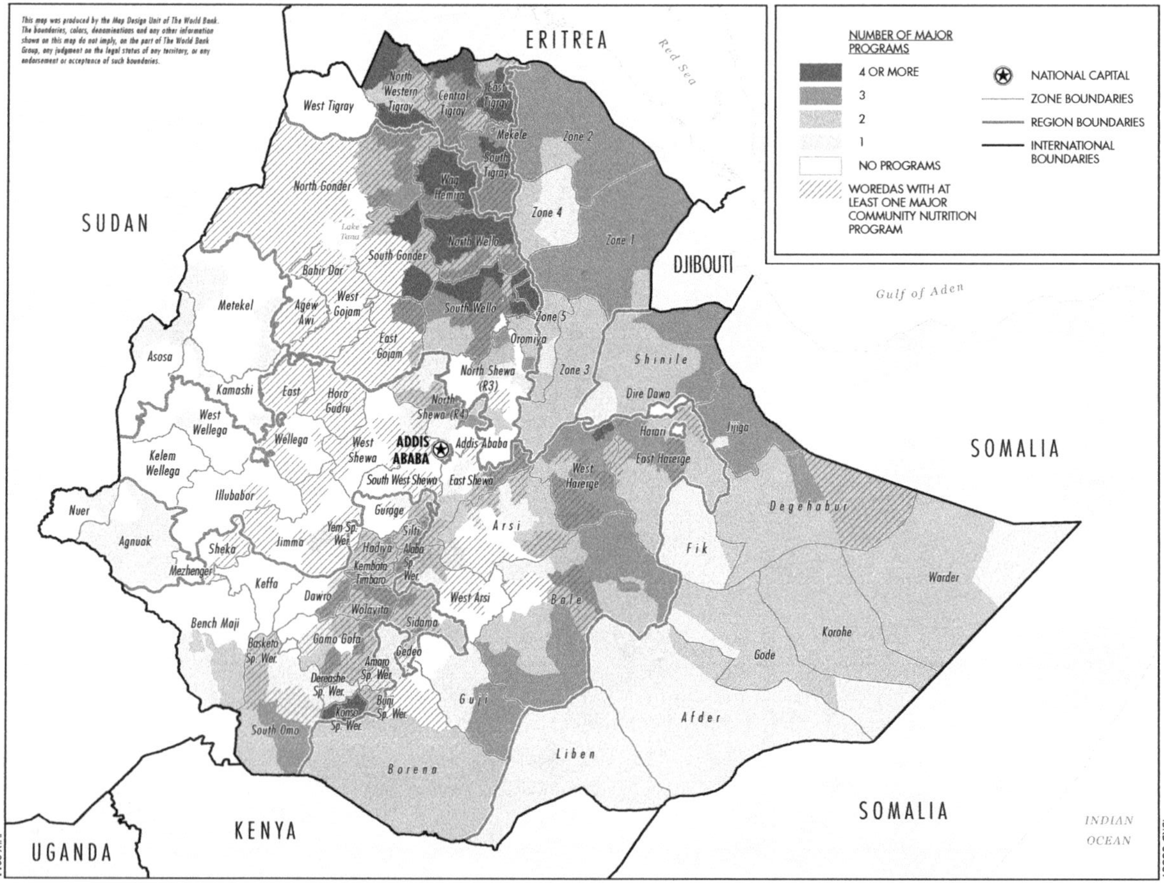

Source: Generated from program data.

Note: Among the programs considered (see table 5.6), ESHE, Pathfinder International, and Child Growth Promotion are the ones with a strong community volunteer focus.

Map 5.3 Wasting Prevalence in Ethiopia, at Zonal Level, 2004

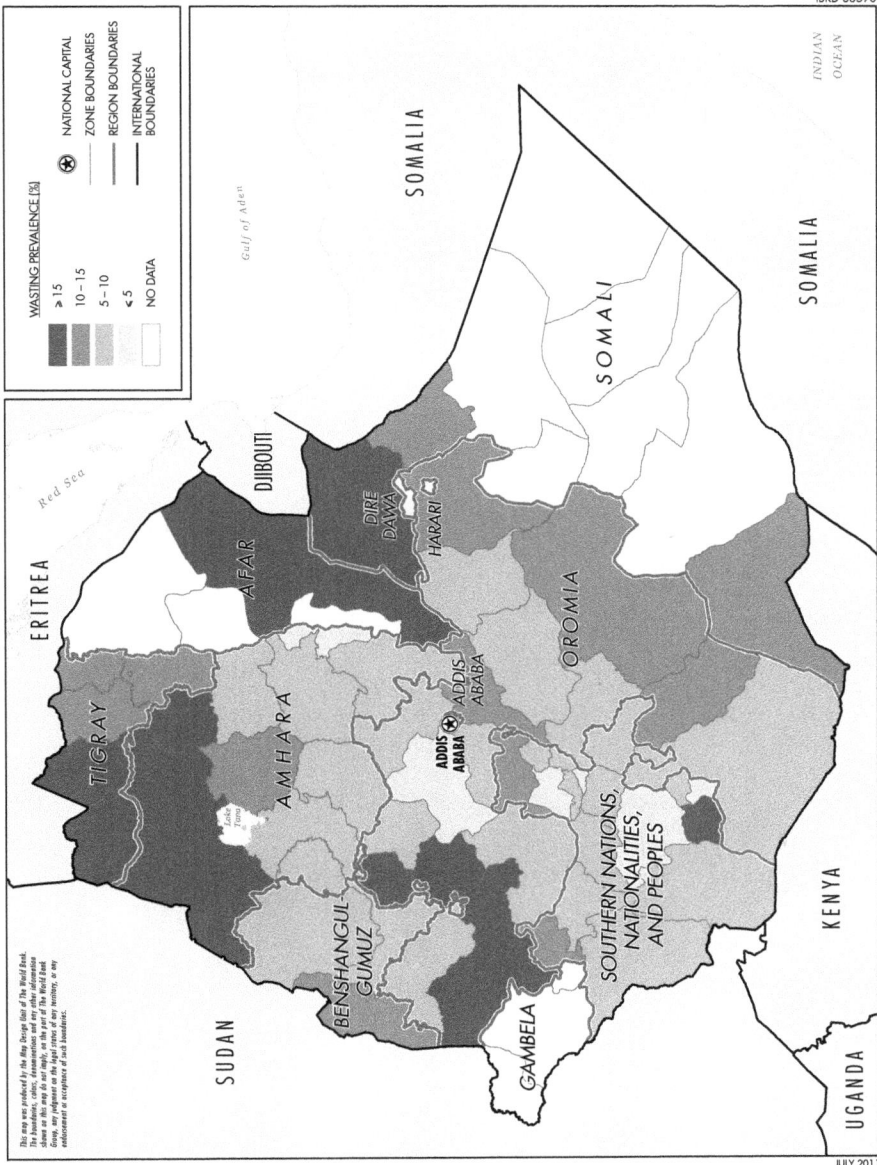

Source: Estimates generated from data from the 2004 Welfare Monitoring Survey (CSA 2004).

Map 5.4 Stunting Prevalence in Ethiopia, at Zonal Level, 2004

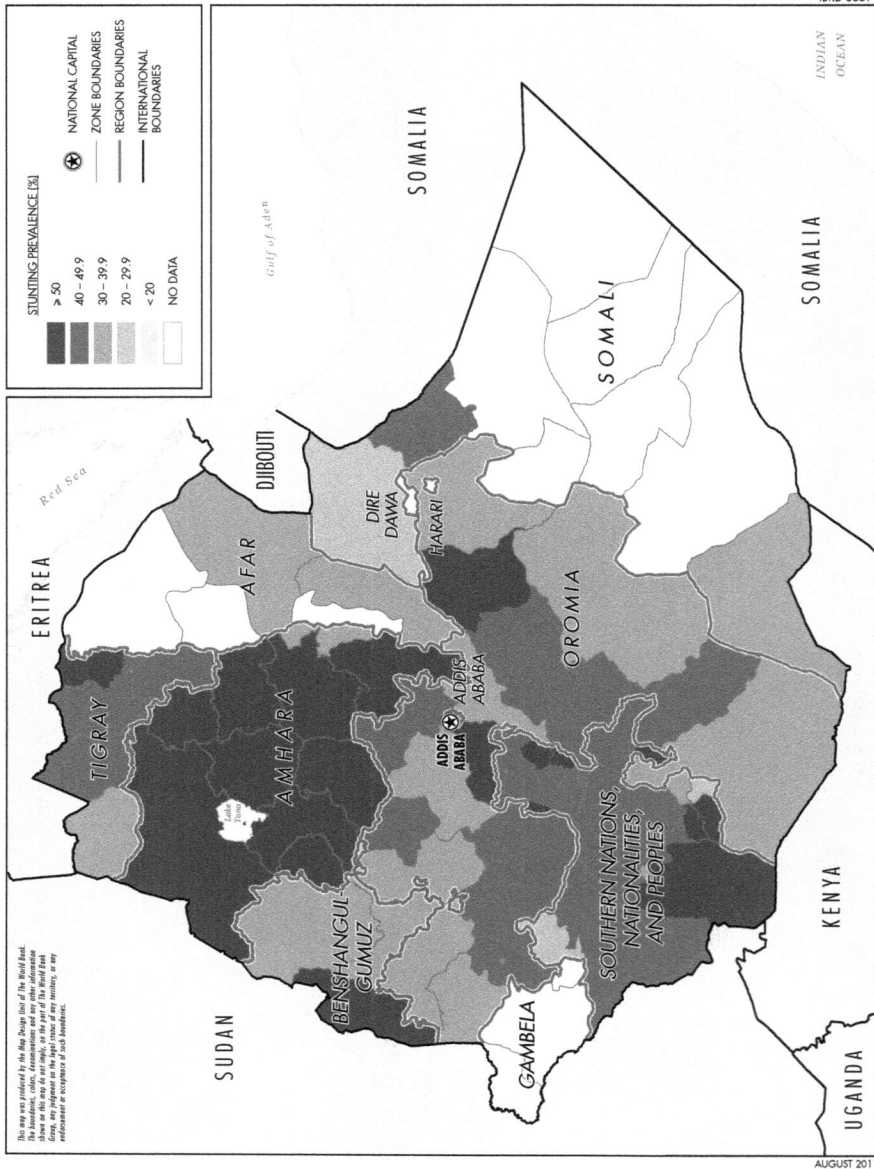

IBRD 38591

AUGUST 2011

Source: Estimates generated from data from the 2004 Welfare Monitoring Survey (CSA 2004).

Map 5.5   Underweight Prevalence in Ethiopia, at Zonal Level, 2004

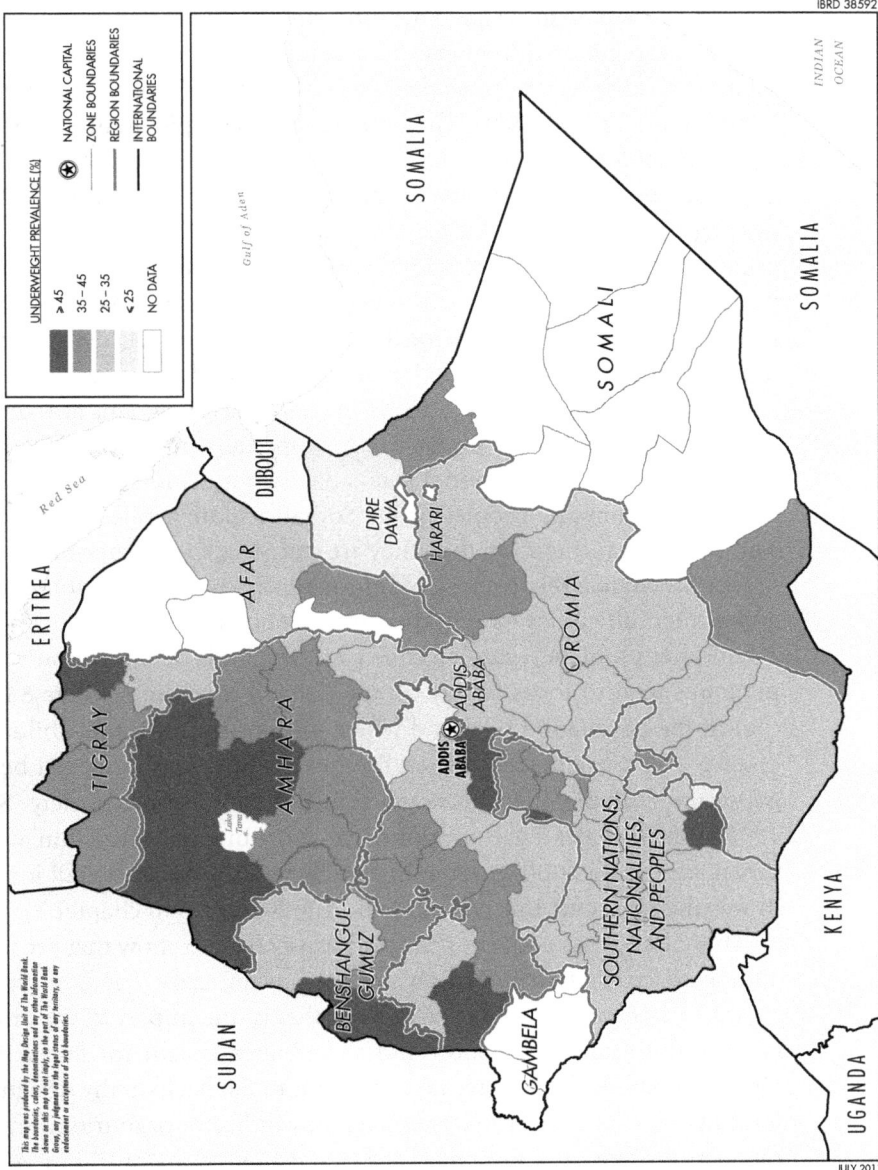

Source: Estimates generated from data from the 2004 Welfare Monitoring Survey (CSA 2004).

The targeting of major programs affecting nutrition clearly could be improved. Large parts of the country that are generally considered food secure (the west, for example) have high malnutrition rates, but a low concentration of nutrition programming or none at all (compare maps 5.3, 5.4, and 5.5 with map 5.1). But the programs with a strong community volunteer focus appear to be better targeted, from a nutritional standpoint, than the food-providing programs, especially if stunting is the indicator of focus (map 5.2; table 5.9). Thus, the maps depict pictorially the results shown in tables 5.7 to 5.9.

Another problem regarding targeting is that, to reduce the unit costs of coverage, programs often locate in larger regions and in areas with denser populations within those regions. Some of the smaller and more sparsely populated regions—such as Benshangul-Gumuz and Somali—have fewer programs, even though some of them have indicators of high malnutrition (see table 5.10). Afar and Somali have the highest wasting rates among all the regions (see figure 2.1 in chapter 2). Programs also tend to avoid the smaller regions because of the especially poor state of updated information on the nutritional status of the populations in these areas, such as the nomadic peoples of the Somali region. While these regions warrant far more attention than they are receiving, the reasons for the lack of focus include a relative lack of information, lower population density, and greater difficulties in delivering interventions.

Another problem regarding choice of location is that nutrition-related programs tend to focus largely on the poor in rural areas where 84 percent of the population lives and where rates of malnutrition, childhood disease, and mortality are higher. But the urban poor should not be forgotten as Ethiopia moves toward a nutritionally secure society. Since 1998, wasting rates have continued to drop in rural areas, but not in urban areas from 2000 to 2004. In fact, there was a slight overall increase in wasting rates over this period (table 1.9; figure 1.8 in chapter 1).

This chapter has used program and survey data to show that programs aiming to combat malnutrition do not always make the best choices regarding beneficiary *woredas*. As noted, this is due in part to gaps in the existing nutrition information and surveillance system for *woreda*-level data. Program designers have no choice but to fall back on the designated food-insecure *woredas* or to develop a proxy indicator of nutrition insecurity, which often does not reflect the true degree of malnutrition. As discussed, other reasons for the poor targeting include the tendency to think of food insecurity as a proxy for nutrition insecurity, inadequacies in the process of food aid targeting, a tendency to focus insufficiently on the smaller regions and urban areas, and a lack of coordination among

Table 5.10 Active Nutrition Programming, by Region, 2007

Region	EOS	TSFP[a]	Productive Safety Net Program[a]	MERET[a]	School Feeding[a]	ESHE	Child Growth Promotion	Pathfinder International	WASH
Tigray	X	X	X	X	X		X	X	X
Afar	X	X	X		X				X
Amhara	X	X	X	X	X	X	X	X	X
Oromia	X	X	X	X	X	X	X	X	X
Somali	X	X	X	X	X				X
Benshangul-Gumuz	X	X							
SNNP	X	X	X	X	X	X	X	X	X
Gambela	X	X							X
Harari	X	X	X						X
Dire Dawa	X	X	X	X					X

Source: Program data.

Note: EOS = Enhanced Outreach Strategy for Child Survival; TSFP = Targeted Supplementary Food Program; MERET = Managing Environmental Resources to Enable Transitions to More Sustainable Livelihoods; ESHE = Essential Services for Health in Ethiopia; WASH = Water, Sanitation, and Hygiene.

a. The program aims to affect malnutrition only or largely through food provision.

different programs. A harmonized method of selecting *woredas* for all programs needs to be devised and urgently implemented. And *woredas* that are not often included in programming on the grounds of their designation as food secure need to be reassessed and considered for programming. A more equitable approach needs to be designed for interventions rather than concentrating on a subset of highly favored *woredas* designated as food insecure.

In the meantime, even with the ostensibly poor targeting of many programs in terms of stunting and wasting, these programs are operating in *woredas* with high rates of malnutrition, as shown in table 5.6. This can be attributed to the widespread nature of malnutrition in Ethiopia. Therefore, despite their less-than-optimal targeting and coordination, those programs possess the potential to have a high impact in their focus *woredas*, even though the maximum potential may not be realized.

Finally, improvements can be made in the way targeting is done within *woredas* and households, not just in the way programs select beneficiary *woredas*. For example, nutrition interventions traditionally have targeted certain groups assumed to be the most vulnerable, such as pregnant and lactating women, children under five years of age, and the elderly. But this assumption is not always correct. Program managers need to research an area's cultural practices before specifying the target group. For example, not all pregnant and lactating women may be at risk, and children under five years of age may be the focus of several programs while adolescents benefit from few programs.

TARGETING: A SUMMARY

A lot of information has been covered in this chapter, and a summary is useful. First, it is important to repeat an important finding from chapter 2, which helps one to understand the findings in this section:

➤ *Summary point 1*. Based on an analysis of household data (from the 2004 Welfare Monitoring Survey) in chapter 2, there is no clear relationship between household food insecurity and child stunting rates. While child wasting rates are higher in households with higher levels of food insecurity, wasting is still high even among households with no reported food insecurity. Thus, large numbers of children suffer from wasting and especially from stunting even in food-secure households, and targeting areas with food insecurity is not the same as targeting areas with high malnutrition or nutrition insecurity.

➤ *Summary point 2.* Although the emergency food aid system in Ethiopia has generally performed well by international standards, it has some drawbacks. These include poor coverage by the Early Warning System in some parts of the country and inflexibility leading to *woredas* often retaining the label of food secure or food insecure according to targeting that was done many years ago, even though circumstances may change from year to year. And the *woredas* labeled as food insecure appear to receive food aid regularly, while those labeled as food secure are much less likely to receive food aid. Yet analysis of the data shows that large proportions of food-insecure people are living in *woredas* designated as food secure, and the difference in the extent of food insecurity between *woredas* designated as food secure and those designated as food insecure is less than may be expected.

➤ *Summary point 3.* Analysis of the 2004 Welfare Monitoring Survey data shows that there is little difference in stunting and wasting rates between the *woredas* labeled as food insecure and those labeled as food secure, even though the former are supposed to have the highest levels of food insecurity. (They also receive the most emergency food aid, as noted in summary point 2.) These results could be attributed to the equalizing effect of emergency food aid and to the fact that nutrition insecurity is not the same as food insecurity; a significant component of both wasting and stunting is attributable to factors other than household food shortages (see summary point 1).

➤ *Summary point 4.* In a country of Ethiopia's size, most nutrition-related programs have to focus exclusively on a subset of the country's *woredas*. Ideally, they would focus on *woredas* with the highest levels of nutrition insecurity. But these are difficult or impossible to identify accurately because of a poor nutrition information system. So instead, programs tend to focus on the *woredas* labeled as food insecure because (a) these *woredas* are supposed to have the highest levels of food insecurity and (b) food insecurity is seen as a proxy for nutrition insecurity. But neither of these assumptions is always valid (see summary points 1 and 2). Indeed, there is little difference in stunting or wasting rates between the *woredas* designated as food insecure and those designated as food secure (see summary point 3). (Some programs use other measures such as "chronic vulnerability" as a proxy for nutrititional insecurity, but as in the case of food insecurity, these are only partially correlated with nutrition insecurity, thus leading to flawed targeting.)

➤ *Summary point 5.* The data show that the major programs affecting nutrition outcomes are, in general, poorly targeted. *Woredas* with one or more major nutrition-related programs in 2007 (except for WASH and emergency food aid) do not appear to have had much higher stunting rates in 2004 (before most of the analyzed programs began) than *woredas* with no major programs. Wasting rates in 2004 were actually *lower* in the *woredas* with major programs in 2007 than elsewhere. However, among these programs, those with a strong community volunteer focus do seem to be relatively well targeted to the right *woredas*.

➤ *Summary point 6*. Ethiopia's malnutrition rate could probably be much reduced by shifting some of the programs from the *woredas* with a high concentration of major programs into *woredas* with high malnutrition rates but no major programs. There do not appear to be strong complementarities between the programs that would justify a high concentration of programs in some *woredas* and no programs in other *woredas*. A harmonized method of selecting *woredas* for all programs—taking into account the *woredas* designated as food secure as well as those designated as food insecure—needs to be created and urgently implemented.

➤ *Summary point 7*. Some other problems with targeting are evident: (a) a tendency to ignore the smaller, more sparsely populated regions, despite their high malnutrition rates in some cases; (b) a tendency to focus on rural areas and to ignore vulnerable groups in urban areas; and (c) a need for improvements in the methods of targeting programs to the correct population subgroups, households, and members within households.

➤ *Summary point 8*. In the meantime, despite the lack of optimum targeting, the widespread nature of malnutrition in Ethiopia means that programs affecting nutrition outcomes still have the potential to have a high impact in their focus *woredas*, even though the maximum potential may not be realized.

The National Nutrition Program aims to improve the targeting of programs affecting nutrition in the country. Enhancing coordination and linkages among the different programs is a key goal of the program, as is improving the country's nutrition information system to facilitate better program coordination and targeting.

NOTES

1. The names of the disaster prevention and preparedness bureaus have changed in the regions to Food Security Coordination and Disaster Prevention Bureau in Amhara; Disaster Prevention, Preparedness, and Food Security Sector in Tigray and

SNNP; Disaster Prevention and Food Security Bureau in Harari, Afar, and Dire Dawa; Disaster Prevention and Preparedness Bureau in Somali and Gambela; Food Security, Disaster Prevention, and Preparedness Commission in Oromia; and Food Security and Resettlement and Disaster Prevention and Preparedness Office in Benshangul-Gumuz. Additionally, the name of each disaster prevention and preparedness desk at the zonal or *woreda* level has the name of the new bureau with the word "department" added. For example, in the *woredas* in Amhara, they are now called Food Security Coordination and Disaster Prevention Departments.

2. State ministers in Ethiopia are, in effect, deputy ministers.

3. The standard approach to treating severe malnutrition is providing Plumpy'nut, a ready-to-eat substance produced from peanuts and milk powder. While some domestic production exists, it is very limited, and most of the local need is satisfied by importing Plumpy'nut from Nutriset, the main global producer based in France. Work is under way to examine ways of enhancing domestic production of Plumpy'nut-type products and alternatives.

4. For example, if a nationwide household survey is done at time t, one would use data from this survey (household-level data) along with data from the health management information system (facility-level data) to estimate the relationship between the values of facility-level nutrition indicators and the values of community-level nutrition indicators. Using this estimated relationship, one would then use the values of nutrition indicators obtained through the health management information system at time $t + 1$ (facility level)—when no nationwide household surveys are conducted—to obtain a rough idea of the values of household-level indicators at time $t + 1$.

5. Live Aid, organized by Bob Geldof and others, was a multiple-venue rock music concert held on July 13, 1985 to raise funds for famine relief in Ethiopia. It was one of the largest-scale satellite link-ups and television broadcasts of all time, with an estimated 1.5 billion viewers in 100 countries.

6. These factors are mentioned in a paper issued by the Ministry of Economic Development and Cooperation in 1998 as part of the Grain Market Research Project (in which this ministry, among others, was a participant). The paper discusses the reasons for the "lack of flexibility in the food aid system." See Clay, Molla, and Habtewold (1998).

7. The chronic vulnerability index began in 1999 as a result of a multiagency project tasked with developing a *woreda*-level baseline to indicate areas needing assistance. Because of a lack of data, some regions were not represented during development of the index, including Afar and Somali regions. Nine variables were ultimately chosen and used to develop the list of the most vulnerable *woredas*. The list was given to the regional offices, which made the final decision about which *woredas* to include. This list was used in implementing Managing Environmental Resources to Enable Transitions to More Sustainable Livelihoods and the School Feeding Program.

8. "Major" programs were defined by the number of beneficiaries, budget, and objectives. These nine programs were chosen because they all affect nutrition outcomes and all have large coverage.

9. The EOS was left out of this particular analysis because it is neither a major program providing food nor a program with a strong community volunteer focus.

Results from Regression Analyses

Table A.1 Determinants of Wasting among Under-Five Children in Ethiopia

Variable	All children (R^2 = 0.084)		Girls (R^2 = 0.089)		Boys (R^2 = 0.10)	
	Coefficient	t-ratio	Coefficient	t-ratio	Coefficient	t-ratio
Constant	−0.32	−1.44	0.09	0.35	−0.72**	−2.32
Child age (months)						
12–17	−0.75**	−7.30	−0.81**	−6.27	−0.68**	−4.63
18–23	−0.72**	−5.98	−0.63**	−3.49	−0.86**	−5.63
24–29	−0.56**	−5.27	−0.63**	−4.55	−0.49**	−3.45
30–35	−0.44**	−3.90	−0.56**	−3.61	−0.35**	−2.58
36–41	−0.54**	−5.21	−0.70**	−5.14	−0.40**	−2.96
42–47	−0.56**	−5.39	−0.62**	−4.37	−0.48**	−3.46
48–53	−0.54**	−4.92	−0.60**	−4.36	−0.50**	−3.33
54–59	−0.45**	−3.94	−0.47**	−3.50	−0.42**	−2.51
Age of household head	0.00	−0.14	0.00	1.03	0.00	−1.24
Female household head	−0.01	−0.08	0.05	0.51	−0.09	−0.94
Household size	−0.01	−1.10	−0.02	−1.17	0.00	−0.16
Parental education						
Primary	0.09	1.27	0.14	1.53	0.05	0.48
Secondary or tertiary	0.58**	4.75	0.35**	2.62	0.87**	4.84
Iodine in household salt						
None	0.03	0.25	−0.21	−1.24	0.21	1.26
Inadequate (0–15 parts per million)	−0.04	−0.34	−0.23	−1.33	0.09	0.51
Received postnatal checkup	−0.14	−1.00	0.04	0.18	−0.28	−1.35

(continued)

Table A.1 *(continued)*

Variable	All children ($R^2 = 0.084$)		Girls ($R^2 = 0.089$)		Boys ($R^2 = 0.10$)	
	Coefficient	t-ratio	Coefficient	t-ratio	Coefficient	t-ratio
Health of child checked in first two months after birth	−0.19	−1.25	−0.02	−0.11	−0.34	−1.77
Toilet type						
Flush toilet	0.15	0.68	0.16	0.54	0.12	0.54
Pit latrine	−0.04	−0.65	−0.01	−0.11	−0.10	−1.09
Wealth quintile (1 = lowest, 5 = highest)	0.06**	2.72	0.02	0.81	0.09**	3.09

Source: Authors.
Note: These regressions were done by using ordinary least squares with the weight-for-height Z-score as the dependent variable and by using Stata with the 2005 Demographic and Health Survey data set. Each child in the data set is an observation in these regressions (if data are complete for all variables). There are 3,872 observations. The weight-for-height Z-score of a child is an indicator of how large the child's weight-for-height is relative to a global reference population. The higher the weight-for-height Z-score, the less likely the child is to be wasted. Likelihood ratio test justifies separating the regressions by gender. Regional dummy variables are also included in the regressions (although their coefficients are not reported). The mean value of the weight-for-height Z-score (the dependent variable) of the sample is −0.58. The 10th, 25th, 75th, and 90th percentiles are −2.03, −1.36, 0.17, and 0.86, respectively. All right-hand-side variables are dummy variables except age of the household head, household size, and wealth quintile. The omitted categories for the dummy variables are (a) children 0–11 months of age; (b) male head of household; (c) no parental education; (d) adequate iodine in household salt (more than 15 parts per million); (e) no postnatal checkup; (f) no two-month postbirth checkup for child; and (g) other types of toilet (composting, bucket, hanging, no facility, bush, or field).
**$p < .05$ *$p < .10$.

Table A.2 Determinants of Stunting among Under-Five Children in Ethiopia

Variable	All children ($R^2 = 0.14$)		Girls ($R^2 = 0.17$)		Boys ($R^2 = 0.14$)	
	Coefficient	t-ratio	Coefficient	t-ratio	Coefficient	t-ratio
Constant	−0.05	−0.18	−0.04	−0.12	−0.13	−0.3
Child age (months)						
12–17	−0.10**	−7.91	−0.78**	−4.74	−1.23**	−7.25
18–23	−1.62**	−10.05	−1.61**	−8.67	−1.67**	−7.68
24–29	−1.08**	−8.23	−1.32**	−6.10	−0.89**	−5.01
30–35	−1.46**	−10.37	−1.73**	−8.98	−1.26**	−7.08
36–41	−1.20**	−8.55	−1.27**	−6.13	−1.17**	−6.56
42–47	−1.54**	−13.36	−1.82**	−10.07	−1.27**	−7.67
48–53	−1.22**	−9.58	−1.20**	−6.59	−1.29**	−7.91
54–59	−1.69**	−12.41	−1.79**	−9.47	−1.63**	−9.09
Age of household head	0.00	−0.17	0.00	0.19	0.00	−0.17
Female household head	0.02	0.20	−0.17	−1.13	0.25	1.82
Household size	−0.02	−1.02	−0.03	−1.28	−0.01	−0.28

(continued)

Table A.2 *(continued)*

Variable	All children ($R^2 = 0.14$)		Girls ($R^2 = 0.17$)		Boys ($R^2 = 0.14$)	
	Coefficient	t-ratio	Coefficient	t-ratio	Coefficient	t-ratio
Parental education						
Primary	0.23**	2.66	0.27**	2.00	0.15	1.16
Secondary or tertiary	0.52**	3.26	0.70**	3.98	0.16	0.65
Iodine in household salt						
None	−0.02	−0.14	−0.10	−0.56	0.04	0.20
Inadequate (0–15 parts per million)	0.05	0.41	−0.04	−0.21	0.15	0.77
Received postnatal checkup	−0.14	−0.68	−0.14	−0.54	−0.14	−0.45
Health of child checked in first two months after birth	0.14	0.64	−0.07	−0.24	0.20	0.57
Toilet type						
Flush toilet	−0.21	−0.71	−0.56	−1.47	0.46	1.44
Pit latrine	0.18	1.76	0.25	1.84	0.11	0.82
Wealth quintile (1 = lowest, 5 = highest)	0.03	1.00	0.06	1.27	0.03	0.66

Source: Authors.
Note: These regressions were done by using ordinary least squares with the height-for-age Z-score as the dependent variable and by using Stata with the 2005 Demographic and Health Survey data set. Each child in the data set is an observation in these regressions (if data are complete for all variables). There are 3,872 observations. The height-for-age Z-score of a child is an indicator of how large the child's height-for-age is relative to a global reference population. The higher the height-for-age Z-score, the less likely the child is to be stunted. Likelihood ratio test justifies separating the regressions by gender. Regional dummy variables are also included in the regressions (although their coefficients are not reported). See notes for table A.1. The mean value of the height-for-age Z-score (the dependent variable) of the sample is −1.78. The 10th, 25th, 75th, and 90th percentiles are −3.99, −2.95, −0.71, and 0.51, respectively.
**$p < .05$ *$p < .10$.

Table A.3 Determinants of Breast-Feeding in Ethiopia

Variable	$R^2 = 0.10$	
	Coefficient	t-ratio
Constant	22.05	3.35**
Child age (months)	0.03	0.71
Age of household head	0.17	6.08**
Female household head	1.42	1.67*
Household size	−0.56	−4.13**
Parental education		
Secondary	−1.53	−2.36**
Tertiary	−2.18	−2.04**
Received postnatal checkup		
Health of child checked in first two months after birth	1.23	0.47
Distance to health center reported as major problem in getting medical care	0.59	0.98
Wealth quintile (1 = lowest, 5 = highest)	−0.043	−0.19

Source: Authors.

Note: These regressions were done by using Stata with the 2005 Demographic and Health Survey data set and by using ordinary least squares. Each child in the data set who was more than 36 months of age is an observation in these regressions (if data are complete for all variables). By definition, children more than 59 months of age are not included because the relevant survey questions were asked only for children under five years of age. There are 1,693 observations. The dependent variable is the number of months of breast-feeding undergone by each child since birth. Regional dummy variables are also included in the regressions (although their coefficients are not reported). The mean value of the number of months breast-fed (the dependent variable) in the sample is 24. The 10th, 25th, 75th, and 90th percentiles are 11, 16, 31, and 39, respectively. All right-hand-side variables are dummy variables except age of household head, household size, and wealth quintile. The omitted categories for the dummy variables are (a) children 0–11 months of age, (b) male head of household, (c) no parental education, (d) no postnatal checkup, (f) no two-month postbirth checkup for child, and (g) distance to nearest health center not a major problem.
**$p < .05$ *$p < .10$.

Assumptions for the Costing of Nutrition Interventions

The assumptions in this appendix relate to the costing of nutrition interventions used in chapter 5.

Table B.1 General Assumptions

Indicator	Assumption
Population	78,000,000
Average *woreda* size	125,000
Household size	5.2
Under-five mortality rate (deaths per 1,000 births)[a]	119
Infant mortality rate (deaths per 1,000 births)	75
Maternal mortality rate (deaths per 1,000 births)	720
Number of births per year	3,201,000
Children under five years of age as % of population	18.41
Children under two years of age as % of population	7.48
Reproductive-age women as % of population	21.79
Percentage of reproductive-age women who are pregnant	10
GDP per capita (US$)	174
Discount rate (%)	5
Growth (%) of real per capita GDP	0
% of Ethiopia where malaria is endemic	72

Source: Authors.
Note: GDP = gross domestic product.
a. Forty percent of the mortality among children one to five years of age is assumed to occur during the second year and 20% to occur in each of the succeeding years.

Table B.2   Beneficiaries and Costs of Current Interventions and Effect on Mortality

Program or intervention	Indicator
Current intervention	
Productive Safety Net Program	5,664,471 beneficiaries (data set for 2005) located in 208 *woredas*
School Feeding	639,191 beneficiaries (data set for 2006) located in 128 *woredas*
Emergency food aid	3,188,511 beneficiaries, calculated as 15 kilograms of grain per beneficiary per month, six months per year in the program (based on the amount of food distributed in 2006), and located in 457 *woredas*
Managing Environmental Resources to Enable Transitions to More Sustainable Livelihoods (MERET)	363,278 beneficiaries, calculated as 15 kilograms of grain per beneficiary per month, six months a year in the program (based on the cost of food distributed in 2005), and located in 72 *woredas*
Targeted Supplementary Food Program (TSFP)	800,000 beneficiaries located in 264 *woredas*
Treatment of severe acute malnutrition (health center–based institutional approach)	All of the children 6–59 months old who would have died in the areas covered by community-based therapeutic care for all of the years it had been functioning in the *woreda*
EOS (Enhanced Outreach Strategy for Child Survival)/EEOS (Extended EOS): vitamin A	6,650,000 beneficiaries (EOS/EEOS data set for 2006 in Amhara and Oromia for one round)
EOS/EEOS: deworming	6,650,000 beneficiaries
EOS/EEOS: measles	2,160,000 beneficiaries (EOS/EEOS data set for 2006 in Amhara and Oromia for two rounds)
Bed nets	20,000,000 distributed; two nets per household
Expanded Program on Immunization	1,205,389 beneficiaries (the number of fully immunized children and women given tetanus toxoid injections in 2001)
Health extension workers	Entire population
Community health promoters	
Breast-feeding	2,255,613 beneficiaries calculated as the number of pregnant women in areas covered by the program for the years during which the program was active
Hand washing	Same as for breast-feeding
Latrines	28,939,960 beneficiaries calculated as 80% of the total population in the *woredas*
Community-based reproductive health agents	6,240,000 beneficiaries calculated as 120 households for each of the 10,000 community-based reproductive health agents

Costs[a]

Grain — US$400

Supplementary food — US$600

Edible oil — US$1,000

Productive Safety Net Program — US$495 per metric ton

TSFP — US$680 per metric ton

School Feeding Program — Total cost per beneficiary: US$18.89

Community health promoters[b]

Breast-feeding — 30% of total costs

Hand washing — 20% of total costs

Sanitation and hygiene — 20% of total costs

Impacts[c]

Emergency food aid — One-third of beneficiaries 6–59 months of age would have died; 57% of children 6–59 months of age who would have died have lower mortality (95% of those 57% survive; Ethiopia PROFILES and AED 2005[d])

TSFP — Mortality rate among beneficiaries was 4.6 times that of the general population;[e] deaths of moderately malnourished individuals reduced by 70%

Treatment of severe acute malnutrition (health center–based institutional approach) — Coverage: 30%; cure rate: 60% of moderately and severely malnourished

EOS/EEOS: vitamin A — Under-five mortality rate reduced by 20% (Beaton and others 1993)

EOS/EEOS: measles — 4% of child deaths are due to measles (UNICEF 2005, 2006); vaccine efficacy: 90% (Aaby and others 1996)

Bed nets — Under-five mortality rate reduced by 20% (Lengeler 2004)

(continued)

Table B.2 *(continued)*

Program or intervention	Indicator
Community health promoters	
Breast-feeding[f]	Timely initiation of breast-feeding reduces neonatal mortality rate by 16% (Edmond and others 2006); the prevalence of timely initiation of breast-feeding increased 25.3%; exclusive breast-feeding reduces the under-five mortality rate by 13%; the prevalence of exclusive breast-feeding increased 8%; correct complementary feeding reduced the under-five mortality rate 6% (Jones and others 2003); prevalence of correct complementary feeding increased 6%
Hand washing	Deaths due to diarrhea reduced by 40% (Luby and others 2005); hand washing increased in prevalence by 7% (Kolesar and others 2003);[g] under-five deaths due to diarrhea reduced by 17% (Black, Morris, and Bryce 2003)

Source: Authors.

a. Per unit food costs for emergency food aid and MERET, including product, transport, program costs, and a 10% government overhead.

b. Rough estimate of cost breakdown.

c. The cost per death averted and the benefit-cost ratio for child and maternal mortality include a range of +/-10%.

d. Based on estimates, 57% of childhood mortality is related to malnutrition (Ethiopia PROFILES and AED 2005).

e. If this difference were maintained until adulthood, as some studies suggest happens when malnutrition is severe and persistent, it would decrease adult height by about 20 centimeters, if one assumes a standard deviation in adult height of about 7.5 centimeters.

f. Mid-term assessment from ESHE (2006) was used to determine the increase in promoted activities.

g. The increase in prevalence of hand washing could not be determined from the mid-term assessment. Instead, data were used for another program funded by the U.S. Agency for International Development that also used community health promoters to promote hygiene and sanitation. There, hand washing by the primary caregiver increased by 12% over two years. Here we are conservative and assume an increase of about half that.

Table B.3   Costing of Possible Interventions and Effect on Mortality

Indicator	Beneficiaries
Intervention	
Salt iodization and iron in iodized salt	99.9% of the population (CSA and ORC Macro 2006)
Vitamin A in sugar	41% of the population (Mason 2001)
Costs	
Iodizing salt	US$0.05 per kilogram; annual demand for salt: 250,000 metric tons (Yager 2003)
Iron in iodized salt	US$0.45 per capita (Micronutrient Initiative 2004)
Vitamin A in sugar	US$16.00 per kilogram; annual demand for sugar: 200,000 metric tons (Umeta 2005)
Iron and folate capsules	US$0.0024 (Abebe Hailemariam, UNICEF, personal communication, August 2007)
Iron and folate syrup	US$1.10 per 50 milliliters (Risonar and others 2008)[a]
Iodated oil	US$0.24 per capsule (Abebe Hailemariam, UNICEF, personal communication, August 2007)
EOS/EEOS: vitamin A[b]	US$0.02
EOS/EEOS: deworming	US$0.0188 (Abebe Hailemariam, UNICEF, personal communication, August 2007)
Impact	
Iodated oil for pregnant women	Reduces under-five mortality rate by 6% (Mahomed and Gulmezoglu 2002)
Iodizing salt	Reduces under-five mortality rate by the same amount as iodated oil
Iron and folate for children 6–24 months old	Increases the IQ of 30% of anemic children by 7.5 points (Ross and Horton 1998)
Iron and folate for pregnant women	Reduces maternal mortality rate by 22% (Stoltzfus, Mullany, and Black 2003)
Deworming	Reduces six-month mortality rate by 20% (Christian, Khatry, and West 2004)
Zinc	17% of under-five mortality is caused by diarrhea (Black, Morris, and Bryce 2003); reduces under-five mortality due to diarrhea by 50% (Baqui and others 2002)[c]

Source: Authors.
Note: EOS = Enhanced Outreach Strategy for Child Survival; EEOS = Extended EOS; TSFP = Targeted Supplementary Food Program.
a. Pelletier and others (1994) found that the mean relative risk for moderate malnutrition was 4.6. Since the target population of the TSFP is moderately malnourished children, this figure was the increased probability of dying among the beneficiaries.
b. Abebe Hailemariam, UNICEF, personal communication, August 2007. EOS/EEOS costs per supplement do not include distribution costs.
c. Each child is assumed to have three diarrheal episodes per year requiring treatment with zinc.

Table B.4 Impact of Interventions on Productivity

Indicator	Description
General	
Average adult height	160 centimeters
Decrease in earnings for a 1% decrease in height	2.4% (Thomas and Strauss 1997)
Prevalence of low birthweight	13.5% (Ethiopia PROFILES and AED 2005)
Decrease in earnings due to low birthweight	7.5% (Behrman, Alderman, and Hoddinott 2004)
Increase in height due to increase in birthweight	1.2 centimeters for 0.45 kilogram (Li and others 2003)
Prevalence of anemia	50%
Prevalence of iodine deficiency disease	65%
Decrease in earnings as a result of anemia	5% (Ross and Horton 1998)
Impact	
Treatment of severe acute malnutrition (health center–based institutional approach)[a]	Children under two years of age admitted to community-based therapeutic care were, on average, −2.5 Z-scores weight-for-height;[b] after treatment, their height returned to normal.
Emergency food aid	A shock decreases child height by 1.75 centimeters; emergency food aid can mitigate the effect of a shock on the poorest half of children under two years of age (Yamano, Alderman, and Christiaensen 2005).
Bed nets	Low birthweight decreased by 28% (Ter Kuile and others 2003).
Iodine	Birthweight increased by about 50 grams (Mason and others 2002).
Deworming	Birthweight increased by about 60 grams (Christian, Khatry, and West 2004).
Iron and folate	Prevalence of low birthweight decreased by 13% (Cogswell and others 2003).

Source: Authors.
a. Because only children less than two years of age are able to benefit in terms of decreased stunting, this impact applies only to this age group.
b. If this difference were maintained until adulthood, as some studies suggest happens when malnutrition is severe and persistent, adult height would decrease by about 20 centimeters, if one assumes a standard deviation in adult height of about 7.5 centimeters.

Table B.5   Impact of Interventions on Ability

Indicator	Impact
General	
Higher earnings due to change in IQ	10% for a one standard deviation increase (Alderman, Behrman, and Sabot 1996)
Standard deviation of IQ	15 points
Impact	
Iron and folate for children 6–24 months of age[a]	Increase in IQ of 30% of anemic children by 7.5 points (Menendez and others 1997; Ross and Horton 1998)
Iodated oil to pregnant women	Increase in IQ of children with iodine deficiency disorders by 13.5 points (Grantham-McGregor, Fernald, and Sethuraman 1999)
Deworming	Decrease in prevalence of anemia by 50% (Stolzfus and others 2004)

Source: Authors.

a. For both iron and folate for children and iodated oil for pregnant women, it is assumed that the same effect would occur with fortification as with supplementation.

References

Aaby, P., B. Samb, F. Simondon, A. M. Seck, J. Bennett, L. Markowitz, and H. Whittle. 1996. "A Comparison of Vaccine Efficacy and Mortality during Routine Use of High Titre Edmonston-Zagreb and Schwarz Standard Measles Vaccines in Rural Senegal." *Transactions of the Royal Society of Tropical Medicine and Hygiene* 90 (3): 326–30.

Action Against Hunger. 2009. "Feeding Hunger and Insecurity: The Global Food Price Crisis." Briefing paper, Action Against Hunger, New York.

Alderman, H., J. R. Behrman, and J. H. Hoddinott. 2005. "Nutrition, Malnutrition, and Economic Growth." In *Health and Economic Growth: Findings and Policy Implications*, ed. G. López-Casasnovas, B. Rivera, and L. Currais. Cambridge, MA: MIT Press.

Alderman, H., J. R. Behrman, and R. Sabot. 1996. "The Returns to Endogenous Human Capital in Pakistan's Rural Wage Labour Market." *Oxford Bulletin of Economics and Statistics* 58: 29–55.

Baqui, A. H., R. E. Black, S. El Arifeen, M. Yunus, J. Chakraborty, S. Ahmed, and J. P. Vaughan. 2002. "Effect of Zinc Supplementation Started during Diarrhea on Morbidity and Mortality in Bangladeshi Children: Community Randomized Trial." *British Medical Journal* 325 (7372): 1059.

Beaton, G. H., R. Martorell, K. J. Aronson, B. Edmonston, A. C. Ross, B. Harvey, and G. McCabe. 1993. "Effectiveness of Vitamin A Supplementation in the Control of Young Child Morbidity and Mortality in Developing Countries." Nutrition Policy Discussion Paper 13, United Nations, New York.

Behrman, J. R., H. Alderman, and J. Hoddinott. 2004. "Hunger and Malnutrition." In *Global Crises, Global Solutions*, ed. Björn Lomborg. Cambridge, U.K.: Cambridge University Press.

Benson, T. 2006. *An Assessment of the Causes of Malnutrition in Ethiopia: A Contribution to the Formulation of a National Nutrition Strategy for Ethiopia*. Washington, DC: International Food Policy Research Institute, September.

Bhutta, Z. A., T. Ahmed, R. E. Black, S. Cousens, K. Dewey, E. Giugliani, B. A. Haider, B. Kirkwood, S. S. Morris, H. P. Sachdev, and M. Shekar, for the Maternal and Child Undernutrition Study Group. 2008. "What Works? Interventions for Maternal and Child Undernutrition and Survival." *Lancet* 371 (9610): 417–40.

Black, R. E., S. S. Morris, and J. Bryce. 2003. "Where and Why Are 10 Million Children Dying Every Year?" *Lancet* 361 (9376): 2226–34.

Bryce, J., D. Coitinho, I. Darnton-Hill, D. Pelletier, and P. Pinstrup-Andersen, for the Maternal and Child Undernutrition Study Group. 2008. "Maternal and Child Undernutrition: Effective Action at National Level." *Lancet* 371 (9611): 510–26.

Christian, P., S. K. Khatry, and K. P. West Jr. 2004. "Antenatal Anthelmintic Treatment, Birth Weight, and Infant Survival in Rural Nepal." *Lancet* 364 (9438): 981–83.

Christiaensen, L., and H. Alderman. 2004. "Child Malnutrition in Ethiopia: Can Maternal Knowledge Augment the Role of Income?" *Economic Development and Cultural Change* 52 (2): 287–312.

Clay, D., D. Molla, and D. Habtewold. 1998. "Food Aid Targeting in Ethiopia: A Study of Household Food Insecurity and Food Aid Distributions." Grain Market Research Project Working Paper 12, Ministry of Economic Development and Cooperation, Addis Ababa, March.

Cogswell, M. E., U. I. Parvanta, L. Ickes, R. Yip, and G. M. Brittenham. 2003. "Iron Supplementation during Pregnancy, Anemia, and Birth Weight: A Randomized Controlled Trial." *American Journal of Clinical Nutrition* 78 (4): 773–81.

CSA (Central Statistical Agency, Ethiopia). 1983. *Report on the National Rural Nutrition Survey.* Addis Ababa: CSA.

———. 1992. *Report on the National Rural Nutrition Survey.* Addis Ababa: CSA.

———. 1996. *Welfare Monitoring Survey 1996 Analytical Report.* Addis Ababa: CSA.

———. 1998. *Welfare Monitoring Survey 1998 Analytical Report.* Addis Ababa: CSA.

———. 2000. *Welfare Monitoring Survey 2000 Analytical Report.* Addis Ababa: CSA.

———. 2004. *Welfare Monitoring Survey 2004 Analytical Report.* Addis Ababa: CSA.

CSA (Central Statistical Agency, Ethiopia) and ORC Macro. 2001. *Ethiopia Demographic and Health Survey 2000.* Addis Ababa: CSA; Calverton, MD: ORC Macro.

———. 2006. *Ethiopia Demographic and Health Survey 2005.* Addis Ababa: CSA; Calverton, MD: ORC Macro.

CSA (Central Statistical Agency, Ethiopia), USAID (U.S. Agency for International Development), and ORC Macro. 2001. *Nutrition of Young Children and Mothers in Ethiopia: Findings of DHS, African Nutrition Chart Books.* Addis Ababa: Central Statistical Agency; Calverton, MD: ORC Macro.

Development Researchers' Network, Aide á la Décision Economique, Baastel, Eco Consulting Group, and Nordic Consulting Group. 2004. *Joint Evaluation of Effectiveness and Impact on the Enabling Development Policies of the WFP: Ethiopia Country Study.* Vol. 1. Rome: Development Researchers' Network.

Edmond, K. M., C. Zandoh, M. A. Quigley, S. Amenga-Etego, S. Owusu-Agyei, and B. R. Kirkwood. 2006. "Delayed Breastfeeding Initiation Increases Risk of Neonatal Mortality." *Pediatrics* 117 (3): 380–86.

EHNRI (Ethiopian Health Nutrition Research Institute). 2005. *Iodine Deficiency Disorders National Survey in Ethiopia.* Addis Ababa: EHNRI.

ESHE (Essential Services for Health in Ethiopia). 2006. "Community Assessment in Selected ESHE Focus *Woredas* in Amhara, Oromia, and SNNP Regions." ESHE, Addis Ababa.

Ethiopia, Federal Ministry of Health. 2007. *Expanded Programme on Immunization: Policy Guideline.* Addis Ababa: Federal Ministry of Health.

———. 2008. *National Nutrition Strategy.* Addis Ababa: Federal Ministry of Health, January.

Ethiopia, Ministry of Finance and Economic Development. 2007. *Ethiopia: Building on Progress; A Plan for Accelerated and Sustained Development to End Poverty.* Vol. 1: *Main Text.* Addis Ababa: Ministry of Finance and Economic Development, January.

Ethiopia PROFILES and AED (Academy for Educational Development). 2005. "Why Nutrition Matters." PowerPoint presentation on the Ethiopian PROFILES analysis, Ethiopia PROFILES, Addis Ababa; Academy for Educational Development and LINKAGES (Breastfeeding, Complementary Feeding, and Maternal Nutrition Program) Project, Washington, DC.

Fiedler, J. L., and T. Chuko. 2008. "The Cost of Child Health Days: A Case Study of Ethiopia's Enhanced Outreach Strategy (EOS)." *Health Policy and Planning* 23 (4): 222–33.

Grantham-McGregor, S. M., L. C. Fernald, and K. Sethuraman. 1999. "Effects of Health and Nutrition on Cognitive and Behavioural Development in the First Three Years of Life. Part Two, Infections and Micronutrient Deficiencies: Iodine, Iron, and Zinc." *Food and Nutrition Bulletin* 20 (1): 76–99.

Gwatkin, D. R., S. Rutstein, K. Johnson, E. Suliman, A. Wagstaff, and A. Amouzou. 2007. "Socio-economic Differences in Health, Nutrition, and Population within Developing Countries: An Overview." *Nigerian Journal of Clinical Practice* 10 (4): 272–82.

Hall, A., and T. Khara. 2006. *Mission Report: EOS/TSF for Child Survival Interventions; November 23 to December 12, 2006.* New York: UNICEF.

Hotz, C., and K. Brown. 2004. "Assessment of the Risk of Zinc Deficiency in Populations and Options for Its Control." *Food and Nutrition Bulletin* 25 (1, supplement 2): S94–203.

Jamison, D. T., J. G. Breman, A. R. Measham, G. Alleyne, M. Claeson, D. B. Evans, P. Jha, A. Mills, and P. Musgrove, eds. 2006. *Disease Control Priorities in Developing Countries.* Washington, DC: World Bank.

Jones, G., R. W. Steketee, R. E. Black, Z. A. Bhutta, and S. S. Morris. 2003. "How Many Child Deaths Can We Prevent This Year?" *Lancet* 362 (9377): 65–71.

Kolesar, R., E. F. Kleinau, M. P. Torres, C. Gil, V. de la Cruz, and M. Post. 2003. *Combining Hygiene Behavior Change with Water and Sanitation: Monitoring Progress in Hato Mayor, Dominican Republic.* Washington, DC: U.S. Agency for International Development.

Kuhl, J. J. 2006. *Nutrition and Its Determinants in Southern Ethiopia: Findings from the Child Growth Promotion Baseline Survey.* Washington, DC: World Bank and United Nations Children's Fund.

Lengeler, C. 2004. "Insecticide-Treated Nets for Malaria Control: Real Gains." *Bulletin of the World Health Organization* 82 (2): 84.

Li, H., A. Stein, H. Barnhart, U. Ramakrishnan, and R. Martorell. 2003. "Associations between Prenatal and Postnatal Growth and Adult Body Size and Composition." *American Journal of Clinical Nutrition* 77 (6): 1489–505.

Lloyd, S., M. Asegid, B. Desalgn, G. Egata, and E. Regassa. 2007. "Child Caring Practices as Underlying Causes of Young Child Malnutrition in Rural Ethiopia." World Food Programme, Rome, February.

Luby, S. P., M. Agboatwalla, D. R. Feikin, J. Painter, W. Billhimer, A. Altaf, and R. M. Hoekstra. 2005. "Effect of Hand Washing on Child Health: A Randomized Controlled Trial." *Lancet* 366 (9481): 225–33.

Mahomed, K., and A. M. Gulmezoglu. 2002. "Maternal Iodine Supplements in Areas of Deficiency." Cochrane Library 4, Update Software, Oxford.

Mason, J. B. 2001. *The Micronutrient Report: Current Progress and Trends in the Control of Vitamin A, Iodine, and Iron Deficiencies.* Ottawa: Micronutrient Initiative.

Mason, J. B., M. Deitchler, K. Gilman, M. Shuaib, K. Hotchkiss, K. Mason, N. Mock, and K. Sethuraman. 2002. "Iodine Fortification Is Related to Increased Weight-for-age and Birth Weight in Children in Asia." *Food and Nutrition Bulletin* 23 (3): 290–308.

Mason, J. B., D. Sanders, P. Musgrove, P. Soekirman, and R. Galloway. 2006. "Community Health and Nutrition Programs." In *Disease Control Priorities in Developing Countries*, ed. D. Jamison, J. Breman, A. Measham, G. Alleyne, M. Claeson, D. Evans, P. Jha, A. Mills, and P. Musgrove. Washington, DC: World Bank.

Menendez, C., E. Kahigwa, R. Hirt, P. Vounatsou, J. J. Aponte, F. Font, C. J. Acosta, D. M. Schellenberg, C. M. Galindom, J. Kimario, H. Urassa, B. Brabin, T. A. Smith, A. Y. Kitua, M. Tanner, and P. L. Alonso. 1997. "Randomised Placebo-Controlled Trial of Iron Supplementation and Malaria Chemoprophylaxis for Prevention of Severe Anemia and Malaria in Tanzanian Infants." *Lancet* 350 (9081): 844–50.

Micronutrient Initiative. 2004. "Activity Highlight: Double Fortification of Salt." Micronutrient Initiative, Ottawa.

Pelletier, D. L., K. Deneke, Y. Kidane, B. Haile, and F. Negussie. 1995. "The Food-First Bias and Nutrition Policy: Lessons from Ethiopia." *Food Policy* 20 (4): 279–98.

Pelletier, D. L., and E. A. Frongillo. 2003. "Changes in Child Survival Are Strongly Associated with Changes in Malnutrition in Developing Countries." *Journal of Nutrition* 133 (1): 107–19.

Pelletier, D. L., E. A. Frongillo Jr., D. G. Schroeder, and J. P Habicht. 1994. "A Methodology for Estimating the Contribution of Malnutrition to Child Mortality in Developing Countries." *Journal of Nutrition* 124 (10 supplement): 2106S–22S.

Risonar, M. G. D., L. W. Tengco, P. Rayco-Solon, and F. S. Solon. 2008. "The Effect of School-Based Weekly Iron Supplementation Delivery System among Anemic School Children in the Philippines." *European Journal of Clinical Nutrition* 62 (8): 991–96.

Ross, J., and S. Horton. 1998. *Economic Consequences of Iron Deficiency*. Ottawa: Micronutrient Initiative.

Sazawal, S., R. E. Black, M. Ramsan, H. M. Chwaya, R. J. Stoltzfus, A. Dutta, U. Dhingra, I. Kabole, S. Deb, M. K. Othman, and F. M. Kabole. 2006. "Effects of Routine Prophylactic Supplementation with Iron and Folic Acid on Admission to Hospital and Mortality in Preschool Children in a High Malaria Transmission Setting: Community-Based, Randomized, Placebo-Controlled Trial." *Lancet* 367 (9505): 133–43.

Stolzfus, R. J., H. M. Chway, A. Montresor, J. M. Tielsch, J. K. Jape, M. Albonico, and L. Savioli. 2004. "Low Dose Iron Supplementation Improves Iron Status and Appetite but Not Anemia, Whereas Quarterly Antihelminthic Treatment Improves Growth, Appetite, and Anemia in Zanzibari Preschool Children." *Journal of Nutrition* 134 (2): 348–56.

Stoltzfus, R. J., L. Mullany, and R. E. Black. 2003. "Iron Deficiency Anaemia." In *Comparative Quantification of Health Risks: Global and Regional Burden of Disease Attributable to Selected Major Risk Factors*, ed. M. Ezzati, A. Lopez, A. Rodgers, and C. Murray. Geneva: World Health Organization.

Ter Kuile, F. O., D. J. Terlouw, P. A. Phillips-Howard, W. A. Hawley, J. F. Friedman, S. K. Kariuki, Y. P. Shi, M. S. Kolczak, A. A. Lal, J. M. Vulule, and B. L. Nahlen. 2003. "Reduction of Malaria during Pregnancy by Permethrin-Treated Bed Nets in an Area of Intense Perennial Malaria Transmission in Western Kenya." *American Journal of Tropical Medical Hygiene* 68 (4 supplement): 50–60.

Thomas, D., and J. Strauss. 1997. "Health and Wages: Evidence on Men and Women in Urban Brazil." *Journal of Econometrics* 77 (1): 159–85.

Umeta, M. 2005. "Technical Report on the Status of the Pre-feasibility Study of Sugar Fortification with Vitamin A in Ethiopia." U.S. Agency for International Development, Addis Ababa, Ethiopia.

UN ACC-SCN (United Nations Administrative Committee on Coordination, Subcommittee on Nutrition) and IFPRI (International Food Policy Research Institute). 2000. *Fourth Report on the World Nutrition Situation: Nutrition throughout the Life Cycle.* Geneva: ACC/SCN in collaboration with IFPRI.

UNDP (United Nations Development Programme). 2010. *Human Development Report 2010: The Real Wealth of Nations; Pathways to Human Development.* New York: UNDP.

UNICEF (United Nations Children's Fund). Various years, 1997–2009. *The State of the World's Children Report.* New York: UNICEF.

WHO (World Health Organization). 2001. *Macroeconomics and Health: Investing in Health for Economic Development.* Report of the Commission on Macroeconomics and Health. Geneva: WHO.

———. Various years. Global Database on Child Growth and Malnutrition. Geneva: WHO.

World Bank. Various years, 1995–2009. *World Development Indicators.* Washington, DC: World Bank.

———. 2007. "Capturing the Demographic Bonus in Ethiopia: Gender, Development, and Demographic Actions." Report 36434-ET, World Bank, Washington, DC.

Yager, T. R. 2003. *The Mineral Industries of Djibouti, Eritrea, Ethiopia, and Somalia.* Washington, DC: U.S. Geological Survey.

Yamano, T., H. Alderman, and L. Christiaensen. 2005. "Child Growth, Shocks, and Food Aid in Rural Ethiopia." *American Journal of Agricultural Economics* 87 (2): 273–88.

Index

Figures, maps, notes, and tables are indicated with *f*, *m*, *n*, and *t* following the page number.

ECO-AUDIT
Environmental Benefits Statement

The World Bank is committed to preserving endangered forests and natural resources. The Office of the Publisher has chosen to print **Combating Malnutrition in Ethiopia** on recycled paper with 50 percent post-consumer waste, in accordance with the recommended standards for paper usage set by the Green Press Initiative, a non-profit program supporting publishers in using fiber that is not sourced from endangered forests. For more information, visit www.greenpressinitiative.org.

Saved:
- 5 trees
- 2 million BTUs of total energy
- 578 lbs of CO_2 equivalent of greenhouse gases
- 2,606 gallons of waste water
- 166 lbs of solid waste

green
press
INITIATIVE

www.ingramcontent.com/pod-product-compliance
Lightning Source LLC
Chambersburg PA
CBHW080329270326
41927CB00014B/3151